MULTINATIONALS IN THE GLOBAL POLITICAL ECONOMY

Also by Lorraine Eden

MULTINATIONALS AND TRANSFER PRICING (*editor with Alan M. Rugman*)

MULTINATIONALS IN NORTH AMERICA

RETROSPECTIVES ON PUBLIC FINANCE (*editor*)

TRANSFER PRICING, TAXES AND FREE TRADE IN NORTH AMERICA

Multinationals in the Global Political Economy

Edited by

Lorraine Eden
Professor of International Affairs
The Norman Paterson School of International Affairs
Carleton University, Ottawa

and

Evan H. Potter
Doctoral Candidate in International Relations
London School of Economics and Political Science

150th YEAR
M

St. Martin's Press

First published in Great Britain 1993 by
THE MACMILLAN PRESS LTD
Houndmills, Basingstoke, Hampshire RG21 2XS
and London
Companies and representatives
throughout the world

A catalogue record for this book is available
from the British Library.

ISBN 0–333–57752–3

Printed in Great Britain by
Ipswich Book Co Ltd
Ipswich, Suffolk

First published in the United States of America 1993 by
Scholarly and Reference Division,
ST. MARTIN'S PRESS, INC.,
175 Fifth Avenue,
New York, N.Y. 10010

ISBN 0–312–09632–1

Library of Congress Cataloging-in-Publication Data
Multinationals in the global political economy / edited by Lorraine
Eden and Evan Potter.
p. cm.
Includes bibliographical references and index.
ISBN 0–312–09632–1
1. International business enterprises.   2. International economic
relations.   I. Eden, Lorraine.   II. Potter, Evan H.
HD2755.5.M8454   1993
338.8′83—dc20
93–13
CIP

Contents

Preface

In the study of multinational–state relations, scholars of international relations, public policy, political science, economics and business studies rarely have the opportunity – save at the occasional inter-disciplinary conference – to trade ideas in a public forum. Rarer still is finding a forum where scholars in different disciplines from *both* sides of the Atlantic are brought together to discuss the future of MNC (or MNE or TNC) relations with the nation-state. It is this latter rarity that the present volume addresses.

The origins of this book can be traced to a panel session on bringing the firm back into the study of international political economy that was organised by Lorraine Eden for the International Studies Association annual meetings in Vancouver in March 1991. Evan Potter at that time was the editor of *Millennium*, a journal of international studies published out of the Department of International Relations at the London School of Economics and Political Science. Seeing the benefit of having the papers of an interdisciplinary panel appear in an interdisciplinary journal, Potter approached Eden about submitting some of the panel papers to *Millennium* for publication.

The proposal then became a bit more ambitious: Why not have a special section on multinational–state relations in *Millennium* that would look not only at how far the study of this relationship had evolved since the publication of Raymond Vernon's seminal *Sovereignty at Bay* but also where this relationship was going. Vernon agreed to provide an introduction to the special section and, following a comprehensive review process that included referees on both sides of the Atlantic and an editorial board at the LSE, a select number of panel papers as well as new papers were accepted for publication in the summer 1991 edition of *Millennium*.

Upon publication, this issue of the journal began to be used quite extensively for teaching and research purposes at a number of universities in the United Kingdom, Canada and the United States. With this positive response we began to think about the possibility of putting together a book that would invite other scholars to contribute full length research papers. The next step was to contact other leading researchers about contributing to this book. Alan Rugman, Magnus Blomström, Robert Lipsey, Robert Kudrle, Louis Wells Jr and Alvin

Wint were all enthusiastic about expanding the focus of the research into a book-length compilation of related works on multinational–state relations from a variety of perspectives and disciplines. These discussions led to further conversations with Clare Wace of Macmillan, and to our joint decision to go ahead. We hope this new volume will stimulate discussion by students, researchers and policy-makers on the emerging new diplomacy in MNE–state relations.

LORRAINE EDEN
EVAN H. POTTER

Notes on the Contributors

Magnus Blomström holds the chair in economics in the Stockholm School of Economics, Stockholm, Sweden, and is a Fellow of the National Bureau of Economic Research, New York, New York, USA.

John H. Dunning is ICI Professor of International Business, Department of Economics, University of Reading, Reading, Berkshire, UK, and State of New Jersey Professor of International Business, Graduate School of Management, Rutgers University, Newark, New Jersey, USA.

Lorraine Eden (co-editor) is Visiting Professor and Fellow, Centre for Business and Government, John F. Kennedy School of Government, Harvard University, Cambridge, Massachusetts, USA, and Professor of International Affairs, Norman Paterson School of International Affairs, Carleton University, Ottawa, Ontario, Canada.

Raphael Kaplinsky is a Fellow at the Institute of Development Studies, University of Sussex, Brighton, UK.

Robert T. Kudrle is Associate Dean for Research and Director, Freeman Center for International Economic Policy, Hubert Humphrey Institute of Public Affairs, University of Minnesota, Minneapolis, Minnesota, USA.

Sanjaya Lall is Lecturer at the Institute of Economics and Statistics, Oxford University, Oxford, UK.

Robert E. Lipsey is Professor, Queen's College and the Graduate Center, City University of New York, and a Fellow at the National Bureau of Economic Research, New York, New York, USA.

Evan H. Potter (co-editor) is a doctoral candidate in International Relations at the London School of Economics and Political Science, London, UK, and the editor of *Canadian Foreign Policy*, a foreign affairs journal.

Alan M. Rugman is Professor of International Business, Faculty of Management, University of Toronto, Toronto, Ontario, Canada.

Susan Strange is Professor in the Department of Political Science, European University Institute, Florence, Italy.

Raymond Vernon is Clarence Dillon Professor of International Affairs Emeritus, Centre for Business and Government, J.F. Kennedy School of Government, Harvard University, Cambridge, Massachusetts, USA.

Louis T. Wells Jr is Herbert F. Johnson Professor of International Management in the Graduate School of Business Administration, Harvard University, Cambridge, Massachusetts, USA.

Alvin G. Wint is Assistant Professor of International Business in the College of Business Administration, Northeastern University, Boston, Massachusetts, USA.

1 Thinking Globally – Acting Locally: Multinationals in the Global Political Economy

Lorraine Eden

INTRODUCTION

This month (August 1992), IBM is running a two-page magazine advertisement entitled 'Thinking globally?' which shows a map of the world dotted with blue pins representing IBM offices. The advertisement says that the world is getting smaller so people are thinking bigger; however, since cultures still differ, international firms face a paradox – how to think global and act local at the same time. IBM thinks local, according to the advertisement, by having offices around the world and manufacturing products that are customised for local markets; it acts global by treating all the offices as part of the same team and by offering consistent services around the world to its customers.

The paradox faced by multinational enterprises (MNEs) – that of negotiating with nation-states so as to balance local tastes and desires for national responsiveness by governments against economic pressures to centralise and integrate functions and products across borders – is at the heart of this book. We live in a global world, one with global products, firms and markets; yet we remain divided into national units, each with its own laws, customs and cultures. National borders are changing, some moving outward (for example, the North American countries sign bilateral and multilateral agreements encouraging freer intra-continental trade and investment flows), some moving inward (for example, Eastern European nations fragment into smaller, often ethnically based, units). Triadic economies are emerging, around which smaller countries cluster (UNCTC, 1991). Where are the borders of a country when information travels instantaneously around the world, when financial capital is completely mobile, when interregional

1

trade barriers are disappearing? Yet cultures continue to differ while rising incomes promote the desires for differentiated products, implying that acting local still matters.

The borders of the firm are also changing as new forms of investment such as strategic partnering and contract manufacturing replace the wholly-owned subsidiary as the main vehicle for penetrating foreign markets. 'Who is us?', asks Robert Reich, when multinationals are global webs made up of firms from many countries, with products and factors flowing around the world. Who is them? What is a domestic MNE, a foreign MNE? Which offers more benefits and fewer costs to a nation, the domestic firm that produces most of its output outside the country or the foreign firm that hires local factors?

Multinationals now function in a global, political economy: global because borders are disappearing between markets, political because national politics and policies still matter. In fact, the increased competitiveness of firms on a global scale as they contend for shares of the world market has forced nation-states to reconsider their policies *vis-à-vis* MNEs. States have moved from confrontation to co-operation with the global firms in their midst, from regulating to encouraging entry, from taxing to subsidising, from opposition to partnership.

The politics of national economic competitiveness in the 1990s has given the term 'sovereignty at bay' a new twist. While the term in the 1970s was (mis)understood to mean that MNEs and nation-states were warring actors locked in a battle where global firms had the upper hand, in the 1990s MNEs and nation-states are now seen as partners in the race to engineer competitive advantage and move up the value chain to higher value added and more technically sophisticated products.

This book deals with the changing relationships between multinationals and nation-states over the 1980s and 1990s, and the research and policy agenda these imply for the upcoming decade. The book takes an international political economy (IPE) approach to state-MNE relations, focusing on the interdependencies, both conflictual and co-operative, between these two primary actors in the global economy. As Raymond Vernon in his chapter, 'Sovereignty at Bay: Twenty Years After' says, '[MNEs and states are] two systems ... each legitimated by popular consent, each potentially useful to the other, yet each containing features antagonistic to the other'. In what follows, we provide a road map for the reader, outlining the structure of the book, summaries of the individual chapters, and the book's main themes.

STRUCTURE OF *MULTINATIONALS IN THE GLOBAL POLITICAL ECONOMY*

This book consists of eleven chapters written by experts on multinationals and organised around several issues and policy dilemmas in MNE–state relations. Chapter 2 by Raymond Vernon, 'Sovereignty at Bay: Twenty Years Later', sets out the overall theme of the book: the changing nature of state–MNE relations in a global political economy where both the state and the multinational enterprise are key actors. This chapter is followed by Lorraine Eden's 'Bringing the Firm Back In' which reviews the existing theory of the multinational enterprise, as outlined in the international political economy and international business studies literatures, and argues that, in a globalised world, MNE–state relations require a closer examination by both sets of scholars. The 'Confrontation to Co-operation?' chapter by John Dunning expands on the MNE–state relation theme by arguing there has been a shift away from states regulating to co-operating with MNEs as a result of the new competitiveness agenda adopted by nation-states. Alan Rugman's chapter on 'Borders' reinforces Dunning by arguing that the borders of the firm and the nation-state have become more amorphous, creating a paradox for firms, whether to go global or be nationally responsive, and for states, whether to regulate or co-operate with MNEs in their midst.

The next set of chapters focus more specifically on challenges for developing countries. 'Big Business and the State' by Susan Strange looks at the confrontation–co-operation issue, concluding that state regulation of MNEs is less desirable or effective as the underlying production and finance structures have shifted more power to globalised multinationals. Raphael Kaplinsky's chapter 'TNCs in the Third World' provides evidence on the underlying structural shift in production from Fordism to Post-Fordism and what this shift means for multinationals and LDC nation-states. Sanjaya Lall in 'MNEs and LDCs', looks at the shift to more co-operative relations between LDCs and multinationals, and concludes that, given the pervasiveness of market failures in developing countries, regulation of MNEs may be necessary to ensure nations receive net benefits from inward foreign direct investment (IFDI), particularly in the area of high technology. He argues that regulating IFDI can be useful if it is accompanied by pro-market competitiveness policies.

The last three chapters are empirically oriented, providing evidence in support of the themes advanced by the other authors. Magnus

Blomström and Robert Lipsey in 'Competitiveness of Countries and their MNEs' differentiate between sources of competitiveness for countries and multinationals. Since firms combine mobile firm specific advantages with immobile country specific-advantages, and globalisation has made MNE production more mobile, the authors conclude that the balance of power has shifted from the nation-state to the multinationals. Robert Kudrle's chapter, 'No Entry', harks back to the confrontation theme. He examines regulations restricting IFDI in the OECD countries and finds that the primary justification is lobbying by vested interest groups, making it more difficult to liberalise closed sectors. The last chapter, 'Marketing Strategies', by Louis Wells and Alvin Wint, discusses the policy shift from regulating IFDI to image building and investment promotion by state agencies. They ask, when all countries are trying to attract IFDI, which policies are most successful, concluding that personal contact works best. We now turn to more detailed summaries of the individual chapters.

INDIVIDUAL SUMMARIES OF CHAPTERS

Raymond Vernon, 'Sovereignty at Bay: Twenty Years After'

In Chapter 2, Vernon looks look back twenty years to his well-known book *Sovereignty at Bay* first published in 1971 and looks forward to the relationship between multinationals and nation-states in the future. Vernon notes, somewhat wryly, that the book title has become a misnomer, taken to mean the inevitable decline of the state and rise of the global corporation. The purpose of the book, however, was to explain the motivations behind the growth of US multinationals and to explore MNE–state friction points. Rather than asserting the decline of the nation-state, the book argued that MNEs and nation-states were two legitimate systems with potential benefits and conflicts inherent in their mutual existence. Vernon still holds this view.

Twenty years later, in looking at state policies towards MNEs, Vernon notes that the attempts by the OECD and United Nations in the 1970s to develop multilateral codes of conduct for MNEs are still failures. Bilateral treaties, primarily in the tax area, are now the major instrument used to define MNE rights and obligations. Unilaterally, the United States is adopting more restrictive legislation, such as the Exon-Florio Amendment which allows the US president to restrict inflows of foreign direct investment on national security grounds. While the United States is tightening IFDI, most other governments have been liberalising capital markets. This liberalisation has been partly due to the shortage of IFDI in developing countries, already hurt by the debt crisis, but also due to the growing interdependence of national economies which necessitates multilateral co-operation.

Vernon argues that governments are now gradually becoming reconciled to a narrower concept of sovereignty. Points of friction still remain, such as the need to define the rights and assess the obligations of global businesses. As international alliances and mergers increase among the largest MNEs this assignment grows more complicated. At the same time nation-states are demanding more in terms of performance from the firms within their borders. As a result, he believes multilateral approaches are the only way to reduce the 'inescapable tensions' of future MNE–state relations; unilateral approaches, on the other hand, are likely to damage both state and firm interests.

Lorraine Eden, 'Bringing the Firm Back In: Multinationals in International Political Economy'

In 'Bringing the Firm Back In', Lorraine Eden looks at the treatment of multinationals in the international political economy (IPE) literature, summarises current thinking about MNEs by scholars in international business studies (IBS), and then addresses the implications of the IBS literature for state–MNE relations as they are characterised in IPE.

Eden examines 'five faces' of the multinational in the international political economy literature: the product life cycle, sovereignty at bay, the obsolescing bargain, the law of uneven development, and the changing international division of labour, noting that the first three faces were explored by Raymond Vernon in *Sovereignty at Bay*. Eden then turns to the international business studies literature and reviews the OLI (Ownership–Location–Internalisation) paradigm, strategic management theory, the international value chain, and their implications for MNE organisational and locational decisions. She concludes that these 'new style' multinationals are 'giant firms, linked by equity and non-equity relations in clusters, engaged in two-way flows of products, investments and technology within the Triadic economies'.

Eden then addresses 'bringing the firm back in', asking how each of the five faces of the multinational in the IPE literature is altered by the new style MNEs of the 1990s. She argues that insights from the IBS literature imply that IPE must pay more attention to the specificities of global corporations: their goals, strategies, structures and locational choices. The chapter concludes that a clearer focus on the multi-national as an institutional actor with goals, strategies and structures is necessary to understand state–MNE relations in the 1990s.

John Dunning, 'Governments and Multinational Enterprises: From Confrontation to Co-operation?'

John Dunning's chapter examines the changing nature of systemic interactions between governments, as they promote national welfare, and MNEs, as they seek global profits, and the future directions of these interactions. His chapter makes three arguments. First, he contends that in the past state policies designed to influence MNEs have not been explicitly related to wider political strategies, either because MNEs were perceived as a small part of the economy or because states believed the consequences of regulating FDI were minor. Secondly, Dunning asserts that governments are now treating the competitive advantage of country resources as a 'national economic objective in its own right', both because economic structures in the OECD countries are converging so that trade is primarily intra-industry, and because global corporations are now more footloose. Thirdly, Dunning argues that MNE locational decisions are increas-ingly affected by state policies to advance social goals rather than by policies directed at MNEs; these social policies now tend to have an impact on the transactions costs facing MNEs rather than direct production costs.

Direct production costs are defined as the opportunity costs of the resources used in production in the absence of market failure in intermediate product and factor markets, whereas transactions costs arise from the extra costs of organising relationships when markets fail. Dunning identifies two basic types of market failure: structural market distortions arising from anti-competitive activities of market agents, and endemic or intrinsic market failure arising from uncertainty, market externalities, natural monopoly, public goods, and market rigidities. Both structural and endemic market failures generate transactions costs.

When multinationals replace external markets by hierarchical structures, the purpose may be to increase market power (creating a structural distortion) or replacing a missing or imperfect market (reducing endemic market failure). As a result, when states intervene to reduce market distortions they may be undertaking actions which MNEs see as conflictual (for example, anti-trust policies to break up monopoly power) or complementary (for example, pro-market interventions to reduce endemic transactions costs). Dunning argues that over the past thirty years MNE–state interactions have shifted from primarily conflictual, as states sought to reduce anti-competitive behaviour by firms, to co-operative, as states now see MNEs as the means by which national competitive advantage can be generated and sustained. In the 1990s, he sees the main cause of market failure in the OECD countries as not structural distortions but endemic distortions due to unstable, integrated and interdependent markets. State policies, as a result, are now focusing on reducing endemic transactions costs.

Up until the 1980s, Dunning argues, most countries treated inward and outward FDI flows as unrelated economic phenomena. In terms of IFDI, states sought to remove or lessen the perceived adverse effects of oligopolistic foreign MNEs, focusing on their structural market power. In terms of outward FDI, there was much less concern and policies primarily focused on double taxation, dividend repatriation and extraterritoriality issues. In the 1980s, however, globalisation and technological advances have meant that most developed economies are both inward and outward investors and multinationals are increasingly mobile, major actors in national economies. This has had three consequences: it has lessened the desire and ability of both firms and states to adopt policies that raise structural market imperfections, increased MNE bargaining power relative to nation-states, and caused governments to reappraise the political consequences of FDI policies and modify their treatment of MNEs.

States are therefore shifting from a focus on removing domestic structural distortions to facilitating the supply capabilities of their domestic firms through lowering endemic transactions costs. Governments are starting to play a positive and co-ordinating role in upgrading industry resources and capabilities. Inward and outward FDI are seen as complementary to domestic investment. As a result, states are developing policies to encourage IFDI and to improve the competitive advantages of domestic MNEs in foreign markets. A fundamental reorientation of the role of government appears to be occurring, one that changes MNE–state relations from confrontation to co-operation. States now see the creation of domestic competitive advantage as a pressing national policy goal, and state regulation of

MNEs is increasingly being driven by the competitiveness agenda. As a result, state policies are now more generic, applying to both domestic and foreign firms, creating a symbiotic relationship between governments, hierarchies and markets.

Alan Rugman, 'Drawing the Border for a Multinational Enterprise and a Nation-State'

In his chapter, Alan Rugman poses the questions: 'What is sovereignty? What is a multinational enterprise?' He argues that globalisation forces are blurring the borders of the nation-state, creating the three regional economic blocs now known as the Triad. At the same time that economic integration is occurring, however, there is increasing political fragmentation. As a result the relevant borders for MNEs are now being defined by cultural areas rather than national boundaries.

Globalisation forces are also causing MNEs to lose their home country identity as they move towards integrated production strategies within each Triadic bloc. He argues that Triadic and non-Triadic multinationals will emerge, with the Triadic MNEs distinguished primarily by their differing cultures and social-political-historical roots rather than by their behaviour. For all firms the most important business decision will be the trade-off between thinking global (i.e. focusing on economic efficiency) and acting local (i.e. being responsive to non-economic issues).

Rugman provides three current examples of the trend towards decentralisation: the shift of power from Canada's federal government to its provinces; the fragmentation of economic power in the United States as the US government becomes more protectionist and responsive to special interest groups; and the revolution and restructuring in East Europe; and contrasts these cases to the centralised home market economy of Japan. He concludes from these cases that sovereignty is of growing importance in the Triad.

Decentralisation of political power in the Canadian case, Rugman argues, raises the costs of doing business and can lead to MNEs investing where climates are more congenial and simpler. Rising economic nationalism, as in the US case, requires foreign multinationals to be sensitive to neoprotectionist restrictions. While national responsiveness is required in the European Community, Rugman contends that efficiency, not sovereignty, will attract IFDI in Eastern Europe. Lastly, the centralised home market of Japan facilitates integrative strategies by Japanese multinationals, making them less aware and perhaps less sensitive to sovereignty issues abroad. He concludes that the most successful multinationals in the 1990s will balance the trade-off between thinking globally and acting locally.

Susan Strange, 'Big Business and the State'

In this chapter, Susan Strange addresses two puzzles associated with MNE–state relations. The first puzzle is a theoretical one: why has international relations theory not incorporated the MNE into the analysis of the international system? She notes that MNEs are treated as an addendum in most textbooks, and argues that solving puzzles in international relations theory requires putting the MNE, together with the state, at the centre of theory. The question of power in the world system, who has it, who does not – all central issues in international relations – demand a focus on big business as an international actor.

The second puzzle is a normative one: how should states respond to big business? The state does have the power to regulate MNEs within its borders, to give or withhold domestic market access. However, this is only a negative power since 'the gate can be barred, but when open, it is up to the TNCs, not the state, to decide whether they should enter. Therein lies the rub'. Strange notes that over the 1980s states have become more accommodating towards the MNEs in their midst. She argues this is not a temporary policy shift due to LDC indebtedness but rather a permanent response to changes in underlying world production and finance structures. The technological revolution and integration of capital markets are more closely interlinking developing countries and multinationals and 'the genie cannot be put back in the bottle'.

She contends that saddling the MNEs with controls is more likely to damage the long-run health of developing countries than to be a successful development strategy. LDCs with fewer controls over FDI have done better than highly protectionist states. Noting that 'protectionism is like smoking cigarettes. It is apt to be habit forming and it does risk damaging your health', Strange concludes that the policy shift towards liberalised treatment of MNEs is permanent. 'The [new] game of diplomacy is triangular', with bargains being struck between states, between big business, and state to firm. As a result, both states and firms need to better understand the web of international bargains through which they are linked in the globalised economy of the 1990s.

Raphael Kaplinsky, 'TNCs in the Third World: Stability or Discontinuity?

In this chapter, Raphael Kaplinsky addresses the changing role of FDI in the Third World in the manufacturing sector. He looks at the dynamics of international competitiveness, the economic and political determinants of location, scale economies, and the unevenness in the world economy.

Kaplinsky argues that the dynamics of international competitiveness are shifting as manufacturing firms move from Fordist to Post-Fordist strategies in the 1990s. In the 'golden age' Fordist period of 1945–73, firms used mass production methods where products were standardised, the division of labour pursued, work organised hierarchically, machines used for special purpose automation, and interfirm relations conducted at arm's length. For production stages where unskilled labour was a major cost determinant, MNE affiliates or local firms in low wage economies were subcontracted to produce labour intensive intermediate products. This export-oriented FDI, located in developing countries, came to be known as 'the new international division of labour (NIDL)' since developing countries were integrated into MNE global strategies via their roles as sources of low-cost labour inputs. The success of the newly industrialising countries (NICs) encouraged many states to reorient their development policies to replicate NIC strategies in the 1980s.

Kaplinsky notes, however, that just as LDCs were engaging in this policy reorientation, the basis of global competition in manufacturing was shifting from Fordism (competition on price) to Post-Fordism (competition on product innovation). Post-Fordism requires product flexibility, which necessitates work flexibility and thus a multi-skilled labour force. At the same time product flexibility requires flexible automation techniques, just-in-time inventory systems, and simultaneous engineering. In Post-Fordism, the economics of location are different. Proximity and reliability of supply are more important than low labour costs, thus reducing the need to spread production across the globe. Product flexibility also allows firms to fine tune their products for final markets, implying greater benefits from locating in those markets. Labour is no longer 'seen as cost of production which has to be minimised (the essential premise of the NIDL), but rather as a central resource whose potential has to be maximised'. As a result, the Fordist strategy of producing standardised world products in low wage world factories is becoming obsolete, paradoxically just as developing countries are reforming their IFDI policies to encourage Fordist inflows. The 'open door' policies of many LDCs are also being offset by the changing politics of location, as the proliferation of managed trading arrangements and non-tariff barriers erected by the First World makes it even more difficult for LDCs to follow successful NIDL-based strategies.

Kaplinsky believes that Post-Fordism offers both opportunities and potential pitfalls to developing countries. Since economies of scale at the level of the plant are less important, there are new possibilities for niche strategies and renewed import substitution industrialisation. On the other hand, Post-Fordism is less labour and natural resource intensive, two of the traditional comparative advantages of the Third World, and a new drive for market oriented FDI is causing MNEs to shift production from LDCs to First World final markets. This shift, while generally unfavourable to LDCs, will be nuanced by increased South–South trade and regional differences as MNEs favour some LDC sites close to members of the Triad (for example, Mexico to the United States). Kaplinsky concludes that the gap between the newly industrialising countries and the least developed countries is likely to widen.

Sanjaya Lall, 'Multinationals and Developing Countries: Some Issues for Research'

Sanjaya Lall notes the warmer climate MNEs face in developing countries over the past decade and offers several explanations for this warming trend: developments in the theory of the MNE, historical experience, better LDC negotiation skills, the debt crisis, faster technological change, and a greater belief in market efficiency. In the 1990s he sees greater liberalisation of capital markets being accompanied by more state controls designed to offset market failures. Lall argues that examples of missing and fragmented markets, high transactions costs, poor information, economies of scale, risk and uncertainty plague developing countries. Multinationals may have conflicting effects on such markets, improving efficiency of some while worsening it in others. In the 1990s he expects there to be an offsetting reaction to the excessive free market ideology of the 1980s as LDC states realise that market failures are widespread and costly if left untreated.

Lall states that the MNE literature, particularly the theory of internalisation, emphasises the beneficial impacts of the transfer of capital, resources and technology that accompany MNE entry into LDCs. However, while such benefits clearly exist, the potential for the internalised markets of globalised multinationals to distort or retard development also exists. He illustrates his thesis with reference to technology, arguing that MNEs can transfer either 'know-how' and/or 'know-why' knowledge to LDCs. While 'know how' enables countries to master existing operational procedures, 'know-why' capabilities are crucial for upgrading the long-run technological capabilities of developing countries. MNEs generally transfer the former but much less often the latter, causing Lall to argue that a strategy based on IFDI restrictions, accompanied by other market-strengthening policies, may be a superior policy mix to total liberalisation of FDI regulations. He concludes that policy-makers should adopt a more pragmatic attitude towards multinationals, look for domestic market failures rather than taking market efficiency for granted, and allow for the possibility of efficient government intervention instead of assuming governments are incompetent.

Magnus Blomström and Robert Lipsey, 'The Competitiveness of Countries and their Multinational Firms'

Magnus Blomström and Robert Lipsey deal with the comparative advantages of countries relative to the competitive advantages of firms. Countries are geographic entities, but multinational firms have head-quarters in one country and produce in many countries. Thus the basis for comparative advantage for a country is its immobile factors; whereas the basis for a multinational is its firm specific advantages, which are mobile throughout the corporation, in conjunction with the immobile country-specific advantages of the various locations in which it produces.

The authors test the differences between national comparative advantage and MNE competitive advantage, using data on manufactured exports from the United States, Sweden and Japan over the 1965–89 period. In each case they compare exports by the countries with exports by multinationals headquartered in these countries.

They find that countries and their multinationals have different comparative advantages. First, MNE shares and country shares of world exports behaved differently over 1965–89: the export shares of the United States and Sweden fell while Japan's rose; export shares for Swedish and Japanese MNEs rose while the US MNEs share rose until 1985 and then declined. Blomström and Lipsey argue that multinationals can shift production out of high cost home countries to lower cost host countries, and thus protect their competitive advantage by moving offshore. This was true for both US and Swedish MNEs; the parent firm's export share fell while that of their offshore affiliates rose. In Japan after the appreciation of the yen in the mid-1980s this also happened with Japanese MNEs.

The authors then look at the impact of technological intensity on export shares and competitiveness. They find that the United States comparative advantage is shifting out of medium-tech to high-tech exports, while its comparative disadvantage in low-tech exports increased over the 1966–86 period. US multinationals, on the other hand, had much higher shares of world exports than did the United States as a whole, and the MNE share of high-tech exports rose over the period. One reason for this could be that MNEs are less sensitive to exchange rate changes than are all US firms, and the authors provide some evidence in support of this, particularly for high-tech products.

Blomström and Lipsey conclude that the competitiveness of US multinationals is due to different factors, or to the same factors in different degrees, than is the competitiveness of the US economy as a whole. This they attribute to the firm specific assets of US multinationals which are mobile and thus not part of the comparative advantage endowment of the United States. US competitiveness, they argue, depends on immobile factors and macroeconomic policies; firm competitiveness depends on firm specific assets and the country-specific advantages where MNE affiliates locate. Thus parent firms and their foreign affiliates may have differing sources of competitive advantage; firm specific assets are the same, but their country based advantages differ.

The implications of this research relate to our overall themes of MNE–state relations and the shift from confrontation to co-operation. Blomström and Lipsey conclude that 'the balance of power has shifted away from governments' as the flexibility of firms increases relative to nation-states. States are less free to impose regulations on MNEs and are more likely to engage in competition to attract inward FDI. A second implication is that measures to increase national comparative advantage should focus on immobile factors that are part of the national endowment, not on mobile advantages specific to multinationals. For example, subsidising R&D may increase the competitiveness of high-tech local firms, which then shift production offshore if other complementary assets for production are not available locally, raising the MNE's competitiveness but not overall country comparative advantage.

Robert Kudrle, 'No Entry: Sectoral Controls on Incoming Direct Investment in the Developed Countries'

Robert Kudrle's chapter focuses on the conflictual relations between states and multinationals, looking specifically at state regulations in the developed market economies which close or explicitly control IFDI in so-called key sectors. He asks, 'What are the commonalities and differences among the developed countries in their restricted sectors? What are the characteristics of those sectors most commonly restricted? What are likely future developments in international co-operation?'

Kudrle notes that several motivations for sectoral restrictions have been discussed in the literature. These include national security, infant industry protection, control of the national patrimony, and mercantilism. He contends that most protected sectors have nothing to do with national security; simple producer protection, as sought by vested interest groups, is the main reason why restricted sectors exist.

He reviews the statistical data on IFDI restrictions among the OECD countries and then narrows the data to six clusters: (1) banking, insurance and finance, (2) broadcasting, (3) post and telecommunications, (4) other public utilities and energy production, (5) transportation, and (6) land and natural resources. After reviewing each of these clusters, he concludes that national security is not an important reason for the existence of closed sectors. A few regulations, such as Canadian and Australian media controls, do appear to be generated by national autonomy motivations. On the other hand, most of the controls do relate to national prosperity grounds; however, since vested producer groups play important roles in policy formation it is hard to distinguish national from producer prosperity motivations. Even if the motivation is national prosperity, Kudrle notes that deadweight economic losses usually follow from such IFDI restrictions.

Kudrle's policy conclusions are provocative. He argues that unilateral pursuit of liberalising IFDI restrictions is unlikely to go very far since the benefits to vested interests are concentrated while the costs to consumers are diffuse. A GATT code on IFDI he also sees as unlikely given differing national attitudes towards FDI inflows, the complexity of IFDI policies and fears of free riding in the GATT. Bilateral reciprocity, however, is seen as 'fair' by many industries around the world and particularly so in the United States. Hence he concludes that sectoral reciprocity – 'I'll open my sectors if you open yours' – is the only feasible route for liberalising sectoral restrictions on inward FDI flows. Thus IFDI flows are most likely to be liberalised within regional trading blocs, as a result of agreements like the Canada–US Free Trade Agreement, the proposed North American Free Trade Agreement and EC 1992.

Louis Wells Jr and Alvin Wint, 'Marketing Strategies to Attract Foreign Investment'

Noting the new shift from confrontation to co-operation between multinationals and nation-states, the chapter by Wells and Wint focuses on government attempts to attract inward foreign direct investment and what makes some attempts successful and others failures. They ask: 'If states and MNEs are to co-operate what policies should state agencies adopt to attract IFDI? What policies work for first time investors? repeat investors?'

They note that states use three basic types of IFDI-attracting techniques: investment incentives, improvements to the general investment climate, and marketing techniques. This chapter focuses on the third strategy, marketing or investment promotion techniques. The purpose of investment promotion is 'to inform investors about a country's potential as an investment site, and to persuade them to set up operations in that country'.

During their research, Wells and Wint interviewed investment promotion agencies in ten countries: Britain, Ireland, Scotland, Canada, Costa Rica, Jamaica, Indonesia, Malaysia, Singapore and Thailand. They also interviewed managers from US multinationals about thirty investment decisions made in these ten countries. The interviews were used to determine what investment promotion techniques were used, and why, by the country agencies, and then to compare these results with the firms' views on what factors influenced their locational choices.

Wells and Wint found that agency marketing techniques have three short-run objectives: image building, investment service activities, and investment generating activities. The agencies tend to concentrate their promotional activities on either the first or third objective. Six of the ten agencies studied started with image building and then shifted to investment generation.

The authors argue that image building is an impersonal, informa-
tion-providing technique, whereas investment generation by necessity
involves direct contact between agency representatives and MNE
investors. From their interviews with US multinational managers,
Wells and Wint conclude that personal promotion techniques are most
useful in influencing firm investment decisions, particularly when the
investment is for export promotion reasons. They conclude that, where
all states are now attempting to attract inflows of FDI, governments
that want to be successful at attracting and expanding multinational
investment should view the marketing of a country as a type of
industrial marketing and use personal contacts with firms to encourage
the development of co-operative MNE–state relationships.

MAIN THEMES OF *MULTINATIONALS IN THE GLOBAL POLITICAL ECONOMY*

From the chapter outlines we can see at least five themes that are
carried throughout the book. The first theme is *the shift to more co-
operative MNE–state relations over the past decade*. How have they
changed? Why? Is this a permanent or temporary shift? The chapters
all conclude that relations between governments and firms are now less
confrontational and more co-operative than in the past. This theme is
explicitly drawn in Dunning's chapter, but also appears in the Vernon,
Eden, Rugman, Strange and Lall pieces. Dunning traces the direction
of this shift from the 1970s to the present, arguing that governments
are now more concerned with improving efficiency through reducing
transactions costs rather than with focusing on monopoly distortions.
More co-operative relations are due to states now seeing FDI as
complementary to domestic investment and as necessary for engineering long-run competitive advantage in the world economy. Strange
says that globalisation and technological changes have caused the
underlying production and finance structures to shift permanently in a
way that favours the MNE and requires more co-operative responses
from nation-states. Kaplinsky fleshes out Strange's argument with his
chapter on the shift from Fordism to Post-Fordism. While Lall and
Rugman both observe this trend, they have reservations. Rugman
notes that political fragmentation raises the need for firms to be
nationally responsive, while making it more difficult for states to
develop centralised co-operative policies. Lall wonders whether the

pendulum has swung too far and that MNE–state relations may be less co-operative in the future.

A second theme relates to the *theoretical implications of more co-operative multinational–state relations*. Eden in particular focuses on this topic, but Strange also looks at the MNE in the international relations literature. Both authors argue that insufficient attention has been paid by international political economy (IPE) and IR scholars to the MNE as a powerful actor and institution in the global economy. Both make suggestions for future research directions.

A third theme is *the policy implications for the firm of more co-operative MNE–state relations*. What should the MNE do? How should it strategically manage its assets in the globalised world of the 1990s? Rugman deals explicitly with the paradox facing the MNE: choosing a strategy that is globally efficient (that is, economics dominates) versus one that is nationally responsive (that is, politics dominates). Eden explains how this can affect multinational choices for locational decisions (such as product range, plant function, intra-firm trade, investment choices) as well as organisational choices (for example, ownership, degree of vertical and horizontal integration, types and number of strategic alliances). The borders of the firm are changing in both a geographic sense as firms have expanded their core networks of affiliates and do a larger percentage of their business outside the home country, and in a structural sense as they make alliances, mergers and various non-equity investments.

A fourth theme is *the policy implications for the nation-state of more co-operative MNE–state relations.* In terms of policy directions for the nation-state, most authors like Dunning, Rugman, Strange and Lall see a need for states to unilaterally intervene in a pro-market sense to make markets work more efficiently. However this means different things to different people. Dunning focuses on individual countries eradicating transactions costs due to endemic market failures, Strange argues for liberalising capital markets and key sectors, while Lall believes IFDI should continue to be regulated by LDCs as long as such regulation is accompanied by pro-market policies. Kaplinsky notes that LDCs face both opportunities and pitfalls in a Post-Fordist world as both the economics and politics of location are different. Developing countries close to large markets in the developed countries, like Mexico to the United States, may have more options than marginalised LDCs not located near a Triad member.

Kudrle draws our attention to the difficulties of unilaterally liberalising key sectors where vested interests hide behind the skirts of national security. He also notes that treatment of IFDI in the United States is moving in the opposite direction to most other countries, with regulations increasing rather than being liberalised. In terms of the potential benefits to a state if it does liberalise, Wells and Wint offer a caveat. They show that even if a country establishes an open door policy towards IFDI, the policy may not be successful; marketing a country has as many pitfalls as marketing products. Blomström and Lipsey offer an even more telling caveat: if the sources of comparative advantage for a firm and a country are not the same, some policies that appear to be pro-market may in fact make the firms more competitive while production and high valued jobs are transferred offshore. They implicitly suggest, similar to Robert Reich, that engineering country comparative advantage requires attention to nationally immobile factors rather than subsidising firms.

In terms of co-operative policy directions among nation-states, some authors like Vernon continue to support multilateral solutions to the interdependencies generated by the shifting borders of the firm and the nation-state. As states create preferential trading areas and Triadic economic 'hubs' emerge around which smaller countries cluster as the 'spokes' around a wheel, the need for at least regional solutions to the problems Vernon identified in 1971 (for example, double taxation, extraterritoriality, transfer pricing, intellectual property rights) grows stronger. Eden notes that there is some evidence, from the Canada–US Free Trade Agreement at least, that regional groupings may be able to move further in terms of extending the GATT-based rules on arm's length commodity trade to today's issues of services, technology transfer and intra-firm trade. Kudrle also argues that sectoral reciprocity is seen as fair by most countries so that bilateral negotiations may be able to liberalise sectors where unilateral and multilateral solutions are unlikely to work.

The last theme running through this book is the importance of Vernon's *Sovereignty at Bay*. The book not only drew attention to the importance of the multinational enterprise as an actor in the global economy, but also conceptualised MNE–state relations in a bargaining framework that continues to dominate theoretical and policy work in this area. All the chapters in this volume bear relation to the themes developed in this original work, and give testimony to its influence on current and potential scholarship in the field of multinationals in the global political economy.

2 Sovereignty at Bay: Twenty Years After

Raymond Vernon

Twenty years after the publication of *Sovereignty at Bay*, I feel justified in offering a solid kernel of advice to aspiring young authors: If you want to draw public attention to your opus, find an evocative title. But if you want readers to remember its contents, resist a title that carries only half the message.

Sovereignty at Bay did not foretell, as is commonly supposed, the decline of nation-states and the emergence of a world of stateless global corporations. My conviction two decades ago was 'that the manifest technical advantages of large enterprises and of strong governments will lead men in the future to insist on both', I saw two systems, therefore, each legitimated by popular consent, each potentially useful to the other, yet each containing features antagonistic to the other. A considerable literature already existed on how multinational enterprises and national governments had sometimes been enlisted to advance one another's goals, a literature ranging from the oil embargo on Japan which preceded that country's attack on Pearl Harbor to Mexico's pressure on the foreign subsidiaries of international automobile companies to increase Mexican exports. What seemed to be lacking in the literature, however, was a systematic account of the motivations that dominated the strategies of such enterprises, along with an exploration of the points of frictions between such networks and the governments of the countries in which the units of the network were located. The principal objectives of *Sovereignty at Bay*, therefore, were to fill in those lacunae.

The message of the book proved unappealing in many quarters. Managers of large multinational enterprises, juggling the sometimes irreconcilable demands of many different sovereigns, took no joy in being reminded of the difficulties of their assignments. The head of America's largest international bank, Walter Wriston, fulminated in public over academic scribblers who suggested that the interests of multinational enterprises might occasionally be at odds with those of the countries in which they operated.

19

The reception of the book in academia was hardly more friendly. Most economists, having been nurtured by the neoclassical paradigm of a world composed of distinct national economies, each with its separate endowment of land, labour and capital, saw research on the multinational enterprise as largely irrelevant to their discipline; if the operations of the multinational enterprise had to be addressed, it was sufficient to analyse them like any other international investment – for instance, like a Japanese insurance company's purchase of a US Treasury bond.

Political scientists were only a trifle less hostile to the emphasis on multinational enterprises as significant actors in international relations. True, a sometimes lurid literature of an earlier generation had occasionally assigned them a central role as political actors. More recently, some serious studies of their position in international affairs have briefly commanded the attention of specialists in political relations. But as a rule political scientists in the 1970s, having built their models of the political economy on the assumption of the absolute sovereignty of the nation-state, saw the multinational enterprise as an irritating anomaly to be wished away. More appropriate than *Sovereignty at Bay,* suggested one reviewer, might be a book entitled Multinationals at Bay.

As events developed in the middle 1970s, that reviewer's perception of the future seemed rapidly on the way to being realised. The extraordinary success of OPEC's member countries in quintupling the price of oil led many developing countries to believe that they had entered a new era, freed from the hegemony imposed by the multinational enterprises that produced and marketed their oil and minerals. Suddenly, developing countries were found expropriating foreign-owned enterprises by the hundreds. Although foreign-owned manufacturing enterprises were usually spared, those in oil, copper, and other raw materials industries suffered a high mortality rate.

In the years to follow, some developing countries would discover that the ownership of raw materials sources was no guarantee of profits, so long as there was no control of downstream markets as well. But one of the more immediate effects of the expropriations was to interest the governments of some of the advanced industrialised countries in defining the rights and obligations of multinational enterprises, and in reconciling the points of conflict between such enterprises and the governments with which they interacted.

Until that time, efforts to define the rights and obligations of multinational enterprises had been confined to a network of bilateral agreements between governments, whose very name – Treaties of Friendship, Commerce, and Navigation – suggested their anachronistic character. These had purportedly endowed such extensive rights on foreign-owned enterprises and their owners as to carry the seeds of their own impotency. That fact was already obvious in the 1950s and 1960s, as some developing countries began to show signs of hostility toward such enterprises. It became crystal clear in the 1970s, when developing countries took the bit in their teeth and began nationalising foreign properties in large numbers.

Accordingly, the Organisation for Economic Co-operation and Development (OECD), an organisation whose membership was confined to relatively rich industrialised countries, launched an ambitious effort in 1976 to define the rights and obligations of multinational enterprises in terms of some general principles. Even before the mid-1970s, the OECD had sponsored some efforts to clarify the rights and obligations of multinational enterprises; but these efforts had been confined to one or two narrow fields, including notably the reconciliation of national tax codes in their application to the income of foreign-owned subsidiaries. With the support of the multinational enterprises themselves, these efforts had borne fruit in the form of a network of bilateral tax treaties devoted to the objective. The new initiative, its sponsors hoped, would go much further, laying down a set of norms that eventually even the developing countries might be prepared to accept.

But the interest of the governments in the advanced industrialised countries in clarifying the rights and obligations of foreign-owned enterprises through multilateral agreements was short-lived. In 1982, the Mexican government defaulted on its international debt, and with that default developing countries lost their ready access to the international credit market. For the decade following, most developing countries proved eager to accept help from the developed world in almost any form in which such help was offered, including the investments of multinational enterprises.

Not surprisingly, then, business groups and governments in the advanced industrialised countries allowed the OECD code to languish. When developing countries, operating under United Nations (UN) auspices, sought to develop their own version of such a code, the project was never allowed to get beyond the talking stage. Instead, governments in the advanced industrialised countries reverted to the use of bilateral treaties to define the rights of multinational enterprises, notwithstanding that such treaties skirted all the difficult problems in the tensions between enterprises and governments and were demonstrably unhelpful in any serious dispute.

By the 1990s, the issue of reconciling the conflicts associated with the multinational enterprise might safely have been consigned to the 'inactive' file, were it not for the persistent tendency of large enterprises in most countries to create and extend their multinational networks all over the world. The latter 1980s saw a resumption of high growth rates in these networks. And in this wave of growth, in a reversal of earlier patterns, the United States proved to be the principal recipient country, attracting investments from the leading firms of Europe and Japan.

In this unfamiliar role, the US public predictably reacted very much as the French had reacted to the establishment of US-owned subsidiaries in the 1960s, and as Mexico, India and Brazil had reacted to such subsidiaries during most of the postwar period. Foreign-owned enterprises were seen in some US quarters as moles, agents of their home governments, to be used in some unspecified scenario of the future to compromise the interests of the United States. And enterprises owned by Japanese business interests were regarded as especially suspect.

That xenophobic streak has been manifest in many ways, including the unprecedented adoption in the United States of the Exon-Florio amendment to the 1988 trade act, an amendment that empowers the president to block some acquisitions by foreigners of US enterprises. Yet, despite such manifestations of acute unease on the part of the US public, my expectation is that governments in the advanced industrialised countries are unlikely to increase their restrictions on the growth and spread of multinational enterprises.

Gradually, almost imperceptibly, governments are becoming reconciled to a modified concept of sovereignty in the economic field. They are aware, for example, that without international co-operation none of them is any longer capable of ensuring the existence of secure banks or of policing their securities markets against fraud. They accept, however reluctantly, the need for some co-operation among central banks in the maintenance of an orderly foreign exchange market. Under the compelling power of the computer, they are creeping up to creating global standards in the various branches of telecommunications activity. National safety standards, health standards and environmental standards are beginning to converge, the process having been greatly accelerated by the European Community's 1992 exercise. In short, as governments respond to the functional problems that crop up in an increasingly crowded universe, they redefine the scope of the autonomy that sovereignty demands. And as the process goes on, the sovereignty at bay metaphor begins to lose what currency it once possessed.

Yet so far, one must agree, governments have been extraordinarily reluctant to tackle some of the most important points of friction that are associated with the operations of the multinational enterprise. One can sympathise with their reluctance, given the complexity of some of the problems. And the issues are not getting any easier as a result of the new wave of international alliances among enterprises, such as those among the giant producers of telephone equipment and aircraft parts. These alliances, by avoiding transfers of stock ownership, often complicate the process of defining rights and assessing obligations.

Yet the problems of jurisdictional conflict slowly build. Consider the basic question of taxation. By one means or another, enterprise managers must assign the global profits of any multinational enterprise to the various taxing jurisdictions in which the network's units do business. For some multinational enterprises, the allocation presents no serious problems. But for many, there is no escape from the managers making arbitrary decisions in any such allocation. When subsidiaries located in several different countries have collaborated in the sale of a big-ticket item, such as the sale of a supercomputer to a Brazilian buyer, it is not always clear in what tax jurisdiction the sale was consummated. When the parent's expenditures on behalf of all the units in the network, such as expenditures on research, are charged out to each of the subsidiaries, the allocation is inescapably based on arbitrary rules. When products and services that have no open market price are transferred between affiliates in a multinational network, such as made-to-order components or specialised technical services, the price used in the transfer can never be free of challenge in the absence of some agreed rule.

Consider, too, the demands that different governments make on the various units of multinational enterprises. Every government would like to see the units of the network in its jurisdiction export more and import less. The only available response for some multinational enterprises is to engage in an occult game of beggar-thy-neighbour by reshuffling the flows in their logistical networks, expanding their output and jobs in one country and shrinking them in another.

Beyond such obvious issues lies a thicket of other problems: how to generate the information required for governments, consumer groups, labour unions and other stakeholders that have a legitimate interest in the strategies of a multinational network operating on their national turf; how to deal with conflicts of national jurisdiction in such areas as antitrust and export controls; how to define the political rights and responsibilities of the foreign-owned subsidiary in the country whose laws created it, including its rights and responsibilities in relation to the national defence base; how to avoid the destructive effects of competition among governments to attract foreign-owned enterprises, including a kind of Gresham's law in such areas as pollution control and factory safety.

History offers plenty of evidence for the capacity of governments to live with acute ambiguity in their international relations over extended periods of time. It may well be, therefore, that governments will postpone indefinitely any serious effort at collaboration aimed at reducing the tensions associated with the operations of multinational enterprises. On a showing of hands, the enterprises themselves would probably choose indefinite postponement as their preferred course; like the King of Siam when invited to make treaties with the Great Powers, they may find themselves wondering if they might come out at the short end in such collaborative exercises.

Yet it would be folly on the part of enterprises or governments to assume that the endemic tensions associated with their relationships will go away. The communications revolution is inexorably intertwining national economies, confusing national identities and redefining the limits of national sovereignty. As governments try to apply unilateral responses to their emerging problems, they stand an excellent chance of damaging both their own national interests and the interests of the multinational enterprises on which they depend. The challenge is to find the multilateral approaches that can reduce the inescapable tensions to manageable proportions.

3 Bringing the Firm Back In: Multinationals in International Political Economy

Lorraine Eden

The state is based on the concepts of territoriality, loyalty, and exclusivity, and it possesses a monopoly of the legitimate use of force ... [T]he market is based on the concepts of functional integration, contractual relationships, and expanding interdependence of buyers and sellers ... The tension between these two fundamentally different ways of ordering human relationships has profoundly shaped the course of modern history and constitutes the crucial problem in the study of political economy (Gilpin, 1987, pp. 10–11).

INTRODUCTION

International political economy (IPE) is a focus of inquiry that seeks to explain international politico-economic relations and how they affect the global systems of production, exchange and distribution (Tooze, 1984, p. 12; Strange, 1988, p. 18). IPE sees the nation-state as the key actor in the global system, the organiser of the international political order. The state is treated as the alternative to the market which is seen as the organiser of economic relations. As the above quote shows, much of the IPE literature has concentrated on this conflict between 'states and markets'; indeed, Susan Strange has written a book with this very title.[1]

The concept of states versus markets is, however, flawed because the market is a structure, not an actor, and hence a poor counterpoint to the state. The appropriate counterpoint is the multinational enterprise

(MNE), the key nonstate actor dominating both domestic and international markets. The largest 600 MNEs now generate worldwide sales of over one billion dollars each and together produce one-quarter of world gross domestic product (UNCTC, 1988, ch. 1). The crucial problem in the study of political economy as we move into the twenty-first century is the tension between states and multinationals, not states and markets. It is time to bring the firm, i.e., the multinational enterprise, back into IPE.

Multinationals are studied in the IPE literature; however, their presence is often implicit rather than explicit, or segregated from other questions.[2] Some IPE perspectives devote more attention to multinationals than others (e.g., dependency versus regime theories). Indeed, the terms used by various authors to identify this international organisational structure (e.g., multinational enterprise (MNE), multinational corporation (MNC) and transnational corporation (TNC)) often reveal the perceptions of multinationals within different paradigms or disciplines.[3]

However identified, all IPE perspectives need to take account of the 'new style MNEs' of the 1990s in thinking about global issues and problems. These new style firms, or global corporations, operate with worldwide strategies, investments and sales, making them the chief vehicle for increasing interdependence among national economies.[4] IPE must come to terms with the globalisation of markets through multinational enterprises.

The purpose of this chapter is to further the process of 'bringing the firm back into IPE'. The chapter first reviews the treatment of multinationals in various strands of the literature, arguing that IPE traditionally focuses on five faces or images of the MNE: the product life cycle, sovereignty at bay, the law of uneven development, the obsolescing bargain, and the changing international division of labour. A review of these faces is followed by a summary of current thinking in the international business studies (IBS) literature on global multinationals, focusing on the Ownership–Location–Internalisation (OLI) paradigm, the international value chain, and strategic management of MNEs.[5] The last section of the chapter deals with implications of multinationals for the concept of states versus markets, and for the five faces multinationals traditionally assumed in IPE. The chapter concludes that a clearer focus on the MNE as an institutional actor with goals, strategies and structures is necessary for a better understanding of state–MNE relations in the 1990s.

FACES OF THE MULTINATIONAL ENTERPRISE IN IPE

Each of the major perspectives in IPE – liberalism, nationalism and Marxism – has a different view of the MNE (Frieden and Lake, 1987; Gill and Law, 1988, chs 3–7, 11; Gilpin, 1975, ch. 6; 1987, chs 2, 6; Heininger, 1986; Isaak, 1991, ch. 6; Leyton-Brown, 1990; Mckinley and Little, 1986, pp. 97–8, 130–36, 154; Spero, 1990, chs 4, 8; Strange, 1988, pp. 10, 74–87). The liberal perspective views multinationals as an integrating force in the world economy. Because MNEs transfer resources between countries according to comparative advantage, they are a force for progress, increasing wealth and lessening income inequalities between developed and developing countries. MNEs are seen by liberals as generally beneficial in their role as promoters of a more integrated world order, offsetting the mercantilist tendencies of nation-states. The nationalist and neomercantilist perspectives perceive MNEs as potential threats to the power of the state. Because MNEs respond to global profit motives, conflict between state goals and MNE goals is inevitable. MNEs need to be regulated, both by national governments and internationally, according to the nationalist perspective, to ensure that state autonomy and sovereignty are maintained. The important question is how to manage multinationals to ensure that they enhance domestic industrial capacity, national sovereignty and state security. Lastly, the Marxist critiques, particularly the Latin American dependency writings, view MNEs as oligopolistic transnational capitalists that systemically exploit and promote underdevelopment in the periphery and semiperiphery. MNEs act at the behest of their home states, enhancing imperialism and permanently creating global income inequalities. Radical theorists argue that MNEs make alliances with transnational elites such as domestic capitalists in the semiperiphery, but that such development is stunted because it remains dependent on relations with the core.

While IPE perspectives have different underlying views of the MNE, five faces or images are covered in all the paradigms and in the major IPE texts.[6] Three of these faces (the product life cycle, sovereignty at bay and the obsolescing bargain) were developed by Raymond Vernon (1966; 1971; 1977; 1979; 1981) the other two images (the law of uneven development and the international division of labour) by Stephen Hymer (1971; 1979). The first three faces of the MNE as outlined above fall within mainstream perspectives in IPE (liberal, nationalist); the latter faces within the radical IPE approach (Marxist). The first three faces take the world order as it exists and try to make the state–MNE relationship work more smoothly; they are thus exercises in problem-solving theory. The next two faces take an historical approach, appraising the changing role of MNEs and the need to change the existing world order, and are therefore exercises in critical theory.[7] Two of the faces (i.e., sovereignty at bay and the obsolescing bargain) explicitly focus on the conflict between multinationals and states, and therefore are more attentive to the MNE as an actor within markets than most of the IPE literature. A brief summary of the five faces of MNEs in IPE follows.

The Product Life Cycle Model

Products have a life cycle where they move from being new to mature to obsolete. New products need frequent product and process changes in their pre-paradigm stage. As a result the production process is unstandardised, labour intensive and high cost, and needs to take place close to consumers. As product design matures, production becomes more capital intensive. Eventually significant economies of scale are achieved through mass production of standardised products.

The product cycle model as developed by Vernon (1966) explains the rise of MNEs from particular home countries in terms of the life cycle of the manufactured goods these firms produce. New products, developed first in the US, were exported to Europe once product designs had stabilised. As the technology matured and foreign demand increased, US firms established branch plants to supply foreign demand and the profits from overseas production were used to generate new products. Vernon later revised the model to argue that foreign direct investment (FDI) was caused by the desire of oligopolistic MNEs to erect barriers to entry in foreign markets in order to maintain their market share (Vernon, 1971, pp. 65–112; 1977, pp. 89–101; 1979). In the later version, MNEs respond to local demands based on incomes and factor scarcities (e.g., energy in Japan). Once the oligopoly becomes mature, the members use economies of scale in production, marketing and research and development as entry barriers to new firms. The oligopolists match each other move for move, generating a bunching of FDI. Eventually the oligopoly becomes senescent, the barriers fail to deter entry and cost competitiveness becomes key to survival. In this phase, MNEs shift production to the lowest cost locations and export products back to the home countries.

The product cycle model has lost its significance with the end of the technological gap and the narrowing of per capita income differentials within the Triad (i.e., the US, Japan and the European Community). However, the model is still used to point out the essential market seeking character of FDI, the importance of technology in MNE activities, the flow of (albeit mature) technology from the parent firm to its subsidiaries, the rents that MNEs earn on overseas sales and production, and the substitutability between FDI and trade.

Sovereignty at Bay

The phrase 'sovereignty at bay' has become a metaphor for the eventual decline of nation-state in relation to MNEs that are above state control (Gilpin, 1975). However, this was not the message of the book. As Vernon wryly notes, 'practically every reader remembers the title of the book; but scarcely anyone will accurately recall its context ... the label (but not the contents) became generic' (Vernon, 1981, p. 247). The original argument was that MNEs were used by home governments to extend their jurisdictional reach beyond their territorial limits; the US in particular practised this extraterritoriality (Vernon, 1971, pp. 231–47). Host governments also attempted to restrain and direct foreign subsidiaries located within their borders. The conflict between the ·social goals of states and the profit goals of MNEs generated significant tensions that were exacerbated by the shrinkage in international space, the narrowing gap in consumer tastes and the higher levels of international trade and capital flows. Vernon argued that nation-states would have to take action to constrain MNEs, facing the inherent conflicts in their 'double personality'. This would involve sorting out the problems of overlapping jurisdictions, double taxation, and their innate global reach.

In a later assessment of the sovereignty at bay theory, Vernon concludes that the three assumptions underlying the theory remain accurate: (1) host states want the benefits FDI can bring; (2) the policies of foreign subsidiaries reflect the overall strategic interests of the MNE; and (3) MNEs can serve as a conduit through which one state attempts to affect other states. While the 1971 book failed to predict the vast wave of nationalisations in the 1970s by Least Developing Country (LDC) governments, the problem of multiple jurisdiction still remains, and in fact has worsened since the 'number of players and intensity of the game' have risen (Vernon, 1981).

The question of whether states or MNEs are 'at bay' remains unsettled. Vernon and Spar (1990, pp. 109–39) argue that, although the 1980s were a relatively peaceful period of MNE–state relations, the problem of overlapping jurisdictions and states' capacities to monitor and control MNEs still exist. As long as the United States insists on its right to regulate affiliates of US multinationals, Vernon and Spar foresee continued tensions. Moran (1985, p. 274), on the other hand, concludes from the case studies in his book that multinationals are at bay, not states. State demands on the firms within their borders are escalating, paralysing MNEs caught between competing jurisdictions.

The Obsolescing Bargaining

Kobrin (1987, p. 610) calls the obsolescing bargain model the 'currently accepted paradigm of Host Country–MNC relations in international political economy'. The model was developed by Vernon and has spawned an enormous literature.[8] These publications are among the best studies of MNEs in international political economy since they usually contain extensive analyses of particular industries, MNE global investment strategies, and the constraints these pose for state development policies.

The bargaining-power model explains the development of host country–MNE relations over time as a function of the goals, resources, and constraints of each party. The model assumes that: (1) each party possesses assets valuable to the other; (2) each party has the ability to withhold these assets, thus giving it potential bargaining power with regard to the other; (3) each party is constrained in its exercise of this power; (4) the party with the larger actual bargaining power gains a larger share of the benefits; and (5) the game is positive sum so that both parties can win absolutely, although only one can win in relative terms.

The key argument of the model is that MNE–host state relations are dynamic and evolve over time. Prior to the entry of the MNE, the host government is assumed to be in a weak bargaining position. Given the uncertainty of investing in a new country, and the number of options open to the MNE, the state must offer concessions in order to attract entry. However, once the investment has been made, bargaining power shifts towards the host state. Over time, the uncertainty dissipates; the MNE commits more and more immobile resources that can be used as hostages; and the host country becomes less dependent on the MNE for capital, technology and access to markets as the FDI resource package diffuses throughout the economy. Thus the host state is likely to insist on renegotiating the bargain to capture more of the benefits. The MNE must either keep the host country dependent on it for new technology, products or access to export markets, give in to state demands, or exit.

The obsolescing bargain model has been applied to many extractive (mining, petroleum) and manufacturing (autos, computers) industries. Kobrin (1987, pp. 634–7) concludes that manufacturing is not subject to the structurally based obsolescence of depletable resource industries. Where the foreign subsidiary is part of a globalised industry or where technology is rapidly changing, the bargain may not obsolesce, and so the model may be inappropriate. Moran, however, notes that competition among MNEs for host country markets can strengthen the position of LDC governments, and concludes more optimistically that LDC states can use FDI to improve their developmental prospects over time (Moran, 1985, pp. 264–9).

The Law of Uneven Development

The first of the critical (in Cox's sense) faces of the MNE is developed by Hymer who posits two laws of monopoly capitalism (Hymer, 1971; 1979; Radice, 1975). The first, the law of increasing firm size, documents the growth in size and complexity as the organisational structures of firms changed from local workshops to MNEs. He argued that MNEs create a spatial division of labour across the globe that corresponds to the vertical division of labour within the MNE. The corporate hierarchy becomes divided geographically into three divisions: top management in the largest core cities, white-collar co-ordination in smaller core cities, and blue-collar production distributed globally. As a result, the core becomes progressively more developed and the periphery less developed. This provides the second law, the law of uneven development. The oligopolistic behaviour of MNEs and their large size further exacerbates uneven development through tax avoidance, erosion of state power, and footloose production sites.

Hymer's uneven development argument is part of a broader dependency perspective that sees multinationals as the agent of external process that produce underdevelopment in the periphery.[9] One recent extension of Hymer's international class hierarchy is made by Cox who argues that as production and exchange became more internationalised in the 1970s, social forces mobilised and a transnational historic bloc emerged (Cox, 1981; 1987). The members of this bloc – MNEs, multinational banks and internationalist institutions – are linked by transnational forces and have a shared ideology. Whereas Hymer focuses on a three level pyramid of production, Cox sees world classes being formed with the highest world class being a managerial class made up of labour and capitalists who work in the transnational historic bloc.

The Changing International Division of Labour

The division of labour has been a subject of inquiry since Adam Smith first discussed the advantages of specialisation in a pin factory.[10] Throughout the twentieth century the primary method of production has been Fordism (Frobel *et al.*, 1978, pp. 843–58; Hoffman and Kaplinsky, 1988). The Fordist production process is based on the increasing division of tasks, the separation of skilled from unskilled labour, the mechanisation of skilled tasks, Taylorist methods of control, the assembly line and just-in-case inventories. Fordism is a capital intensive system, designed to achieve economies of scale through mass production of standardised products.

Hymer (1979) was the first to integrate the concept of the MNE with the concept of Fordist production to develop a theory of the international division of labour (IDL). The IDL had four components, according to Hymer: firm expansion (the law of increasing firm size), hierarchy (the creation of a world hierarchy of classes), class conflict (conflict between the international managerial class and domestic classes), and the internationalisation of production (the movement of capital abroad through foreign direct investment). Throughout the 1860–1970 period, MNEs went abroad to gain access to raw materials in the periphery, exporting these materials for processing in the core. This old international division of labour was perceived by both Marxist and *dependencia* scholars to be exploitative of the South.

In the 1970s, however, the type of FDI exported to the periphery states began to change. US multinationals, following the logic of the product cycle, began to search for cheaper labour sites and to move the production of mature technology products to developing countries. This new IDL, or NIDL, characterised the spread of FDI to the periphery from the early 1970s to the present. Asian and Latin American developing countries encouraged the inflow of this new type of foreign investment by setting up export processing zones with cheap, docile labour forces, tax incentives and minimal regulations

(Yuan and Eden, 1992). Most recently, the NIDL appears to be changing again (the new NIDL) as MNEs adopt knowledge intensive methods of production, reducing the labour and materials content of production processes and outputs. This shift, referred to as post-Fordism, systemofacture or lean production, is reflected in the adoption by MNEs of new information technology products and Japanese flexible production processes.

In summary, the IPE literature views MNEs as oligopolistic firms that control and organise production facilities in two or more countries. The firms are usually in manufacturing or resource industries, have parents headquartered in the US or Western Europe, and expand abroad through wholly-owned foreign affiliates. MNE relationships with their home countries are usually assumed to be amicable, whereas host country relationships are more adversarial. Developing countries are used by multinationals as sources of raw material and/or cheap labour inputs. FDI provides a package of capital, technology and management skills to host countries; however, FDI also brings a loss of sovereignty and the ability of home states to influence host development. In this writer's opinion, the political economy model that best captured host country–multinational relationships is the obsolescing bargain model. The analyst's view of the future of MNE–state relations depends on the IPE perspective that is adopted: there may be a sovereignty at bay world where MNEs dominate states, a mercantilist version where states dominate, or a dependency version where the periphery remains permanently dependent on the transnational capital from core states.

Let us now turn to the current thinking about global MNEs in the international business studies (IBS) literature and see how this literature differs from the five faces of the MNE in international political economy.

MULTINATIONALS IN INTERNATIONAL BUSINESS STUDIES

Within international business studies (IBS), research on multinationals falls into three time periods: the 1950s to mid-1970s, the mid-1970s to mid-1980s and the mid-1980s onwards (Dunning, 1990a). The focus of inquiry has shifted from a macro approach to FDI, to an examination of the firm as an institution, to a focus on the value adding activities of MNEs. Regardless of the focus, the perspectives all fall broadly within what IPE scholars would define as liberalism. All are exercises in problem solving and little attempt is made to examine MNEs from a critical perspective. While the work of neomarxists such as Hymer are known to IBS scholars, only contributions in a liberal context are carried over to IBS.[11] There are crossovers between IPE and IBS. Vernon's contributions are well known; the product cycle, sovereignty at bay and the obsolescing bargain are discussed in the IBS textbooks. Similarly, the obsolescing bargain is considered by IBS scholars, as well as by IPE scholars, to characterise host country–MNE relations. Most IPE scholars are aware of John Dunning's work on multinationals, and his explanation for the growth of MNEs, the OLI (ownership, location and internalisation) paradigm, is covered in several IPE texts (e.g., Gill and Law, 1988; Strange, 1988). The existence of research centres on MNEs (e.g., Vernon and his colleagues at Harvard and Dunning and his colleagues at the University of Reading), has facilitated interchange between scholars from different disciplines. The UN Centre on Transnational Corporations (UNCTC) has also encouraged this. Kindleberger's work on FDI and Chandler's work on the business history of MNEs are known to both groups.[12]

However, in spite of these crossovers it is clear that the IBS focus on multinationals differs from that of the IPE scholars, with IPE scholars generally taking the more critical view. In addition, the IPE literature, with the exception of recent work on the international division of labour, lags behind IBS research on global multinationals. The outline of current IBS research given below has not crossed over into mainstream IPE thinking on multinationals. The complexity of international value adding activities of MNEs in the 1990s and its implications for states and markets remain to be explored.

Explaining MNEs: The OLI Paradigm

International business studies has taken three approaches to the study of the MNE. Initially the IBS literature took a macro approach, examining issues such as the substitutability of FDI and international trade, the effects of FDI on host countries, the composition and location of FDI, and the US as the largest home country (Kindleberger, 1969; 1970). While various definitions of the MNE existed, the simplest was that MNEs were enterprises that owned and managed production establishments in more than one country. In the mid-1970s the focus shifted from looking at the act of FDI to examining the institution making the investments abroad.[13] The MNE is now seen as an institutional structure that co-ordinates activities across borders. While there are many individual theories about the MNE, the generally accepted paradigm containing the various theories for understanding the existence, patterns and growth of the MNE is the eclectic or OLI paradigm developed by John Dunning.[14]

The OLI paradigm argues that MNEs form and grow because they possess three sets of advantages relative to other firms. These advantages of ownership, locational and internalisation are sometimes referred to as the OLI tripod. All three sets of advantages must be taken into account simultaneously in order to explain the existence of multinationals and the reasons for their growth and success in certain sectors or countries. These advantages can also be used to analyse MNE decisions about locating, expanding or divesting abroad.[15]

Since the mid-1980s there has been another shift, this time to thinking about the international value adding or production activities of the MNE rather than the firm's institutional structure. This shift in focus to international production by MNEs has several motives. First, the work done by Michael Porter and other IBS scholars in the United States on strategic management of MNEs, along with new concepts such as the value chain (more on this below), have infiltrated the OLI model. Second, there has been an enormous increase, since the early 1980s, both in cross-border alliances between firms in the same industry within the Triad economies and in alternative contractual arrangements such as subcontracting in the LDCs. The focus on the firm as a single entity has therefore been broadened to examine clusters of firms and non-equity investment relationships.[16] Third, the increasing use by states of aggressive industrial policies in high-technology sectors designed to increase national competitiveness has focused attention on the role states can play in engineering long-run competitive advantage.[17] Fourth, the technological revolution that has been occurring as information technology and biotechnology transform production and distribution methods has generated more attention to cross-border technology, service and data flows.[18] Fifth, the move of Japanese firms from exporting to setting-up production plants in the United States and Europe has drawn attention to process technology changes (e.g., just-in-time, flexible automation) that are affecting the value adding strategies of MNEs (Eden, 1991; UNCTC, 1988; van Tulder and Junne, 1988). Sixth, the rapid rise of MNEs in services such as banking, business services and retailing has shifted attention away from manufacturing and natural resource multinationals and toward explaining international production of services. All of these factors have influenced the definition of an MNE in the international business studies literature. Dunning's new definition for a global MNE is:

> an orchestrator of production and transactions within a cluster, or network, of cross border internal and external relationships, which may or may not involve equity investment, but which are intended to serve its global interest (Dunning, 1988, p. 327).

These new style MNEs have ownership, locational and internalisation advantages which explain their growth and success in international markets.

Ownership Advantages

MNEs have ownership advantages on which they can earn rents in foreign locations and which allow MNEs to overcome the cost disadvantage of producing in foreign markets. These advantages are usually intangible, based either on knowledge or oligopoly, and can be transferred relatively costlessly within the MNE. Knowledge advantages include product and process innovations, marketing and management skills, patents, brand names, *etc.* whereas oligopolistic advantages include economies of scale and scope, and privileged access to various resources. Ownership advantages arise from one of three sources: (1) the firm's size and access to markets, resources and/or intangibles; (2) the firm's ability to co-ordinate complementary activities (e.g., manufacturing and distribution); and (3) the 'global scanning' ability, which allows MNEs to exploit differences between countries. These core competencies provide potential access to a wide variety of markets, contribute significantly to customer satisfaction, and are difficult to imitate (Prahalad and Hamel, 1990, pp. 78–91). However, they are not fixed for the firm; ownership advantages require identification and continuous investment to prevent their dissipation and/or obsolescence. The advantages can be lost if firms do not understand and invest sufficiently and effectively in their areas of competency. Some of the most recent work on MNEs is now turning to this problem, focusing on issues such as: (1) the core competencies of various MNEs in the same industrial sector and why they vary across countries;[19] (2) the underlying structures which states can provide to help generate successful firms;[20] (3) how technological advantages can be generated, appropriated and sustained over time;[21] (4) the role of entrepreneurial culture as an advantage;[22] and (5) whether firm-specific advantages are necessary to explain the existence of MNEs.[23]

Internalisation Advantages

Internalisation advantages arise from exploiting the differences among exogenous imperfections faced by MNEs in external markets. Exogenous imperfections are of two types. The first group are inherent to certain types of markets, arising, for example, from the public good aspect of knowledge, from uncertainty and from the existence of transactions costs in all external markets. Through using markets internal to the firm, the MNE can reduce uncertainty and transactions costs and generate knowledge more efficiently. The second type are state-generated imperfections (such as tariffs, foreign exchange controls and subsidies). State policies in the internalisation literature are considered as inefficient policies to be arbitraged by MNEs, implying that internalisation is a welfare improving activity. MNEs with global horizons are thus seen as efficient actors, offsetting the inefficient activities of states with their national horizons (a very different perspective from IPE scholars!). Internalisation theory therefore predicts that hierarchy (the vertically or horizontally integrated firm) is a better method of organising transactions than the market (trade between unrelated firms) whenever markets are imperfect. By replacing an external or missing external market with an internal, hierarchical control structure, the impact of market failures can be reduced.

Internalisation advantages can also be generated by exploiting oligopolistic rivalry among competing MNEs, when the firms themselves create or worsen market defects.[24] Oligopolistic imperfections include exertion of monopoly power, cross-subsidisation of markets and opportunistic exploitation of suppliers or buyers. IPE scholars have tended to emphasise endogenous imperfections created by MNEs as international oligopolists, starting with Hymer's laws of uneven development and increasing firm size. Most internalisation theorists, however, have de-emphasised this aspect, focusing on MNEs as efficient internalisers of market imperfections (Cantwell, 1990, p. 13; Rugman *et al.*, 1985, pp. 104–8). Some IBS scholars do take exception, arguing that internalisation is not just a passive response to market failure but also one of the rules of the game for firms trying to avoid risks by creating barriers to entry for competitors (Chesnais, 1988).

Internalisation helps prevent the dissipation of, and increase the rents from, the core competencies of the MNE. The early internalisation literature of the late 1970s and early 1980s assumed that it would be more profitable for MNEs to earn rents on their ownership

advantages and service foreign markets through wholly-owned subsidiaries than by exporting or licensing to foreign markets. More recent
work has extended the OLI model to other arrangements such as joint
ventures and subcontracting, and has shown that FDI is not always the
most effective choice for the MNE (Contractor and Lorange, 1988).
Firms face a wide range of options in contractual arrangement for
transacting goods, services and factors across borders. The range
extends from the polar case of markets – buying or selling to unrelated
firms at arm's length in external markets (this is considered low
control, but has a high risk of dissipation of ownership advantages)
– to the polar case of hierarchies – all transactions take place between
wholly-owned affiliates in an internal market where the firms are
related and not at arm's length (this is a high control, low risk
option).[25] There are a variety of contractual arrangement options in
between, offering varying amounts of control and risk to the MNE.
Internalisation theory predicts that MNEs compare the costs and
benefits of alternative modes and select the most profitable (Anderson
and Gatignon, 1986, pp. 1–26).

Contractual relationships within the MNE have varied historically.
Until the mid-1970s most MNEs preferred the wholly-owned subsidiary; more recently MNEs have increasingly moved to non-equity
contractual arrangements. State strategies for import substituting
industrialisation in the 1950s and 1960s encouraged MNEs to choose
the wholly-owned subsidiary as a vehicle for entry into developing
countries. However, the rise in host regulations and wave of nationalisations in the 1970s encouraged MNEs to switch to non-equity
investments. Low interest rates and easy bank loans also facilitated
this move. Non-conventional MNEs and new MNEs without ready
access to financial capital also often chose what we can call the foreign
minority investment (FMI) route in preference to FDI. The situation
changed in the early 1980s as real interest rates rose and bank lending
to LDCs dried up. Given the shortage of FDI inflows into developing
countries, many have been forced to liberalise their investment policies
to attract capital. Structural adjustment policies endorsed by the World
Bank and the International Monetary Fund are also encouraging this
policy change. While developing countries are now more willing to
allow inflows of FDI, multinationals have come to realise that foreign
minority investments have their own advantages. MNEs can earn rents
on their ownership advantages without owning or financing investments in developing countries by concentrating on supplying technology, marketing and management skills while the host country partner

puts up the equity capital and does the actual production. Thus more of the risk but also more of the potential gains are shifted to the host country. Oman notes that small or latecomer MNEs (e.g., from the four Asian tigers) use minority investment more than the FDI route, and that even the largest multinationals will use this strategy in protected or isolated markets (Oman, 1990).

Locational Advantages

The third advantage possessed by MNEs is their access to factors of production in foreign countries, that is, locational or country-specific advantages. Ownership advantages must be used in combination with immobile factors in foreign countries to induce foreign production. These country specific advantages determine which countries are hosts to MNE foreign production. Locational advantages can be broken into three categories: economic, social and political factors, all of which can be expected to change over time. Country risk analysis is used by MNEs and multinational banks to estimate the advantages of different locations. Economic advantages are based on a country's factor endowments of labour, capital, technology, management skills and natural resources. In addition, market size and transportation and communications can make a host location more or less economically attractive. Non-economic or social advantages include the psychic distance between countries in terms of language, culture, ethnicity, and business customs. Political advantages include general host government attitudes towards foreign MNEs and specific policies that affect FDI and production such as trade barriers and investment regulations. Foreign production is expected to move to countries that are geographically close and have similar incomes and tastes to the home country, and have good factor endowments and low factor costs.[26]

Dunning has recently argued that IBS scholars need to pay more attention to the role of locational advantages as underlying factors affecting the core competencies of the MNE (Dunning, 1990a). In fact, the impact of political factors on all three elements of the OLI tripod has been underestimated. The lack of coverage of MNEs in the IPE literature is matched by the lack of coverage of the state in international business.[27] Some work has been started in this area. Ostry focuses specifically on the political economy of policy-making in the United States, the European Community and Japan, looking at the role MNEs have played in the Uruguay Round of the GATT and in the development of national policies for high-technology industries (Ostry,

1990). Rugman and Verbeke (1990) examine the interactions between government trade policies and MNEs using a series of two-by-two matrices to characterise firm strategies.

The OLI paradigm traditionally has focused on the why, how and where questions: Why do firms go abroad? How do they choose modes of entry? Where do they go? The management of these firms once abroad has received less attention. In this regard, the American strategic management literature, based on the concept of the value chain, is an essential prerequisite to understanding the new style MNEs of the 1990s.

Strategic Management and the International Value Chain

The theory of strategic management was developed initially in the United States (Porter, 1980; 1986; 1987; 1990a; Doz, 1986; Bartlett and Ghoshal, 1989). Strategic management theorists model firms engaging in a range of activities called the value chain. The value chain consists of primary activities (functions involved in the physical creation of the product such as extraction, processing, assembly, distribution, sales and service) and support activities (functions that provide the infrastructure necessary to support the primary activities such as research and development, finance, marketing). Each firm must decide the shape and length of its value chain, i.e., the number of products it produces, the number of value adding activities in which it engages, and the number of geographical areas in which these activities take place. These decisions depend on the firm's overall management strategy. The choice of overall strategy for the MNE affects its choice of structure and location.

The international value chain concept recognises that MNEs have additional strategies that are not available to domestic firms. MNEs can locate stages of the value chain in different countries, or have several plants at the same stage of the value chain in different locations. MNEs can adopt differing positions depending on the country location and the position of the affiliate within the MNE. According to Porter global strategies for MNEs fall into one of four categories: global cost leadership or differentiation (selling a wide range of products globally); global segmentation (selling a narrow range of products worldwide or, alternatively, a wide range in a subset of countries); protected markets (seeking shelter from foreign competition markets are protected by host governments); and national responsiveness (developing products that meet local needs in particular countries) (Porter, 1986, pp. 46–9).

MNEs can adopt a wider range of strategies than can domestic firms by taking advantage of economic, political, geographic, social and cultural differences among countries (Doz, 1986; Negandhi and Savara, 1989).

The combination of the OLI paradigm and the value chain thus provides a simple explanation for the existence of vertically and horizontally integrated MNEs. A horizontally integrated MNE produces the same product or product line (i.e., at the same stage of the value chain) in two or more plants located in different countries. A basic motivation for horizontal integration is the additional rents in the foreign location that can be earned on the MNE's firm-specific assets. Usually horizontal integration occurs at the final assembly and sales stages for market-driven manufacturing MNEs as states demand nationally responsive MNEs or MNEs seek shelter behind protectionist barriers erected by states. A vertically integrated MNE, on the other hand, controls and co-ordinates two or more different value adding activities such as resource processing and manufacturing. The basic motivation for vertical integration is the avoidance of exogenous transactions and governmental costs associated with external markets. Uncertainty and incomplete futures markets combine to raise barriers to contract making between unrelated firms, particularly in natural resource industries and industries where quality control is essential (Casson, 1982; Porter, 1986; Grimwade, 1989). Government barriers can be avoided through such techniques as transfer pricing of intrafirm trade and financial flows, and leading and lagging of payments (Eden, 1985).

Managerial Structures of Global Multinationals

The managerial structure of a firm describes its executive lines of authority and responsibility, lines of communication, information flows and how they are channelled and processed (Robock and Simmonds, 1989). There are many kinds of international managerial structures available to MNEs.[28] In the 1970s most American multinationals followed nationally responsive or shelter strategies based on supplying products to segmented national markets. MNEs decentralised day-to-day operations to national subsidiaries, but used centralised service staffs for headquarters functions such as financial planning and policy-making (Drucker, 1988, pp. 45–63). Hymer's vision of the three-level pyramid of decision-making within the MNE was an accurate characterisation of the command and control structure of most MNEs.

Information technology is changing this, however (Grimwade, 1989, pp. 143–215). Telecommunications networks can be used to link MNE affiliates worldwide, providing centralised corporate data bases for use by both headquarters and affiliates. This improves centralised control by the parent firm and creates new information channels within the organisation. The parent firm can monitor foreign operations more effectively with fewer middle managers to analyse and relay information. In addition, information technology is homogenising tastes through increasing the mobility of consumers and information. International brand recognition (e.g., Sony, Gucci) is increasing. The advantages of moving to a global cost leadership or differentiation strategy are encouraging the integration of local and international planning. The more integrated the structure, the less the local autonomy of the affiliate and the greater the centralisation and co-ordination functions of the parent. MNEs are moving to organisational structures that more effectively promote global planning objectives. As a result, the tension between the national objectives of states, both home and host governments, and the global goals of MNEs is more likely to increase in the 1990s.

Locational Choices of Global Multinational

In the general OLI framework outlined above, the ownership advantages of the multinational enterprise give it advantages over domestic firms in going abroad. The internalisation advantages imply that the MNE can best profit from its advantages through a hierarchy of vertical and horizontal intra-firm equity and non-equity linkages. However, neither of these two factors determines where the MNE invests. Location, like structure, tends to follow strategy, i.e., the particular location selected by the MNE depends on the strategic role that the affiliate is to play within the multinational. MNEs go abroad for many reasons: gaining access to low-cost foreign inputs such as natural resources and labour, being close to foreign markets, earning rents on ownership advantages, and pre-empting competition by rival firms. The list can be reduced to three general categories that influence plant location: securing natural resources, reducing costs, and gaining access to foreign markets. Locational decisions determine initial FDI and subsequent trade patterns; both horizontal and vertical FDI have resulted in substantial growth in intra-firm trade flows in the post-war period.[29] Locational advantages are the key to determining which countries become host countries for the MNE, and depend on whether the purpose of the investment is resource seeking, cost reduction, or market access. In setting up a foreign plant, global MNEs can choose among several different types of locational structures. Given the basic purpose behind the investment, some structures are more likely than others. Since states often want to influence the nature of the foreign investments offered by an MNE, it is clearly crucial for states to know what the underlying purpose of the investment is. Strategies designed to encourage more local production of R&D may be useless if the foreign factory has been set up simply to take advantage of low labour costs. The various locational structures available to the MNE fall into three categories corresponding to the three strategies, resource seeking, cost reducing and market access. These are outlined below and illustrated in Figure 3.1.

Resource seeking strategic investments. *Extractors* secure natural resources essential to the production process. The key factor driving location is the need to be close to raw materials. *Processors* turn raw materials into fabricated materials through refineries, smelters and fabricators. If the weight-to-value ratio is high, economies of scale at the two stages similar, and foreign tariffs on processed imports low, extracting and processing may occur in the same plant.

Cost reducing strategic investments. *Offshores* use cheap local inputs such as low wage labour to produce components or assemble inputs which are then re-exported to the MNE for further assembly. Many investments in export processing zones are of this type. As wage rates rise, footloose offshores move from country to country searching for lower cost sites. *Source factories* provide access to low-cost inputs, but also carry responsibility for developing and producing specific components for the MNE. Sources are globally rationalised plants where the factory produces subcomponents for final assembly and sale elsewhere. These factories are tightly integrated into MNE networks since output is sold within the MNE.[30]

Market access strategic investments. *Importers* facilitate MNE sales in a host country by providing marketing, sales, service and warehousing facilities. Most Japanese early investments in Europe and North America were importer factories. *Local servers* are also designed to service local markets, but they normally assemble subcomponents for domestic sale (e.g., bottling plants, drug packaging). Where state regulations require MNEs to maintain a local presence, local servers are normally chosen as the choice of location. *Focused factories* are globally rationalised firms that produce one or two product lines in mass production runs for final sale in local and foreign markets, exchanging these product lines for those produced of other focused factories within the MNE family. They are relatively autonomous and nationally responsive units with some process technology facility.

Miniature replicas are plants that assemble and sell a full range of products, similar to the parent in the local market, generally due to a shelter strategy adopted by the MNE in response to host country trade barriers. Miniature replicas are likely to be costly, inefficient plants in domestic markets which are small. *Lead factories* are equal partners with the parent firm in developing new technology and products for global markets. Lead factories are placed in strategic locations within the Triad and are insiders in each of their major locations. *Outposts* are R&D intensive investments set up by MNEs from one of the Triad countries in the other Triad markets to source knowledge worldwide and to act as a window on technology developments. MNEs are now moving abroad to improve access to technology and share research and development costs with strategic partners such as universities, governments and rival firms. Programmes such as ESPRIT in Europe are encouraging the formation of outposts.

Figure 3.1 illustrates both the concept of the MNE's value chain and the range of strategic locational choices available to the firm. Each investment is placed in the appropriate part of the MNE's value chain depending on whether the general motivation for foreign production is resource seeking, cost reduction or market access. The higher the vertical placement, the greater the amount of technological innovation expected from the factory.

In summary, each MNE, depending on the length of its value chain and the nature of the industries in which it competes, consists of a set of foreign affiliates, strategically located according to their underlying resource, cost or market function. These affiliates are part of the firm's direct value chain if they are owned and controlled by the parent firm. They become part of the MNE's indirect value chain if the foreign factories are linked to the MNE through contractual arrangements or strategic alliances.

The choice of location strategy is partly dependent on the age of the affiliate (Ferdows, 1989). Firms may first go abroad by setting up extractors, offshores or importers. As the plant matures, a growth in functions is likely. Extractors may take on processing functions, offshores become sources, and importers become focused factories.

Figure 3.1 Locational strategies of multinationals

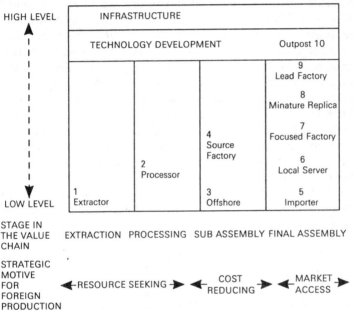

Locational factors can influence this upgrading. Cascading tariff structures in Triad countries deter offshore processing and assembly. In mature industries such as automobiles, global MNEs follow integrative strategies that are cost driven, using source factories to divide production among affiliates and subcontractors, assembling the final products locally to meet domestic content requirements. Government-controlled industries such as telecommunications and aircraft, on the other hand, tend to adopt more nationally responsive strategies, e.g., miniature replicas and focused factories (Doz, 1986).

The revolution in information technology (IT) is also affecting the locational choices of MNEs. Natural resources and unskilled labour are being eliminated as sources of competitive advantage, while highly skilled workers are in increased demand. Given the global mobility of capital, MNEs are moving to set up factories in Triad cities to gain access to new technology. With the short product life cycles that the IT revolution has partly generated, access to the latest technology becomes more important. Just as in the 1970s, the MNEs set up offshore factories to take advantage of cheap labour through source factories, in the 1990s MNEs are setting up outposts and lead plants to take advantage of cheaper and newer sources of knowledge (Mytelka, 1987). In the 1990s, knowledge-intensive production requires world-wide access to knowledge and this is replacing the search for cheap labour as the driving force behind MNE's foreign location strategies.

In summary, the field of international business studies is a rapidly growing area, where the focus of inquiry has shifted from explaining the act of FDI, to analysing the firm making the investments, to examining the international value adding activities of MNEs. The key ideas behind IBS are the OLI paradigm, the value chain and strategic management as tools explaining the organisational and locational structures of the new style MNEs of the 1990s. While there have been some cross-overs between IBS and IPE scholars, particularly the work of Raymond Vernon, the concepts of the OLI tripod and the international value chain and their implications for states and markets have been little discussed by IPE scholars. In this last section, we turn to bringing the firm back into IPE.

BRINGING THE FIRM BACK IN: MULTINATIONALS IN IPE

As outlined above, IBS scholars have tried to understand and explain the new style MNEs of the 1990s. They are giant firms, linked by equity and non-equity relations in clusters, engaged in two-way flows of products, investments and technology within the Triadic economies. What implications does the IBS literature have for the faces of the MNE portrayed in the IPE literature? First, we examine some implications for the concept of states versus markets, and then for the five faces of MNEs in the IPE literature.

Bringing the Firm Back In: MNEs, Markets and Globalisation

IPE scholars argue that increasing interdependence or globalisation in the 1980s has exacerbated the tension between states and markets as neomercantilistic states jockey for competitive advantages in a shrinking world. However, if one examines the concept of globalisation more closely, the dominance of multinationals in this process becomes clear.

The globalisation of markets has been well documented (Doz, 1986, ch. 6; Investment Canada, 1990; UNTC, 1988, Pt 1). It is a multifaceted phenomenon with at least three components. The first, *convergence*, refers to the trend within the Triad countries for the underlying production, financial and technology structures to approach a common average standard. For example, the technology gap between the United States and Europe and Japan has substantially lessened. Per capita income differentials have narrowed considerably. Although some would argue that the United States is still the global hegemon, it clearly acts in a multipolar world. Consumer tastes within the Triad countries have become more homogeneous, leading to the development of global markets and global products. OECD tariff rate differentials, both among countries and among product classifications, have narrowed, as have corporate tax differentials, further encouraging the globalisation of markets.

The second measure of globalisation, *synchronisation*, refers to the increasing macroeconomic tendency for the Triad economies to move in tandem, experiencing similar business cycle patterns. This has partly been hastened by the G-7 states agreeing after the Plaza Accord to synchronise their economies more closely through monetary, fiscal and exchange rate policies. Increasingly, states are also using similar microeconomic and structural policies, e.g., liberalisation, deregulation, privatisation, to encourage development and growth.

The third component, *interpenetration*, has received the most attention. It refers to the growing importance of trade, investment and technology flows, both inwards and outwards, within each domestic economy. Trade and investment flows have grown faster than world GDP consistently since the 1950s, and this trend has accelerated since the mid-1980s. Two-way or intra-industry flows dominate intra-OECD patterns (Erdlick, 1985; Grimwade, 1989, ch. 1; Investment Canada, 1990; OECD, 1987c; UNCTC, 1988).

A closer look at these three measures of globalisation, however, makes clear the importance of multinationals as the engineers or agents of this increasing interdependence. Statistics document the overwhelming importance of MNEs in today's markets (Investment Canada, 1991; OECD, 1987c; UNCTC, 1988). While only a portion of MNEs are truly global, the 500 largest account for about 80 per cent of all foreign production and have sales turnovers of at least $US100 billion (Dunning, 1988, p. 328). Investment, trade and technology flows within the Triad economies are increasingly dominated by MNEs with global strategies. Eighty per cent of MNE activities are now within Triad countries, mostly two-way flows in similar industries (Dunning, 1990a, pp. 24–5; Grimwade, 1989).

MNEs now dominate all the underlying structures of the global economy: production, finance, technology, security, energy and trade. Let us now turn to the five faces of MNEs in IPE and attempt to show how these faces need to be modified for the new style MNEs of the 1990s.

Bringing the Firm Back In: Faces of the MNE in IPE

The Product Life Cycle

The problems with the product cycle model of FDI are well known, with Vernon himself arguing that it has become obsolete (Vernon, 1977; 1979). The first version of the model suffers from several problems. In the first place, its single focus on the market seeking motive for FDI and inattention to the choices of foreign factories available to the MNE, is too limited. The model assumes that firms set up abroad once foreign demand is high enough to justify the additional costs of producing in a foreign location. However, as argued above, global MNEs have at least three motives for going abroad: resource seeking, cost reduction and market access. Second, the model assumes that MNEs produce technologically sophisticated goods initially developed in their home markets. MNEs are viewed as the creators of technology, transferring it outwards to foreign affiliates. However, with the elimination of the technological gap, the homogenisation of tastes and the ease of international communications among the Triad economies, global MNEs now have lead plants and outposts in the major Triad markets in order to take advantage of domestic technology. Thus the parent firm is importing products and technology from its foreign affiliate abroad in a reversal of the model's prediction. In addition, the product cycle model cannot explain where or when particular products are developed in the Triad, or why there are mutual cross investments by MNEs in each other's markets.[31] The focus on manufactured goods rather than services is also problematic. The increasing volume of trade and FDI in services such as banking and engineering services does not fit the model well.

Vernon's second product cycle model, where the firms are strategic rivals engaged in battles over global market share does, however, describe today's oligopolistic global MNEs. It is surprising that the second version of the model still receives less attention than the first.

Interpreted in a Triad–non-Triad framework where product cycles are short and research and development costs high, only the largest firms can afford to be technological leaders. Thus strategic alliances are increasingly being used in the Triad among global MNEs to exchange complementary technologies (Mytelka, 1987). These alliances strengthen the position of global MNEs versus other firms, and the position of Triad countries versus other nations. Note that the creation of knowledge through strategic alliances is not itself the problem; problems arise because global MNEs operate in oligopolistic world markets where ownership advantages can be exploited to earn oligopolistic rents. However, the second product cycle model argues that the oligopoly itself becomes mature and obsolescent. With the information technology revolution, even mature products are undergoing rejuvenation. It is hard to argue that markets are maturing, and with the wide range of products which global MNEs produce and sell, generalisations about obsolescence are hard to justify. Thus the utility of the product cycle model in explaining today's global MNEs is somewhat limited.

Sovereignty at Bay

This is the twentieth anniversary of Vernon's sovereignty at bay thesis. Vernon and Spar (1990) argue that the model, interpreted as conflicts between states and MNEs, remains an accurate portrayal of MNE–state relations. Extraterritoriality is still a problem as long as home countries such as the US maintain their rights to enforce domestic regulations on overseas affiliates of domestic MNEs. Two trends may check this somewhat. First, the trend to substitute foreign minority investments for FDI means that 'quasi-affiliates' may not be subject to the same home regulations. With the limits of the firm becoming less discernible (e.g., are cross licences, subcontracts and joint ventures part of the MNE?), it becomes more difficult for home and host states to enforce regulations such as transfer pricing and taxation rules. Second, the inflow of foreign investments is turning the United States into a host country. Its domestic policies for MNEs (antitrust, tax, national treatment, patent laws) were set up when the United States was a home country. With cross-cutting investments, US goals can be expected to change, albeit slowly, as foreign subsidiaries press for more favourable treatment in the United States.[32]

Vernon's three assumptions should also be modified to accommodate the global firms of the 1990s. First, states want economic, social and political benefits from the MNEs in their midst. With Triad countries being both home and host states simultaneously, pressures will be put on both domestic and foreign MNEs. Second, MNEs are caught between internal pressures for a globally integrative strategy and external pressures for a nationally responsive strategy. Different MNEs, depending on their structures and locational choices, will choose different mixes of integration and national responsiveness. Third, minority investments allow a more nationally responsive strategy while reducing the risks and costs involved in foreign production. Fourth, states are increasingly using domestic firms to further national competitiveness and strategic goals. Thus states, while now less attentive to the ownership of a particular plant, are demanding more contribution to national competitiveness.

An obvious extension, given the escalating demands for competitiveness by home states, is to apply the obsolescing bargain model in the home country–MNE situation. It is clear that Triad states are demanding more from the MNEs within their midst (Cohen, 1990, pp. 261–81; Ostry, 1990; Richardson, 1990, pp. 107–35). The usual assumption is that home states and MNEs have common interests. However, given the cross-hauling of investments and the intra-industry nature of trade and investment flows, it becomes difficult to identify global MNEs in terms of their ownership. Nationality may be becoming a technical or legal term without real meaning. When firms are allied to each other through webs of co-operative arrangements, it becomes difficult for them to identify which firms are rivals, and where their national allegiance lies. MNEs are likely to respond in different ways to pressures depending on the rapidity of change they face and the homogeneity of firms in the industry (Milner and Yoffie, 1989). Their willingness to co-operate with home country policies should vary depending on their value chains, their locational and organisational structures and the equity and non-equity arrangements to which they are tied.

While both MNEs and Triad states appear to have more options, both groups face increasing pressures: MNEs from other global rivals, states from domestic interest groups. Domestic regulation of MNEs has little effect unless accompanied by information exchanges among states. International regulations of MNEs remain toothless and non-binding. One possible regulatory regime might emerge from the Uruguay Round. If the General Agreement on Tariffs and Trade (GATT) is extended to cover more investment issues (intellectual property rights, trade related investment measures), there may emerge codes of conduct which like-minded states can sign, effectively creating an international club within which MNEs are regulated (Eden and Hampson, 1990). It is unlikely that developing countries would be willing to join such a club; however, with substantial two-way flows of investments, Triad states may find it to their mutual benefit to regulate MNE actions regionally. The inclusion of FDI measures within the Canada–US free trade agreement is one signal of this possible trend in state–MNE relations.

The Obsolescing Bargain

The theory of global MNEs adds further complications to the obsolescing bargain model. On the one hand, host states are faced with a shortage of savings, both domestic and international, with which to finance investments. Thus the need for inflows from MNEs has never been higher and host country bargaining power probably never less, particularly for the least developed countries in sub-Saharan Africa. In addition, with more MNEs following global strategies focused on knowledge intensive production, the country-specific advantages of many developing countries are not high enough to attract global MNEs. The declining resource and labour intensity of production and the need to locate upstream suppliers close to final production are causing some MNEs to shift production from the South to the North (Junne, 1987). Lastly, with well defined locational strategies, MNEs locate foreign plants in order to achieve particular purposes. The ability of host states to demand these affiliates move up the value chain and add more value locally becomes difficult. Host states need to understand the overall strategy of global MNEs and how their affiliates fit into this strategy. While the host state and domestic interest groups may see foreign firms as levers of change and adopt strategies that target particular MNE policies, affiliates vary in their will and capacity to respond.[33]

On the other hand, as MNEs delink foreign production from ownership, more firms that are willing to unbundle the FDI package – for a price. As Oman notes, while host countries may call such inflows foreign investments, in many cases the foreign firm is really engaged in exporting (e.g., turnkey plants) (Oman, 1990). When the MNE is a seller of access to its core competencies, the divergence of interests between the MNE and the host state is more profound since the two are effectively locked in a bilateral monopoly. As an investor, however, the MNE has a shared interest with the host state in maximising the overall profit on the project, even though they differ over the relative gains. Thus host LDCs now may face more options in terms of foreign inflows but minority investments may not be as attractive in the long-run.

The Law of Uneven Development

Hymer's concern with the inequity of the FDI process, its tendency to concentrate wealth and highly paid jobs in the North, remains a present concern of IPE scholars. The focus of international business studies on the MNE as an efficient international unit, arbitraging markets and state-generated imperfections, is not one for which critical IPE theorists have much sympathy. Although it should be stated that movement is occurring in both directions. IBS scholars are becoming more concerned about the oligopolistic tendencies of global MNEs; while IPE scholars are faced with the graduation of some Asian countries to income levels above certain members of the Triad, demonstrating that periphery states can engineer their own movement up the development ladder using foreign investment.[34]

The new-style MNEs of the 1990s, however, may play out the law of uneven development by widening the income gap between the richest and poorest countries. With FDI almost occurring totally within Triadic economies and strategic alliances among Triad MNEs producing most technology, the technology gap between the North and the poorest countries of the South (e.g., sub-Saharan Africa) is likely to widen. While lead plants may be located in more than one country (decentralising Hymer's top management jobs), they will only be found within the Triad. As the newly industrialising economies graduate to more capital and knowledge intensive production plants, the poorest LDCs may well be left with only resource seeking and cost reducing foreign investments. Without a more open trading order that encourages LDC exports of labour intensive manufactured products to the North and attracts MNE investments, uneven development – a wealthy core, fast-growing semiperiphery and stagnant periphery – may well continue.

The Changing International Division of Labour

It is on this face that IPE and IBS scholars are closest. Nevertheless, while both groups have focused on technological change, they have also had quite different concerns. IPE scholars, worried about the impact on developing countries, have generally taken a critical view of the worldwide sourcing strategies of MNEs and have also feared the movement of production from the South to the North under post-Fordism. Most IBS scholars, on the other hand, have been interested in the impact of technological change on cost savings and competitiveness for the Triad economies. Both groups agree, however, that the tendency to uneven development may be exacerbated by information technology.

Changes in product and process technology are encouraging the introduction of flexible manufacturing systems in manufacturing plants. Low-cost labour is no longer the focus of MNE worldwide sourcing. Sourcing new products and processes from other Triad partners is now key for the new-style MNEs. Offshores are therefore likely to be more footloose in the 1990s, moving back to the OECD countries. As some authors have argued, the newly industrialising economies may have difficulty retaining their share of MNE value added unless they increase their locational advantages.[35]

Nevertheless the impact of post-Fordism on service sector MNEs has been little studied by either group; nor has there been much examination of the effects on the various MNE locational strategies.[36] If MNEs secure natural resources through non-equity investments and are less attentive to labour costs, there are still a number of factors that will determine the choice of location. Further research on the impact of choices on LDCs is needed.

In conclusion, the new five faces of the MNE outlined above differ from the general ones presented in the IPE literature. The international business studies literature calls for more attention to the specificities of global MNEs: their goals, strategies, structures and locational patterns. The key characteristics of the new style MNEs are their clusters of equity and non-equity relationships, the increasing importance of access to foreign knowledge rather than resources or labour inputs, and their complicated patterns of international value chains. From the brief outline presented here, we conclude that more work on upgrading the five faces is necessary; IPE scholars need to 'move up the value chain' in their analyses of the multinational within IPE.

CONCLUSIONS

The purpose of this chapter was to examine the ways in which multinationals are treated within international political economy and to document the need to 'bring the firm back in'. The chapter reviewed the faces which multinationals assume in the IPE literature, contrasted these with the research on MNEs within international business studies, and made a first attempt to integrate the new developments in the business literature into IPE theory.

Just as Evans *et al.* (1985), assert that 'critique and prescription have tended to overshadow and constrain analysis' of the state within international relations, so too has the IPE literature boxed the MNE into the undifferentiated concept of the market. Critique and prescription within IPE have constrained analysis of the MNE. Whereas IPE takes a general approach that focuses on foreign direct investment as a process, the IBS literature has opened the box in order to understand the MNE as an institution and as an actor that engages in international productive activities. As markets have become increasingly globalised and dominated by large firms, a clearer focus on the MNE as an institutional actor with goals, strategies and structures is needed in the study of international political economy. MNEs are an increasingly dominant actor in both domestic and international markets and in international politics. Without a better understanding of this actor's goals, structures and institutional processes, our comprehension of the sources and uses of power in international political economy remains imprecise. More careful analyses of the causes and consequences of MNE responses to state actions can lead to a better understanding of the efficacy of state policies, and of state–MNE relations. Nuanced and sophisticated studies of the MNE are needed, both in terms of the underlying structures – production, finance, technology, security, trade, energy – of the global economy, and of the web of bargains that drive world efficiency, equity, development and growth. The crucial problem for the study of IPE as we move into the twenty-first century is the tension between states and multinationals, the two key actors in the global economy, not between states and markets. It is time to bring the firm – the MNE – back into international political economy.

Notes

An earlier version of this chapter was presented at the annual meetings of the International Studies Association in Vancouver, 19–24 March 1991, and was subsequently published in *Millennium: Journal of International Studies*, vol. 20, no. 2 (1991). Research assistance was provided by Jeremy Byatt and Susan Olsen. I would also like to thank Derek Baas, Michael Dolan, Richard Higgott, Barbara Jenkins, Christopher Maule, Maureen Molot, Lynn Mytelka, Angela Nembavlakis, Tony Porter, Yimin Qi, Susan Strange, Raymond Vernon, the students in my MNEs course, the outside referees and the editors of *Millennium* for helpful comments. I assume responsibility for any remaining errors and for the views expressed in this chapter.

1. Strange (1988). Strange has more recently argued that IPE must be looked at from the viewpoint of the MNE because multinationals exercise power and the aim of IPE is to look for sources and effects of power. See Strange (1991, pp. 40–9).
2. For example, the following books cover multinationals in one chapter (Spero devotes two) but pay little attention to MNEs outside these pages: Gill and Law (1988), Gilpin (1987), Isaak (1991), Spero (1990, 4th edn), McKinley and Little (1986), and Strange (1988). Each explicitly discuss MNEs or foreign direct investment over about 20 pages. I take these books as representative of current IPE texts.
3. For example, political scientists have historically used the term MNC. Economists tend to use MNE, arguing that all multinationals are enterprises but not all are incorporated. There may also be a regional bias, with American scholars using MNC and British scholars using MNE. UNCTAD and the UNCTC use the term TNC on the grounds that MNE or MNC implies multinational ownership whereas most multinationals are owned by residents of one country, according to Heininger (1986). The term MNF has been dropped since a multinational may consist of several firms. Fieldhouse (1986) documents the history of the term multinational corporation since its first use in 1960, arguing that the concept has been taken up and misused by a variety of interest groups.
4. The term new style MNEs is used by Dunning (1988, ch. 13); Ostry (1990) refers to them as global corporations.
5. In both cases page length must make our examination somewhat cursory; interested readers are directed to the bibliographies and summaries cited here and in these readings for more extensive treatments.
6. Kudrle (1985) argues that host countries see the multinational enterprise as having three faces: extension (as an extension of the home country), rival (as a rival to the host country), and resource (as a resource transfer package to the host country). All three of these faces fall within one of the five faces of MNEs of IPE: the obsolescing bargain model. In addition, the extension and rival faces are captured in the sovereignty at bay argument.
7. On the differences between problem solving and critical theory see Cox (1988, pp. 126–55).
8. Vernon (1971, pp. 46–59; 1977, pp. 151–73). See Moran (1985, ch. 1), the citations in its footnotes and the case studies for a review of the literature to the mid-1980s. See also Samuels (1990, Ch. 1 and the bibliography) for an update.
9. The arguments are not developed in detail here. See, for example, Amin (1976); and Newfarmer (1985).
10. See Caporaso (1987), Chapter 1, for a theoretical overview of the literature on the international division of labour. Casson (1986, Ch. 2) relates this literature to the economic theory of the vertically integrated MNE.

11. For example, Hymer's early work on the oligopolistic advantages of
    MNEs that allow them to cover the costs of foreigness in going abroad is
    a key component of the OLI paradigm outlined below. However, his later
    neomarxist writings are not discussed. *Dependencia* views are almost
    totally ignored.
12. Kindleberger (1969). See Chandler (1986; 1990). The early work on the
    MNE as an actor was developed in Stephen Hymer's 1960 doctoral
    dissertation, written under Charles Kindleberger. See Hymer, *The
    International Operations of National Firms: A Study of Direct Invest-
    ment* (PhD, Thesis, MIT; published by MIT Press under the same title in
    1976). Their works on oligopolistic motives for FDI are now known in
    IBS as the Hymer–Kindleberger approach.
13. Good summaries of the various theories can be found in Cantwell (1990),
    and Dunning (1988, chs 1, 2, 12). For a short summary see Dunning
    (1989a).
14. There are many references but several of the best known are gathered
    together in Dunning (1988). See also Dunning (1989a) for a concise
    summary of the development of the OLI model; Dunning (1989c, pp. 411–
    36) for current directions in IBS; Dunning (1990a) on globalisation,
    MNEs and competitiveness; Casson (1986, 1987) and Cantwell (1990).
15. Cantwell (1990) argues that the eclectic paradigm can be analysed at the
    macro (economy), meso (industry) or micro (firm) level. Dunning (1989a,
    pp. 68–9) shows how these advantages can vary at each level. For an
    application of this model to the pharmaceutical industry see Eden (1989).
16. Contractor and Lorange (1988) and Oman (1990) document the growing
    non-equity linkages among MNEs. Charles Kindleberger, 'The 'New'
    Multinationalization of Business', *ASEAN Economic Bulletin* (November
    1988), pp. 113–24, argues, however, that many of these so-called 'new
    forms of international business' are not new (e.g., joint ventures) and may
    not be efficiency based.
17. On international competitiveness strategies see Porter (1990a; 1990b,
    pp. 73–93), Ostry (1990) and Rugman and Verbeke (1990).
18. See Eden (1991a), UNCTC (1988), and van Tulder and Junne (1988) on
    information technology and its potential impacts on MNE organisational
    and locational structures.
19. See Giddy and Young (1982, pp. 55–78), on the ownership advantages of
    'nonconventional' MNEs. They argue that multinationals from LDCs
    and small countries tend to rely more heavily on non-equity joint
    ventures, do not have innovation based advantages, and tend to be
    imitators, fast followers or niche players. See also Oman (1990).
20. The key work initiating this study is Porter (1990a). A much shorter and
    more readable summary can be found in Porter (1990b). Porter argues
    that home states can generate sustainable competitive advantages in
    domestic firms by encouraging the development of a domestic competi-
    tiveness diamond. This diamond has four points: (1) factor conditions, (2)
    related and supporting industries, (3) demand conditions, and (4) firm
    strategy and industry structure.
21. At a micro level, Teece (1987, pp. 185–219) is most useful in identifying
    the roles of the initial innovator, the fast followers and the owners of

specialised and co-specialised assets. At a macro level, Cantwell (1989) develops a model of the MNE and technological competence.

22. Casson (1990) examines the economic and cultural determinants of firm performance, arguing that culture-specific transactions costs explain most performance differences. He examines the roles of the entrepreneur as a risk taker, problem solver and global scanner. Determinants of entrepreneurial culture are discussed, applied in case studies of the United States and Japan, and then extended to examine joint ventures and the impacts of MNEs on LDCs.

23. This last issue has caused some considerable internal debate among the British IBS scholars. See the summary in Cantwell (1990).

24. Dunning (1990a, p. 60) calls these internalisation advantages arising from properties structural market failure.

25. Markets versus hierarchies theory, referred to as the new institutional economics, was recently linked to IPE in Yarbrough and Yarbrough (1989, pp. 235–59). For an application of the theory of governance to international regimes, see Eden and Hampson (1990). It is interesting that the IPE literature sets up its polar cases as states versus markets, whereas the IBS literature uses markets versus hierarchies. In both sets of literature markets are the alternative to the primary unit of analysis.

26. Schneider and Frey (1985, pp. 161–75). Dunning (1988) divides locational advantages into environmental, systemic and policy factors. While the interpretations are somewhat similar, the triad of economic, social and political factors is easier to differentiate.

27. Dunning (1988) contains approximately 40 pages on the state and state policies. Just as the major IPE textbooks pay insufficient attention to the MNE, so do the major MNE textbooks provide too little study of the state. One recent exception is a new book on government-business relations by Behrman and Grosse (1990).

28. Business International (1988) identifies seven generic types: (1) the international division where one unit within the MNE is responsible for all international operations; (2) worldwide regional where the MNE's affiliates are divided into regional divisions; (3) national subsidiaries where each host country constitutes a division; (4) worldwide product divisions where the MNE is organised into several domestic businesses each of which is responsible for its own worldwide operations; (5) worldwide functional divisions based on major functions, e.g., administration, manufacturing, research and development; (6) matrix structures that focus on two characteristics (product function, region), providing a dual chain of command; and (7) mixed where the MNE combines two or more of the above structures. Business International concludes that the mixed and matrix structures, due to their synergistic properties, are likely to dominate MNE organisational structures in the 1990s. See also OECD (1987b).

29. For more discussion of these locational strategies in the context of technology and trade policy changes facing US multinationals with Canadian affiliates, see Eden (1991a). This paper adds an additional locational strategy (the world product mandate) which is not considered here due to its specific Canadian context.

30. Gary Gereffi, in 'International Subcontracting and Global Capitalism: Reshaping the Pacific Rim', presented at the PEWS conference on Pacific-Asia and the Future of the World System, University of Hawaii at Manoa, 28–30 March 1991, refers to offshores as 'export processors' and source factories as 'component suppliers', pp. 5–8.

31. The link to Porter's (1990a, b) diamond of competitive advantage may provide a clue; that is, sophisticated consumers and strong competitive rival firms in the home country can generate an explosion of new products. Thus, as Porter argues, individual countries may have a comparative advantage in particular industries such as Northern Italy in textiles. See also Erdlick (1985).

32. Milner (1988) and Milner and Yoffie (1989, pp. 239–72). One obvious example of this change is the Exon-Florio amendment which requires the Committee on Foreign Investment in the United States (CFIUS) to review large inward FDI projects for their national security effects. The CFIUS has been around for some time. Its functions have been and are likely to be increased, partly to monitor Japanese takeovers of US firms. Another interesting question arises as to whether Japanese and European states will attempt to apply extraterritoriality to affiliates in the United States.

33. Samuels (1990). Some optimism may be provided by Ferdows (1989) who argues that as subsidiaries mature they tend to adopt more technologically sophisticated functions within the MNE, e.g., offshores moving up to source factories. This is already happening in the Mexican *maquiladoras* where the old plants (offshores) tend to be simple, female dominated and labour intensive operations (e.g., in textiles) while the new plants (source factories) are more technology and capital intensive and operate with a higher proportion of male workers (e.g., in autos and advanced electronics assembly). See Gary Gereffi, 'Mexico's Maquiladoras Industries: What Is their Contribution to National Development and Transnational Integration in North America?', presented at the conference Facing North/Facing South: A Multidisciplinary Conference on Canadian–US–Mexican Relations, University of Calgary, 2–4 May 1991.

34. Blomström (1990), UNCTC, (1988) Joel Migdal's (1988) recent book *Strong Societies and Weak States: State–Society Relations and State Capacities in the Third World*, however, documents the difficulties governments in the Third World face in mobilising their resources for development purposes.

35. Junne (1987); Womack *et al.* (1990). Locational advantages can be increased through technological upgrading and/or trade linkages. For example, Womack *et al.*, see small sized auto plants moving to Mexico in response to a North American Free Trade Agreement. See also Eden (1991a).

36. Lavalin, a Canadian engineering MNE, in the mid-1980s shifted its drafting work from Canada to India where unit labour costs were lower. With the introduction of CAD-CAM in Canada, the MNE recently shifted the drafting work back to Canada. This example demonstrates the importance of technological infrastructure for both manufacturing and services in developing countries.

4 Governments and Multinational Enterprises: From Confrontation to Co-operation?

John H. Dunning

INTRODUCTION

There have been many studies of the ways in which governments[1] may directly affect the activities of multinational enterprises (MNEs).[2] Few, however, have attempted to analyse the extent to which outward or inward direct investment – through its effects on the economics of investing or recipient countries – has led governments to modify their existing economic objectives and strategies; or, indeed, of the way in which governments have sought to influence the level and pattern of MNE activity, as part of a package of policy instruments designed to advance a broader set of economic and/or social goals.

It is the purpose of this chapter to highlight some features of the systemic interaction between government and foreign direct investment (FDI) over the past three decades or so; and, to speculate a little on its likely direction in the foreseeable future. By systemic interaction, we mean the interface between the global strategies of MNEs designed to advance corporate profitability and growth, and the strategies of national governments intended to promote the economic and social welfare of their citizens.

There are three main tenets of this chapter. The first is that for most countries, and until very recently, the actions of governments to influence the value added activities of MNEs have rarely been explicitly related to their wider political strategies. This was primarily because, either such activities were perceived to be relatively insignificant (for example, in the case of the US), or because governments believed that they could absorb the consequences of such activities without making any adjustments to their existing modes of conduct (as in the case of several developing countries). A combination of the growing importance of MNE investment in, or by, the economies of most countries, and a realisation (often brought about by hard experience) that, by integrating the use of foreign and domestic resources, FDI inevitably affects the efficacy and flexibility of government actions, has considerably modified this viewpoint.

The second is that governments are being forced to look at the competitive advantage of the resources under their jurisdiction as a national economic objective in *its own right*; and it is here, particularly, that both inward and outward investment are likely to have a pronounced impact. This change in emphasis has occurred for two reasons. The first is the convergence in the economic structure of the leading industrialised economies. Rather than trading different goods and services with each other, countries are increasingly competing with each other in the supply of similar goods and services. Second, the liberalisation of (some) cross-border markets and the increased mobility of resources and capabilities, brought about by lower transportation costs and communication advances, has enabled companies to be more footloose in the location of their value added activities. While this has sometimes led to increasing competition for inward investment – within the European Community (EC) the UK competes with Belgium and France, just as do Maryland, New Jersey, and California within the US – the formation of regional economic blocs, together with some inter-regional protectionism, has led several MNEs to seek a presence, and particularly an innovatory related presence, in each of these territories to protect or advance their global competitive postures.

Our third tenet is that the way in which governments are affecting the resource allocative decisions of MNEs is increasingly by actions taken to advance *other* economic or social goals, rather than by those directed specifically at these companies. Moreover, governments (whether deliberately or not) increasingly are affecting the behaviour of MNEs through their impact on *transaction* costs of organising economic activity, rather than on the direct costs of producing goods and services. Since this is a critical tenet in our analysis and is frequently misunderstood by governments, we propose to explore its implications in more detail in the following section.

THE CONCEPT OF TRANSACTION COSTS

Let us define two kinds of costs incurred in the supply of goods and services, namely production and transaction costs. We define production costs as those costs which have to be incurred to supply a given quantity of goods or services *in the absence of market failure in intermediate product and factor markets*. Essentially, these costs represent the opportunity costs of the resources used, i.e., the price paid for the inputs multiplied by the number of units of each used to produce a given output. In a perfectly competitive market, all firms are assumed to optimise both the combination of inputs needed to produce a given output,[3] and maximise the value-added from any given combination of inputs. In this situation, *private* transaction costs are assumed to be zero, i.e., the market, as an organisational mechanism, is assumed to be a costless mechanism. However, to create and sustain efficient markets, there are always some set-up and running costs which have to be borne by society. These include a legal system designed to ensure that the rights and responsibilities of buyers and sellers are protected, and an insurance industry, the function of which is to spread the risks of individual market transactions over a larger number of such transactors.

Now, let us assume some kind of market failure or imperfection is introduced. Such a failure may occur for two reasons. First it may brought about by the anti-competitive strategies of participants in the market, or by governments intervening in the market to achieve objectives which the market is unable to achieve. This behaviour gives rise to *structural market distortions*. Second, markets may fail because the conditions of demand or supply underlying a particular transaction are such that the market cannot fulfil the tasks ideally required of it. We shall call this failure *endemic or intrinsic market failure*. Both kinds of market imperfections raise supply price above the opportunity costs of the resources used, that is, they result in positive transaction costs.

Let us now give some illustrations. The literature identifies a variety of *structural market distortions*, but the common feature of each is that they confer some degree of monopoly power on the part of the sellers or factor services or intermediate products.[4] The *origin* of this power might be a reduced number of rival firms, or some barrier to market contestability, or the ability of the seller to differentiate his product from that of his competitors.[5] The *outcome* of this power may take various forms, including the charging of a monopolistic price, a reduction or variability in the quality of output, irregularities in the supply of inputs, and increased negotiating costs over employee compensation. Sometimes these market deficiencies show themselves *directly* to the supplying firms in the form of higher input costs; and sometimes *indirectly* through increases in transaction costs associated with the acquisition or utilisation of factor services or intermediate products.

Endemic transaction costs stem from five main kinds of market failure. First, wherever there is uncertainty (e.g., uninsurable risk) associated with the supply or, demand for, goods and services, a simple Pareto optimum condition can no longer exist. Uncertainty is an activity related transaction cost, which may affect a firm's revenue as well as its cost expectations. These costs include the uncertainty over future prices or qualities of inputs, of future demand conditions, and of the behaviour of competitors (Vernon, 1983).

Second, it is assumed that the costs and benefits of markets are borne and received solely by the participants in the market. By itself, the market mechanism is not designed to cope with the consequences of a particular transaction to other economic entities, or to society at large, i.e., market externalities. Where such costs or benefits do arise, it follows that societal costs and benefits of transactions may be different from those incurred or gained by the participants to the exchange.

Third, in perfect markets, it is assumed that all firms can reach their optimum, i.e., least average production costs, where the elasticity of demand for the product being produced is still infinite. Such a situation makes implicit assumptions about the relation between the firm's production capabilities and the size of the market for the product it is supplying. However, in practice, it may well be that the optimum size of output cannot be reached without it becoming sufficiently large to influence market prices.

Fourth, and related to the third condition, in the case of some goods, the marginal cost of production is very low, or even zero, once the good is actually produced; but the start-up or fixed costs are extremely high. This suggests that, *de facto*, the good takes on the characteristics of a public good.

Fifth, perfect markets are assumed to adjust easily, and without cost, to changes in the conditions of demand or supply for the good or service being transferred. In practice, however, there are many markets – notably the market for some kinds of labour and capital goods – in which rigidities of one kind or another inhibit the optimal operation of market forces and sometimes where there are externalities, that of social efficiency as well.

The literature has classified the nature of transaction costs in various ways. Essentially, they arise from the *costs of organising relationships over and above that which have to be incurred in a perfect market.* The costs may be both endogenous and exogenous to firms. Both kinds of costs may vary between *countries, sectors of activity and firms.* Both kind of costs may also contain elements of both structural and endemic market failure.

The transaction costs of endemic market failure will vary according to how economic activity, or changes in that activity, are organised, and the incentives facing firms to minimise such costs. Much of the literature has concerned itself with costs and benefits of using markets or hierarchies as modes of transactions. While not disputing the legitimacy of this approach, it is equally possible to look at the costs and benefits of alternative ways of organising value-added activities. For example, where one firm acquires another firm to exploit the economies of scale or scope, although this is a market replacing activity, it also results in a different organisation of production (i.e., one firm produces what was previously produced by two firms). The question of how production is optimally organised is, then, no less relevant than how transactions are optimally organised.

We have suggested that transaction costs reflect the degree and form of market failure. A perfect market would cause production to be optimally organised. Production in imperfect markets may or may be optimally organised depending upon the nature of the imperfections. Structural market distortions usually result in sub-optimal resource allocation and higher transaction costs for at least some participants in the market. Firms, however, might respond to endemic market failure in a beneficial way by reorganising production so as to lower transaction costs.

In practice, both markets and hierarchies – indeed the private enterprise system itself – are constrained in their ability to minimise transaction and production costs by the political and institutional framework, and the economic and social milieu within which they operate. It is, however, important to distinguish between the kind of internalisation of markets by firms, which is designed to advance or exploit monopoly power, and that intended to promote a more efficient allocation of resources (Teece, 1985, pp. 21–45).

So much for the reasons for endemic market failure, which might cause production and transaction costs to be higher than is socially desirable; and which might justify some kind of action by governments, on behalf of society, to try and reduce these costs. But, it is important to observe that the kind of intervention is very different from that required to remove or reduce structural market distortions; or that in which the state itself believes that planning is a superior organisational mechanism to the market. The kind of interventionism to reduce endemic transaction costs is essentially pro-market and symbiotic with the goals of the firms. It is co-operative and complementary to the actions to the market rather than combative or substitutable. Furthermore, it essentially concerns itself with efficiency rather than distributional questions. Far from forcing firms to behave contrary to their own interests, it helps them to improve their economic performance and to behave as they would if markets were perfect.

In this chapter, we shall be primarily concerned with the organisation of resource allocation to achieve economic objectives. With the risk of oversimplifying a quite complex issue, our theme is that over the past thirty years, the interaction between governments (and particularly governments in advanced industrial countries) and MNEs has changed from being one primarily of conflict arising from the perceived differences in the objectives of the two parties, to being one of co-operation to achieve mutually compatible goals. In the first case, governments intervened (and, or course, still do) to reduce the (perceived) structural distorting consequences of MNE activity. To the MNEs themselves the frequent perception was that governments, by their inappropriate interventionist policies, were more likely to exacerbate rather than cure market failure, and to inhibit rather than enhance the welfare creating effects of FDI.

In the second scenario, governments are increasingly viewing MNEs as a means by which they can advance the efficiency of their own resource usage, and sustain or improve their living standards *vis-à-vis* those of their major foreign competitors. This will occur when outbound direct investment (relative to some other allocation of resources) advances the innovatory capacity and the efficiency of resource allocation of the investing country, and when inbound direct investment increases the innovatory capacity and competitiveness of the resources of the recipient economy. In this scenario, governments and MNEs are seen to co-operate, rather than compete, with each other to promote their respective goals.

POLICIES AFFECTING MNES: 1950–1980

With the above analysis in mind, let us now consider the changing role of governments as they have interacted with MNEs. We shall consider just two periods, namely 1950 to (approximately) 1980 and 1980 to 1990. The next section will then speculate on the possible future direction of the interaction between governments and MNEs.

For the three decades up to 1980, and for most, but not all countries, inward and outward direct investment were treated by policy-makers as two separate and unrelated economic phenomena. In discussing government actions taken, either to influence, or as a result of, these two kinds of MNE activity, a distinction might usefully be drawn between (a) those specifically designed to affect the behaviour of foreign direct investors and their affiliates and (b) those intended to affect the general economic conditions within which both domestic and foreign firms operate. Examples of the former include investment incentives and regulations, performance requirements and controls on capital outflow, and dividend remissions. Examples of the latter include modifications in development, trade, industrial, innovatory or macroeconomic policies, which either influence the locational attractions of countries to both domestic and foreign investors, or the ability of their domestic firms to become MNEs, or increase the share of global markets.

INWARD DIRECT INVESTMENT

While it is difficult to generalise about the actions of host governments towards, or as a result of, inward direct investment, for most of the three decades prior to 1980, it is possible to make two assertions. The first is that, in almost all cases, such actions were directed towards maximising the benefits and minimising the costs of inward direct investment, given the existing political system and economic strategies pursued by these same governments. The philosophy seemed to be that, if the net benefits were not as high as governments perceived they could (or should) be, this reflected the inefficient or anti-competitive behaviour of the foreign investors, rather than an inefficient or inappropriate economic system or set of policy instruments which the host governments were either unable or unwilling to modify.

The second assertion is that, apart from in the case of a few East Asian economies, actions taken to affect the level and structure of inbound direct investment and the behaviour of foreign affiliates were rarely part of a systemic economic strategy of governments. Usually, action was directed towards achieving a particular set of objectives, with little knowledge or understanding of how MNE activity might impact on this goal; or, indeed, of how the actions of governments might, themselves, affect the unique contribution of inward direct investment. Only in the case of Japan and later of Korea, and, to a lesser extent, of Singapore and Taiwan, did governments seek to incorporate inward investment into their broader economic planning. One of the consequences of this partial and fragmented approach was that the governance costs were higher than they would otherwise have been – including the devising, administration, and monitoring of inward investment policy *per se*.

Over the years, an extensive documentation has been amassed on the various strategies and policies pursued by host governments towards inward direct investment, and on the negotiations concluded with MNEs in a variety of sectors.[6] *Inter alia*, a reading of these studies reveals that the laws, regulations and policies towards MNEs have been modified frequently over the last three decades, even by the same country. There has been an iterative learning process, both by MNEs of the economic conditions in host countries and of the ideologies and expectations of their governments, and by the latter of the costs and benefits of different kinds of MNE activity. By the 1980s, except in the case of the poorest countries, most administrations had compiled fairly sophisticated regulations and requirements affecting foreign investors; and most too, offered a medley of incentives and controls that they considered best suited their particular needs. In addition, by drawing on the data, advice and training facilities of such international agencies as the European Investment Bank (EIB), United Nations Centre for Transnational Corporations (UNCTC), and the Foreign Investment Advisory Service of the International Finance Corporation (IFC); and gleaning from the experience of other countries, governments have gradually learned to modify and refine their inward investment policies with respect to changes in environmental conditions, their own macro-management and technological capacity, and to the new opportunities opening up for MNEs.

We have suggested that most actions by government to influence inward direct investment, in the period until the mid-1970s, were intended to achieve two main objectives. The first was to remove, or redress, the adverse effects of the behaviour of MNEs or their affiliates, that were perceived to result from their economic power. Examples include restrictions over sourcing inputs and destination of exports by subsidiaries imposed by parent companies, the transfer of inappropriate technology, transfer pricing abuses, and so on. The second was to promote domestic economic policies which, themselves, were designed to modify the shortcomings of cross-border markets. While, in some cases (e.g., Japan) these were justified in so far as they helped to facilitate long-term comparative advantage; in others, and especially in developing countries pursuing import substitution policies (e.g., India), the result was simply to distort (or further distort) prices and make for a less efficient allocation of resources.

We have mentioned that government action towards inward direct investment until the early 1970s was often dependent on the administration in power. In the latter part of the decade, however, a series of events occurred which caused a shift in the perceptions and actions of most governments. Some of these, such as the world recession following the two oil price hikes, which caused governments to reappraise the costs and benefits of inward investment, could well be of a cyclical nature. Likewise, it is too early to judge whether the contemporary disenchantment with socialist economic regimes and the liberalisation and deregulation of many markets are lasting phenomena. Each of these events has, however, fostered the belief by governments that MNEs, far from distorting internal market structures, may help countries to 'tap into' the international division of labour; and to question the ability of central planning to allocate resources more efficiently than the market.

But, perhaps the most far-reaching and, we believe, irreversible change affecting host government attitudes and policies towards inward investment, has been the tremendous technological advances of the last two decades. These have brought about widespread repercussions both on the demand for and supply of particular resources and capabilities, and on the organisation of economic activity. In turn, these effects have widened the options open to firms in the location of their value-adding activities, as well as altered the significance of many of the parameters affecting their locational decisions.

Together with the rapid growth of some industrialising economies, particularly in East Asia, these events have had three results. First, they have generally lessened the desire and the ability of both governments and MNEs to engage in practices and policies which add to structural market failure. Second, they have increased the bargaining power of MNEs relative to the governments of many host countries. But, third, as the next section will show in more detail, the technological changes have caused a reappraisal by governments of their attitudes towards the internationalisation of value-added activities.

OUTWARD DIRECT INVESTMENT

To begin with, we would reiterate the point made earlier, that in the 1960s and 1970s, the attitudes and actions of most governments towards the foreign activities of their own MNEs were totally divorced from those towards inward investment by foreign MNEs. In some cases, different government departments (or sections of the same department) were responsible for the collection and analysis of data outward and inward investment, and/or for the formulation and implementation of policies towards it.

In the two decades up to 1980, the US, UK, West Germany, Japan and France were the major outward investors, although the relative significance of foreign investment to some smaller developed countries, e.g., Switzerland, Netherlands, Belgium, and Sweden, was even greater.[7] Nevertheless, only in the UK, the US and Japan was there any kind of coherent policy towards outbound MNE activity.

In the former two cases there were four points of concern. The first was to do with the comparative rates of return on foreign and domestic investment. Here the hypothesis was that, since the former represents mainly the profits earned by companies, net of tax on capital invested, while the latter represented the total value added by such investment, gross of the tax, there was a bias against outward investment. If correct, this hypothesis had certain implications for tax policies.

The second disquiet related to the balance-of-payments consequences of foreign production; the third to its employment effects, particularly in stagnant and labour-intensive sectors; and the fourth to its possible erosion of the technological capacity of the home country. Other anxieties, such as the impact of foreign investment on industrial structure and anti-trust policy, were also voiced in the 1970s by economists (Musgrave, 1975; Bergsten *et al.*, 1978).

The implicit assumption underlying most concerns by home governments was that foreign and domestic investment were substitutable for each other, and that because of the loss of taxation to the home country, the social rate of return on foreign investment was normally less than the private rate of return. It was not surprising, then, that attention was primarily focused on export substituting, rather than on resource based, investment, although, later in the 1970s, the growing participation of MNEs in foreign export processing zones further added to the vexation of labour unions in capital exporting countries. Rarely, outside the resource based sectors, was outbound investment perceived to be complementary to domestic investment, or as part of and parcel of a restructuring of domestic resources. The main dissenting view was that of the Japanese Government, who, by the early 1970s perceived the overseas production by its own manufacturing and service firms as a way of exporting lower value added activities, and of redeploying the labour released in higher value added domestic activities.

In spite of these concerns over outward direct investment, the policies of Western governments were largely limited to the implementation of selective controls on the capital exports (which were rarely effective as most MNEs were able to raise the capital they needed from other countries or the international market), and/or on the remission of dividends; and a variety of fiscal provisions, which were designed to neutralise any tax advantages on income earned from foreign investment *vis-à-vis* domestic investment.[8] In addition, governments sometimes imposed extra-territorial restrictions on the exports of certain types of products by their own MNEs to unfriendly powers; and on the conclusion of cross-border mergers, alliances and business agreements, which, had they been undertaken in the home country, would have contravened the anti-trust legislation. Finally, in this period, home governments occasionally intervened to counteract unwelcome actions taken by foreign governments,[9] or negotiated with them to ensure a level playing field for the treatment of inward and outward direct investment.

GOVERNMENT POLICIES IN THE 1980s – AND BEYOND?

Perhaps the most striking development which has affected government attitudes and policies towards MNEs since the 1980s has been the globalisation of the world economy. Such globalisation is shown both by the tremendous growth of all forms of international transactions, and the integrated strategies pursued by firms towards their domestic and foreign production and market activities. It has been coupled with a reaffirmation of the merits of a market economy, the most dramatic expression of which is currently being played out in Eastern Europe. At the same time, a new generation of advances in information and communications technology has had major consequences for both the location and organisation of economic activity.

The increased participation of MNEs in almost all economies has forced governments to re-evaluate, not only their actions taken to influence the behaviour of such firms (or that of their affiliates), but also their general macroeconomic and microeconomic strategies which might affect, or be affected by, inward or outward investment. Moreover, the growing convergence in the structure of economic activity in the advanced industrial economies, and of cross-border intra-industry transactions, has meant that most of these economies are now both major outward and inward direct investors. Within the Triad (US, EC, Japan), the value-added activities of MNEs are now becoming increasingly interdependent and influenced by the same economic factors.

The last decade or more has also seen a change in the economic focus of many nation-states. Though domestic issues still dominate the thinking of the larger industrial countries, the increasing need to be competitive in global markets, or with foreign firms in domestic markets, has become a major catalyst for action. Much of this shift in interest has reflected the economic renaissance of Western Europe – now given an additional boost through the prospects of the completion of the internal market in 1992 – and the growth of newly industrialised developing countries, especially in East Asia. Such inroads into the markets of the leading industrial nations have led governments of these countries to reconsider the factors influencing the competitiveness of their own resources and competencies; and to judge the contribution of MNEs in this light.

These developments have also resulted in a change of the role of national governments as enablers and sustainers of wealth-creating activities. From actions designed to remove structural distortions in domestic markets – especially in the production of goods and services based on natural factor endowments – governments are being increasingly required to examine how they might facilitate the supply capabilities of their own firms, by lowering transaction-related barriers, and by fostering the upgrading and structural redeployment of the assets within their jurisdiction.

To be admitted, this shift of perspective is quite new and, except in Japan, South Korea and Singapore, has not yet been fully translated into practice. Neither the US nor the UK administrations, for example, while acknowledging the need to improve industrial competitiveness, has shown any inclination to adopt a holistic or systemic approach to its long-term microeconomic strategy, or to the role which MNE activity might play in the pursuance of this strategy. To be sure, governments are quick to publicise particular actions they take to improve national competitiveness or rid markets of structural impediments. But, underlying the rhetoric and piecemeal policies, there seems little real appreciation of the positive and co-ordinating role which governments need to play in setting the conditions for firms and markets to operate efficiently, especially in the upgrading of resources and capabilities, and the restructuring of production. To sustain the efficient working of a well-established and stable market is one thing; to create entirely new markets, particularly of goods and services which are jointly demanded or supplied, and to ensure that existing markets can adjust speedily and efficiently to the changes required of them, is quite another.[10]

Michael Porter, in his latest book refers to a 'diamond' of competitive advantage which he suggests all countries may possess to some degree or other (Porter, 1990a). He identifies four facets of the diamond: (1) the quality and structure of indigenous resource endowments and capabilities; (2) the level and quality of domestic demand; (3) the extent to which firms are able to fully exploit clustering or agglomerative economies; and (4) the nature of the strategy of structure and rivalry between firms. Obviously the relevance of the facets will vary between firms, industries and countries; but Porter contends that the extent to which, and the cost at which, countries possess, create or acquire these advantages, will determine their competitive position in the global marketplace.

It is possible – but Porter does not do this – to examine the composition of the diamond of advantage in terms of the extent to which the industry (or country) is internationalised;[11] and in terms of the extent of government influence and what kind of government influence. It is also possible to examine the interaction of these variables from a dynamic perspective. The result of the exercise is confirmed by a very different exercise on the kinds of industrial sectors most likely to be affected by the reduction in market distortions as a result of 'Europe 1992' (see e.g. Cecchini *et al.*, 1988). It is precisely the sectors in which MNEs are concentrated, or are increasing their concentration, which are those whose prosperity is linked to the role played by governments in affecting the structure and social efficiency of markets and, especially, the extent to which they are able to minimise the net costs of endemic market failure.

We may further hypothesise that this is likely to be the main battleground for competition between countries in these and other industries in the 1990s. Such competition shows itself both in the attempts by many governments to attract inward direct investment to help enhance their indigenous innovatory capacity,[12] and to improve the competitive capabilities of their own MNEs in foreign markets. To this extent – and this is the final piece of the jigsaw – inward and outward investment become complementary to, rather than substitutable for domestic investment.

All of this suggests a very different scenario for the way in which MNEs and governments may interact in the 1990s, compared with that in the 1960s and 1970s. Essentially we are suggesting that, whereas in the earlier period, the focus of interest was on the possible conflicts between governments and MNEs,[13] today, it is much more the ways in which the two parties might co-operate to promote their mutual goals; and, in the case of governments, to best promote the restructuring of their own resources and institutions to meet the challenges of the global marketplace. This is not to suggest that all is 'sweetness and light' between governments and MNEs, or that bargaining over the distribution of the benefits of MNE activity is any less combative than it once was. Nor does it lessen the need for an internationally agreed regime, and/or rules of the game (as Vernon has suggested in his earlier article), in which global corporations may flourish efficiently. Moreover, concern over some of the possible non-economic costs of cross-border production (e.g., the export of unacceptable health, safety, and environmental standards, and the erosion of country-specific social norms and cultures) is as pronounced, or more pronounced, as it has ever been (see e.g. UNCTC, 1991). But, in most industrial societies, at least, these have now taken second place to the more pressing need of fostering competitiveness in international markets. Moreover, most of the non-economic issues facing nation-states today have little to do with the multinationality of firms, *per se*, even though MNEs may be transmitters of resources, values, and behavioural patterns which may have a distinctive impact on these issues.

Let us now return to our main theme. The basic thesis of this chapter is that the tasks of governments, as custodians of wealth creating capabilities of the institutions and citizens within their jurisdiction, are currently undergoing a fundamental reorientation as a result of six characteristics of the modern global economy. First, the increasingly important role of created or engineered endowments and capabilities is determining the economic prosperity of most nation-states. Second, the fact that the markets for these endowments and capabilities are often intrinsically imperfect, and that, in many instances, their demand and supply characteristics are directly or indirectly influenced by governments. This especially applies to the markets for human capital and for knowledge-intensive intermediate products. Third, the increasing convergence in the economic structure of the advanced industrial nations, and the growing competitiveness between them in the markets they seek to serve. One sign of this competitiveness is revealed by the dramatic growth in cross-border intra-industry trade and investment (UNCTC, 1991). Fourth, the growing participation by multinational hierarchies in these same economies, and the increasing international mobility of resources, capabilities, and intermediate products. Fifth, the increasingly significant role of government in influencing the production and transaction costs of MNEs, and particularly in the location of innovatory activities (Dunning, 1990c). Sixth, the growing instability of, and interdependence between, the markets for intermediate products; and the complementarity between the role of governments, hierarchies, and markets in creating and sustaining an orderly, flexible, and efficient system of resource restructuring.

Added to these factors are others such as the growing liberalisation of many political and economic systems, the learning experience of both home and host countries of the costs and benefits of FDI. But no less significant is the fact that whereas earlier government measures, intended to affect the behaviour of MNEs, were specifically addressed to such firms, contemporary policies are more generic in their orientation but geared to the recognition that MNEs may be among the firms most affected by such actions. At the same time, there is need for a better understanding by governments that some markets need to be collectively organised and/or administered by hierarchies if other markets – and, indeed, the market system as a whole – are to operate at optimal or near optimal social efficiency.

COMPARATIVE GOVERNMENT POLICIES

A review of the contemporary and changing attitudes and actions of governments, as they seek to come to terms with the globalisation of production and markets, would seem to belie much of the analysis so far presented in this chapter. Few governments currently either adopt, or even acknowledge the necessity to adopt, a systemic strategy towards MNE-related activity, or to the upgrading or restructuring of indigenous resources and capabilities, occasioned by this activity. Views as to the mission of government as a resource creator or as a facilitator of competitiveness, differ considerably between countries (Dunning, 1989b). Until very recently, the philosophy of the UK government, for example, was that this task is almost the exclusive responsibility of the private sector, and that the onus of governments begins and ends with the removal of structural market distortions. By contrast, the Japanese philosophy, as described in the writings of Teretumo Ozawa, is that even if the market were completely free of structural distortions, it would not be capable, by itself, of upgrading resources and responding to the changes demanded of it, at a societal optimal rate.

This philosophy is demonstrated by the very different policies and practices of the UK and Japanese governments, particularly as they affect international business. For many years, the Japanese Government has viewed both outward and inward direct investment as an integral part of its broader microeconomic strategy. In turn, this strategy has been systemic in its objective of improving the long-term competitive advantage of the Japanese economy by reducing the transaction costs facing its firms in their attempts to improve their capabilities and restructure the activities of their firms to meet the challenges of the global marketplace.

Such government interaction has been cohesive and comprehensive, and designed to achieve a set of well-specified and clearly articulated economic goals. Specific policy measures include those directed to personal and corporate savings, education and training, R&D, taxation, environmental issues, transport and communications, the exchange rate, technology transfer and dissemination, and competition; but each is co-ordinated in such a way as to achieve a similar set of objectives, and to do so in a way in which captures the economies of governance.

The promotion of a well conceived, positive, and systemic strategy to reduce endemic market failure, and so improve the long-term competitiveness of Japanese resources and of Japanese MNEs, is in marked contrast to that of the UK government, which might be best described as *neo-laissez faire*. This, however, is not to say that, by its actions or policies, the UK government does not affect the ability of its own firms to compete in foreign markets or the propensity of foreign investors to set up factories in the UK. Indeed, taking a broad brush perspective, it could be argued that the current administration is one of the most interventionist of any administration since World War II.

In each of the areas identified in the previous paragraphs, the UK Government has a distinct, and well articulated, policy, but rarely is it possible to see a link between these policies – or the *raison d'être* for them. There seems to be little clear recognition of the very positive and constructive role which the UK authorities can play in affecting the competitiveness of its resources and capabilities by helping individuals and firms to overcome the obstacles to that competitiveness, which result from endemic market failure. For example, it is strange that, at the time its major competitors are stepping-up their relative expenditures on education, R&D, vocational training, transport and communications and the like, the UK Government (in the belief that such public spending is inherently unproductive) is doing the reverse.

It would be wrong to give the impression that the current administration has not done a great deal to improve the competitiveness of the UK economy or its attractions to foreign companies. In particular, its philosophy and actions have exerted a considerable influence on the ethos of the British people towards competition, work, incentives, and entrepreneurship. But, at least, until the change of leadership in the Conservative Party in November 1990, I for one found its faith in the invisible hand to solve all the economic problems of the UK both naive and disturbing; and quite out of touch with the needs and realities of modern business. Even by the summer of 1991, one sees little evidence of any active coalition between the British Government and the private sector in charting the future course of the UK economy. Nor is there – except in particular situations[14] – a recognition that the kind of variables which most influence international companies in their investment decisions are transaction costs rather than production driven, and are critically influenced by the actions (or non-actions) of governments. If there was one particular piece of advice I would have to offer to the present administration, it is that it should adopt, and be seen to adopt, a holistic and systemic approach to the organisation of economic activity; and to accept that governments, markets, and hierarchies have a complementary and interactive role to play in upgrading the human and physical assets and the restructuring of economic activity continually demanded by the modern global economy. This, I would emphasise, is not government telling firms and markets what to do, or attempting to replace their functions, but government working with firms and markets to achieve mutually beneficial goals.

CONCLUSION

In this chapter, I have sought to demonstrate that the changing character of market imperfections, and the attitudes and actions of governments to these changes, have fundamentally affected both the ability and willingness of domestic firms and MNEs, or increase their degree of multinationality, and the level and pattern of inward direct investment. I have suggested that, for much of the post-war period, governments have either sought to negate the effects of structural market distortions, including those perceived to be created or practised by MNEs or their affiliates; and to intervene in the workings of existing markets wherever the outcome is not in accord with their own political and economic expectations. In general, in the 1960s and 1970s, the actions take by governments to achieve their goals were piecemeal and unco-ordinated; those actions directed to affect the outward and inward direct investment were implemented quite independently of each other. There were few attempts to modify macroeconomic or microeconomic strategies in the light of the growth of international direct investment, or the trade related to it. These strategies generally led to a confrontation between MNEs and governments, as, basically, the latter sought to affect the behavioural pattern of the former so as to increase their share of the economic rent created by them.

In the early 1990s, the main cause of market failure in most industrialised countries is not that of structural distortion but of the transaction costs associated with unstable, integrated, or interdependent markets. In particular, the costs associated with the uncertainty underlying demand and supply conditions, those which result from the externalities of transactions, those which arise from the segmentation of markets where the optimum size of production is very large, and those which stem from the need to ensure that the core competencies of firms are properly and efficiently exploited have each become a more important component of the total costs of economic activity.

The chapter has further argued that the exogenous variables affecting market structure and government behaviour have led to a broad convergence of economic structure in the industrialised countries. This has been accompanied by a growth of intra-industry trade and investment, and an intensification of competition between countries in the production and marketing of a wide range of products. This, in turn, has led governments to reassess their portfolio of strategies to protect or promote their international competitive positions. One of the means by which this can be achieved is by assisting the lowering of the transaction costs of hierarchies or markets over which they (i.e., the governments) have some influence, and by so doing to reduce systemic market failure. Another is to develop a holistic approach to a whole range of policies which, directly or indirectly, affect the competitiveness of the resources within their jurisdiction. Such a need is accentuated not only by the growing ease with which firms can move their need to seek global sales in order to finance the upgrading of their competitive advantages.

All these developments suggest the need for a symbiotic rather than an anti-symbiotic relationship among governments, hierarchies and markets.[15] As yet, the shift away from confrontation, and towards co-operation, has only been fully manifested in some Asian economies, notably Japan. In the West, the 1980s saw a reaction to the interventionist policies of previous Left-wing administrations, and to a restatement of the virtues of the free market system. This has sometimes led governments to the view that any intervention by themselves to affect market forces (apart from that designed to reduce structural distortions) is to be avoided. (On this point see Sanjaya Lall's chapter in this volume.)

No doubt, there are a host of historical, cultural and institutional reasons which explain the differences in the reactions of the Japanese and Western governments (especially the US and the UK) to the global technological and organisational changes affecting the ownership and location of cross-border economic activities. But, as things currently stand, for most countries the age of an integrated competitiveness-led economic strategy, jointly fashioned by the government and the private sector, has yet to come.

Whether it will happen in the next decade, or indeed in the next century, we can only speculate upon. My own judgment is that although there will continue to be country-specific advantages in the perceived organisational role of government, and its interaction with that of hierarchies and markets, all the major industrial economies will be forced to adopt – gradually or otherwise – more integrated and collaborative microeconomic strategies. This has already happened at a macroeconomic level where co-operation between countries is much greater today than most people could have imagined two decades ago. Because of the intra-governmental transactional costs it has not yet occurred at the microeconomic level – and, if and when it does, it will be among governments and firms and hierarchies within a country rather than between governments in different countries.

In a variety of directions, there are signs of this happening. But, a systemic approach is still lacking – and what is no less important – is seen to be lacking. Only, I suspect, the full force of international competition – not only from the Far East but from Eastern Europe and from the revitalised European Community will compel governments to realise that they and the constituents they represent, will either swim or drown together! And, part of this force will undoubtedly be the influence on, or the response of MNEs to, the changing shape of the global village.

APPENDIX

ILLUSTRATIONS OF STRUCTURAL AND ENDEMIC MARKET IMPERFECTIONS AND SOME POSSIBLE GOVERNMENT RESPONSES TO THEM

(A) Structural Market Distortions

Types of Distortion	*Possible Government Response*
Barriers to entry.* Legally restricted access to inputs or final goods markets, possession of proprietary rights (e.g., patents, trademarks) by encumbent firms, restrictive entry requirements (e.g. for some kinds of labour), scale economies, non-contestability of markets.	Disallow proprietary ownership of essential inputs, and/or exclusive dealing with customers; deregulate and/or encourage the contestability of markets; assist new (and small) firms to enter markets; revise patent laws to encourage more innovation.
Oligopoly or monopoly control of output* (leading, e.g., to price hiking), 'X' inefficiency, restrictive business practices, cartelisation, higher transaction costs (e.g., through unreliability of delivery schedules), lack of pressure to innovate, etc.	Break up monopolies and outlaw restrictive business practices and cartels; in case of 'natural' monopolies, enforce accountability and monitoring procedures over performance, and/or introduce price controls.
Excessive product differentiation or market fragmentation (leading to higher unit costs, and/or cut throat competition and lower product standards), excessive marketing (including advertising) expenditure.	Sometimes legally imposed entry barriers may be desirable (e.g., to protect quality standards and/or reduce *excessive* competition), but mainly Government action should be directed to encouraging more *effective* competition, e.g., by removing import barriers which may tend to a proliferation of foreign-owned production units [as in Canada].
Interference with market mechanism by Governments* (e.g., price controls, import quotas, output limitations, performance requirements, employment subsidies, inefficient imposition of health, safety and environmental regulations, immigration laws, discriminatory taxation, *etc.)*	Reduced Government intervention to allow firms to perform more effectively and to encourage domestic competition.

---

* These practices are only structurally distorting if they result in a less than static or dynamic optimal market structure; and/or allow the supplying firms to exploit their privileged positions by engaging in anti-competitive practices for their own gain.

(B) Endemic or Intrinsic Market Failure

Types of Failure	*Possible Government Response*

Failure of markets to take account of costs and benefits of transactions which are external to those transactions. Results in social consequence of markets being different than 'private' consequences. specially noticeable in markets for knowledge, and human capital, and often leads to under-investment in creation of new assets (Brooks, 1982).

A variety of actions which may increase (or reduce) demand and/or supply as the need arises. *A propos* R&D and the upgrading of human capital, action may vary from generic policies to improve educational standards and encourage basic research in universities (often in cooperation with local firms), and treatment of intellectual property rights; to more specific fiscal, labour market and innovation policies designed to promote more (or less) investment in asset creation. These may include the undertaking, or commissioning of R&D, and the dissemination of its results by Government itself. especially in sectors, which tend to be made up of small producers, that cannot economically perform these functions.

Failure of markets to adequately deal with risk and uncertainty. To a varying degree, uncertainty is inherent in most markets. Again, however, the social costs of risk may be greater than the private costs; and Governments have a responsibility to reduce the private costs or increase the (expected) private benefits of risk taking to equate the social and private net returns of uncertainty beating. ·

Encourage private institutions to 'socialize' uncertainty, *e.g.*, by facilitating insurance and future markets; and to protect buyers and sellers from some of the consequences of uninsurable risks (the breaking of commercial contracts). In cases of Government-related risks, to foster or help finance investment, guarantee and/or insurance schemes, e.g., as set up by several Governments to protect their own MNEs from adverse political actions of foreign Governments. To encourage capital markets to be entrepreneurial in the financing of risk-intensive projects, particularly by small firms; where necessary (preferably jointly with the private sector) to help provide a fund of risk capital. To lessen politically related uncertainty by injecting more stability in economic policies. Governments should also encourage a positive ethos to (judicious) risk taking and not to penalise rewards for successful risk taking by excessive taxation. Finally, Governments may help reduce uncertainty by providing more information – again, especially to smaller firms, *e.g.*, with respect to export markets, foreign investment regulations, *etc.*

(B) Endemic or Intrinsic Market Failure (continued)

Types of Failure	*Possible Government Response*
Failure of markets to cope with the public goods characteristics of some products; *i.e., those* which involve very high 'front end' or 'set-up' costs and low or zero marginal costs. Again, many public goods have characteristics of social intermediate or final goods. This uncertainty sometimes reflects a lack of knowledge or information; and in their cases from the difficulty of risk evaluation. Willingness to undertake risks also reflects the structure of rewards and the transaction costs of risk taking. Often, too, the pay-back period of such production is very long indeed (e.g., for highways and airports).	Allow consortia of companies sometimes jointly financed by Governments, even though these result in a monopolistic or oligopolistic market structure. The more the socially generic use of goods, the more they should be funded by Government. Note, however, that the presence or absence and the quality of some public goods facilitates or hinders production by firms. Hence, Governments have a responsibility to increase the supply of these goods, wherever the social rate of return justifies it.
Failure of markets to ensure all firms are price takers and, at the same time, to ensure they produce at the optimum level or output. Technological imperatives may require a concentrated market structure and/or alliances between firms, either along or across value-added chains. In some cases such alliances may involve firms from more than one country.	Some positive response in respect to competition and anti-trust policies. This kind of market failure requires Government to foster the appropriate balance between too little and too much industrial concentration. A constant monitoring and redefining of the concept of workable competition, *i.e.,* that which promotes the market structure, which best combines static efficiency and the dynamic upgrading of resource usage and product quality.
Insufficiency or inadequacy of institutional framework within which markets can operate efficiently. (A good example is the current situation in many east European countries.) Lack of impetus or initiative of producers to innovate or upgrade resources, and of consumers to demand sophisticated and fault-free products.	Responsibility of Governments to set up an institutional and legal framework so markets can efficiently perform their function. Such a framework is more complicated with technologically sophisticated and 'generic' intermediate goods and services than with simple consumer products. Governments can also do much by legislation, persuasion and example to help set the appropriate entrepreneurial and work ethos, and to upgrade consumption standards.
Failure of markets to adjust to changes demanded of them speedily and efficiently, due to extra-market structural rigidities.	To promote, encourage and financially assist in retraining and relocation schemes. Encourage, by tax credits, etc., firms to absorb redundant labour elsewhere in their organisation by appropriately restructuring their portfolios of products and/or markets. Foster a positive attitude towards changes, while helping those who are adversely affected by change to help themselves.

Notes

This chapter is a revised and shortened version of a paper first presented in Tokyo in July 1990 at an international workshop on 'The Multinational Enterprise in the 21st Century'. Previously it was published in *Millennium*, Vol. 20, No. 2, 1991.

1. Although, in this chapter we shall be primarily concerned with the role of central or federal governments, the term 'government' should be taken to embrace subnational and supranational administrations as well.
2. Throughout this chapter we define a multinational enterprise (MNE) as an enterprise which owns or controls value added activities in two or more countries.
3. In the economist's language, the ratio of marginal productivity of each input is proportional to its price, while in the case of each input, the value of marginal productivity will be equal to its price.
4. They may also confer power on the buyers, but in this chapter we shall concentrate on seller power.
5. As described in standard industrial organisation textbooks.
6. These include those compiled by national and regional governments, private consultancies and banks; but perhaps the most comprehensive source is that of United Nations Centre on Transnational Corporations. See especially UNCTC (1989), and Sections III and IV of the *List of Sales Publications of the UNCTC, 1973–1989*, issued by the United Nations in October 1989.
7. For example, expressed as a proportion of GNP, the outward direct capital stock in 1982 was 28.5 per cent in the case of the Netherlands, 41.0 per cent for Switzerland, compared with 6.0 per cent for West Germany, 7.2 per cent for the US and 4.7 per cent for Japan. See Dunning and Cantwell (1987).
8. Sweden was an exception, and by 1974 had enacted fairly comprehensive legislation, in an attempt to ensure that foreign investment by Swedish MNEs was in the best interests of the home country.
9. Bergsten *et al.* (1978) give examples of the US reacting to the policies of some European governments giving exemption from domestic taxation of export income and direct support in their oil MNEs.
10. A good example of the costs of creating (or recreating) a market system is now being played out in Eastern Europe. Here the transitional costs from a centrally-planned to a market-oriented system seems so huge that only by a united international support (rather akin to the US Marshall Plan for West European recovery after World War II) can this change in the macro-governance of economic activity be accomplished relatively smoothly and within a reasonable period of time.
11. For an attempt to do this, see Dunning (1991a).
12. And, by implication, depict their competition for such opportunities. Good examples include those countries comprising the EC and some East Asian economies.

13. See Kindleberger and Goldberg (1970, pp. 295–323). The quotation that 'reduced to its simplest terms, there is an inherent conflict between the objectives of the international corporation and the nation-state' does not ring as true today as it did 20 years ago.
14. For a further analysis, see Dunning (1990a).
15. For an examination of these relationships, see Dunning (1991b).

5 Drawing the Border for a Multinational Enterprise and a Nation-State

Alan M. Rugman

INTRODUCTION

What is sovereignty? What is a multinational enterprise? While Vernon knew the answer twenty years ago it is not clear that we still do today (Vernon, 1971). No longer do US multinationals compete with Japanese multinationals solely for the benefit of their home nations. Even Reich now recognises that multinationals are no longer 'national champions', but contribute to host nation performance, as well as home (Reich, 1992).

But what is a home or host nation? Today the European Community (EC) is emerging as a major economic bloc. Together, the United States, Japan and the European Community account for over 80 per cent of the world's largest 500 multinational enterprises. Yet an EC multinational is different from a US or Japanese one; most of its trade and/or foreign direct investment is intra-firm or intra-industry, that is within the EC. As the directives of the EC's Single Market programme come into effect, the EC multinationals will continue to prosper, but will these economic changes be of political benefit to Britain, Germany, France, Italy and other countries? Presumably not, as their former national champions are being transformed into 'European' multinationals.

Indeed, this is a generic attribute of multinationals. Even the US and Japanese multinationals will gradually lose their home country identity as the forces of globalisation dictate the need to devise successful corporate strategies. Such global strategies will balance economic integration features with the need for national responsiveness, as demonstrated by Bartlett and Ghoshal (1989).

The nature of Triad-based global competitiveness leads the three sets of multinationals to interact with governments in order to secure sustainable competitive advantages. I have argued elsewhere that the successful multinationals will develop efficiency-based firm-specific

84

advantages independent of government support (Rugman and Verbeke, 1990). In contrast, weak and decaying multinationals will seek
shelter-based entry barriers from governments, in the form of protection, subsidies or related discriminatory measures.

Due to cultural factors the implementation of multinational-
government strategies will vary across the Triad. The Japanese-based
multinationals will be the most successful in terms of strategies
requiring economies of scale and scope. This is because business and
government work well together. The US-based multinationals will be
the least successful; this is because the US government is subjected to
conflicting internal lobbies. The EC multinationals will reflect the
confusion of the EC itself; it is an economic powerhouse but a political
pygmy.

These paradoxes are perhaps best illustrated by the state of
confusion surrounding the issue of international competitiveness. In
his remarkably old-fashioned 1990 book Porter argues that a home
nation's 'diamond' is the source of competitive advantages and that
domestic firms which do well in that diamond can then go forth and
succeed as global industries (Porter, 1990a). This is a zero-sum game.
Porter measures success by the export shares of national firms, and
their affiliated 'clusters'. Yet he does not measure the EC as a unit;
instead, he studies the diamonds of the separate nations. This indicates
that Porter does not understand that it is the size of the internal EC
market, and the associated market access for the EC firms, which is the
dominant characteristic; that is, that the 'EC diamond' is now the
source of competitive advantages for an EC multinational, not the
French or German diamond.

If diamonds are not forever, what does this mean for sovereignty? It
suggests that the Triad-based multinationals will continue to dominate
international business. Non-Triad multinationals will need to despe-
rately seek access to Triad markets. It also suggests that the Triads will
give rise to different types of multinationals, reflecting their different
cultures and social-political-historical roots. In contrast to Ohmae,
who sees the globalisation of markets leading to homogeneous
products, it is quite feasible for product diversity and adaptability to
increase, reflecting sophisticated managerial understanding of the need
for national responsiveness (Ohmae, 1990).

To utilise Porter's diamond concept once more, the appropriate
economic and political 'spaces' are flexible upwards and downwards.
At the same time that the Triad encourages multinationals to cross
borders, the corresponding increase in national wealth drives up the

demand for product differentiation and service variations. The national diamond can go up into international space and simultaneously down to regional (sub-national) space. Successful multinationals will operate across all these spaces.

While economists (and some political scientists) have been adept at recognising the upward movement of economic space, they have tended to ignore the recent evidence of sub-national lobbying and increased regionalisation within the borders of nation-states. Examples of the latter include: the recent splintering of the USSR and Yugoslavia; the potential separation of Quebec from Canada; the continued call for independence by Basques and Irish factions, etc. Despite the increased degree of globalisation and economic linkages in the world there is some evidence of political fragmentation rather than political unification occurring at the same time as the economic integration.

When the multinational enterprise adapts its products and services to accommodate such sub-national tastes and values it is providing more responsive management than politicians who attempt to operate in centralised nation-states and flawed diamonds. Because the multinational enterprise is close to the customer, its national responsiveness can become a path for the greater recognition of cultural independence. What is the relevant border? In contrast to twenty years ago, today it is a cultural area rather than a nation-state.

GLOBALISATION AND MULTINATIONAL CORPORATE STRATEGY

The major trend which has affected the thinking of corporate strategists in business and financial services over the last ten years is globalisation. This will continue over the next decade. By globalisation is meant the production and distribution of products and/or services of a homogeneous type and quality on a worldwide basis. The producers and distributors enjoy economies of scale through large volume production of standardised products and services. Most of these goods and services are provided by multinational enterprises operating across national borders.

To an extent, the multinational enterprises homogenise tastes and help spread consumerism. Throughout the wealthier nations of Europe, North America and Japan, there is a growing acceptance of standardised consumer electronics goods, automobiles, computers, electric appliances, and so on. To a large degree, the multinational enterprises have to respond to consumer needs and tastes. The multinational enterprises are successful because there is a demand for their products and services.

Multinational enterprises are in business; they are not social agencies. Yet over the next decade there will be more criticism of the performance and social responsibility of multinational enterprises, including their linkage to the environment. The single goal of efficient economic performance through a simplistic globalisation strategy will be compromised by the need for the multinational enterprises to be more responsive to social needs and national interests. Yet sovereignty will not fade away as globalisation increases. Instead, multinational enterprises will have to deal with the twin goals of globalisation and national responsiveness. By national responsiveness is meant the need for corporations operating across national borders to invest in understanding the different tastes of consumers in segmented regional markets, and the ability to respond to different national standards and regulations imposed by autonomous governments and agencies.

The information technology revolution has helped globalisation. The mass production of cheap personal computers, fax machines and cellular telephones makes information flow faster and deeper across borders and within companies. The greater flexibility and mobility facilitated by information technology enhances the ability of managers and companies to produce and distribute products and services on a global basis.

Most of the action by multinational enterprises is concentrated in the Triad markets of North America, the European Community and Japan. As explained earlier, over 80 per cent of the world's largest 500 multinational enterprises come from these three areas of economic and financial wealth. These 500 multinational enterprises account for 80 per cent of all the foreign direct investment in the world and over half of the world's trade in goods and services (Rugman, 1988).

In the next decade the nature of the Triad markets will change as they become more protectionist. Already there are strong indications of an increase in US protectionist devices, such as the Super 301 trade law, the widespread use of countervailing duty laws, and concern about Japanese multinational enterprises operating in America. There is also some evidence in the European Community of an increase in anti-dumping actions and the possibility of a 'Fortress Europe' emerging by the end of 1992, as the single internal market emerges. However, the global economic interdependence already achieved through the activities of the large multinational enterprises will not be halted. Indeed, a group of new multinational enterprises, from the Asian economies of South Korea, Taiwan and other newly industrialised economies (NIEs) will emerge, largely within the Japanese sphere of influence.

Set against these wealthy economies of the Triad blocs and the NIEs will be the poorer nations of Africa, China, South America, Eastern Europe, the former USSR and other regions lacking access to one of the Triad markets. There will be increasing social and economic discontent in these areas over the next decade because television, newspapers and other media will continue to spread information about more affluent life styles to regions which lack the economic infrastructure, corporate know-how, and supportive political systems to compete in global markets.

The nature of information technology is that it is a two-edged sword. While it helps multinational enterprises in their economic tasks it also speeds social discontent and raises unrealistic expectations in poorer nations. Corporate efficiency is enhanced yet the costs of doing business are also increased. The internal corporate tasks of strategic planning, financial control, research, production, human resource management and marketing are all helped by the efficient design and use of information technology systems. Yet the external environment for doing business is simultaneously complicated. This means that multinational enterprises must learn to tackle both tasks.

To respond to the twin challenges of globalisation and national responsiveness requires new thinking in multinational enterprises and in financial institutions. The days of simple globalisation are limited. Instead, multinational enterprises must face up to making major investments in being nationally responsive, that is, in understanding what makes people tick and why people differ across borders. Cultural understanding is becoming as important as research and development. Globalisation of production and distribution feeds one desire but it also creates a hunger for more individual care and attention, a two-headed monster which needs the response of a two-pronged corporate strategy.

Put more formally, the corporation now faces a basic challenge of transaction costs economics in dealing with the public on a global basis. Since there are literally millions of consumers, yet only a few hundred large multinational enterprises, there exists the problem of asymmetry in information costs, a type of buyer uncertainty. There is no possible solution to this problem by consumers, since it is not in any one individual's interest to make the investment of time and money required to achieve a solution which will satisfy everyone else. But the relatively few large multinational enterprises do have this incentive. The multinational enterprises need to stay in business, so they need to be able to achieve both economic efficiency through globalisation and also keep sovereignty at bay, or at least accommodated to the extent that business does not suffer. In short, the multinational enterprises themselves need to develop management strategies to be nationally responsive as well as globally efficient. It is to the method of achieving this balance that we now turn.

THE TRADE-OFF: GLOBALISATION VERSUS SOVEREIGNTY

Conceptually, the twin issues of globalisation and sovereignty can be analysed through the use of Figure 5.1. This is adapted from Bartlett, where he uses a globalisation/national responsiveness matrix to analyse the strategies of nine large multinational enterprises (Bartlett, 1986). This work was extended and tested on nine multinational enterprises in the Triad by Bartlett and Ghoshal (1989). Here I adapt this framework to consider the nature of corporate strategies in a world with an increasing amount of sovereignty being exhibited.

The vertical axis captures the concept of the need for economic integration, frequently referred to as globalisation. Movement up the axis results in a greater degree of economic integration. Globalisation generates economies of scale as a firm moves into world-wide markets selling a single product or service. These are captured as a result of centralising specific activities in the value-added chain in locations with the strongest perceived country specific advantages. They also occur by reaping the benefits of increased co-ordination and control of geographically dispersed activities.

The horizontal axis measures the need for corporations to respond to sovereignty. Companies need to be 'nationally responsive' to consumer tastes and government regulations in the relevant countries in which they operate. Sovereignty means that corporate activities need to be adapted to local conditions, both in terms of content and process. This may imply a geographical dispersion of activities or a decentralisation of co-ordination and control for individual firms. Corporations and financial institutions need either a low or a high degree of awareness of sovereignty.

On the basis of the two axes of Figure 5.1, four cases can be distinguished. Quadrants 1 and 4 are simple cases. These are two cases where the impact of an exogenous 'environmental' change (such as the

Canada–US Free Trade Agreement or Europe 1992) unambiguously affects the firm's movement towards a higher required responsiveness to one variable and simultaneously decreases the required responsiveness to the other variable. In Quadrant 1, the need for globalisation increases and the need for awareness of sovereignty is low. This focus on scale economies will lead to competitive strategies based on Porter's first generic strategy of price competition (Porter, 1980). Usually mergers and acquisitions will result. The opposite situation is characteristic of Quadrant 4 where sovereignty matters but globalisation is low. There niche strategies must be pursued; companies will adapt products to satisfy the high demands of sovereignty and ignore scale economies as globalisation does not matter very much.

Quadrants 2 and 3 reflect more complex situations. Quadrant 2 refers to those cases where both the need for integration and awareness of sovereignty are low. This implies that both the potential to obtain economies of scale and benefits of being sensitive to sovereignty decline. Typical strategies for Quadrant 2 would be firms and industries characterised by increased international standardisation of products and services. This could lead to lower needs for centralised

Figure 5.1   Globalisation and sovereignty

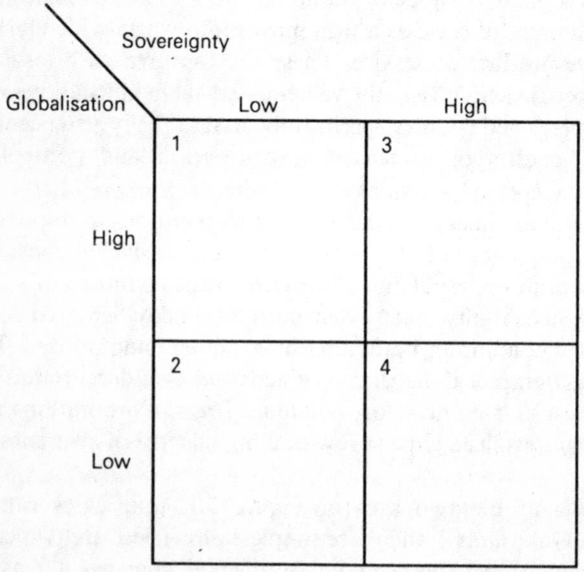

quality control and centralised strategic decision-making, while simultaneously eliminating requirements to adapt activities to individual countries.

Finally, in Quadrant 3, both the needs for integration and sovereignty increase, implying that different activities in the vertical chain are faced with opposite tendencies, for example a higher need for integration in production, along with higher requirements for regional adaptations in marketing. This is the most challenging quadrant and one where many successful globally efficient multinational enterprises must perform. Using this framework, I can analyse the impact of various government policies shocks and trends on different industries, firms, and other private sector institutions.

In this matrix the globalisation only view of Ohmae (1990) is shown in Quadrant 1. Here the overarching commercial and economic interests of the multinational enterprise are paramount and aspects of sovereignty are ignored. It is where misinformed readers of Vernon would conceive sovereignty to be at bay (Vernon, 1987). In contrast, in Quadrant 4, globalisation pressures on the multinational enterprises are less important than sovereignty. Quadrant 4 is one where governments dominate the multinational enterprise. Quadrant 2 is now of minimal interest (it is one where neither globalisation nor sovereignty issues dominate) but Quadrant 3 is the one where the current problems of globalisation and sovereignty co-exist. Quadrant 3 is where Vernon (1981, 1991) says that informed readers of *Sovereignty at Bay* would be positioned.

Figure 5.1 can also be used to re-interpret the literature of international political economy. Quadrant 1 is a case of markets in contrast to Quadrant 4 which is one of states. In between, Quadrant 3 is where both co-exist, as pointed out by Susan Strange (1991) and Eden (1991).

MULTINATIONALS AS TRANSMISSION AGENTS

Lenway and Murta state that the core hypothesis of Vernon (1971) has been obfuscated as most writers misinterpret the title itself (Lenway and Murta, 1991). This misreading of his work was recognised twice by Vernon himself, in 1981 and 1991. The theme of *Sovereignty at Bay* is not that the large multinational corporation has emerged as a direct political rival of states. Rather, it is that the growth of multinational corporations has served to compromise national sovereignty in a particular way. This occurs when the foreign subsidiaries of multinationals serve as vehicles to transmit home country influences to host nations. In a basic textbook on international business, Rugman *et al.* (1985) illustrate the Vernon (1981) point by showing that the transmission of home country values to host nations is stronger than the reverse possibility for the host country.

Both Vernon (1981) and Rugman *et al.* (1985) have suggested the need for home country managers to be less ethnocentric in their management styles and more receptive to the expertise of subsidiary managers overseas. They also argue that the multinational corporation itself can become a valuable tool of domestic policy if its internal transmission network is reversed to bring host country values into the home nations, instead of the traditional one-way flows. Over the last few years the need for such 'national responsiveness' has increased. The paradox is that, while multinationals have improved their internal networks there is still little evidence that home nation governments and institutions see 'their' multinationals as having or needing this capacity.

THE GROWING IMPORTANCE OF SOVEREIGNTY FOR MULTINATIONAL CORPORATE STRATEGY

From the viewpoint of private sector corporations the most important business decision to be made is a judgement about where the tradeoff between globalisation (economic efficiency) and sovereignty (non-economic issues) will fall. By now it should be clear why *both* of these two issues are of concern to business. Today a successful company can no longer afford to ignore sovereignty and just concentrate on globalisation; Quadrant 3 matters. Each business therefore bears the costs of making the decision about the tradeoff itself. Evidence that sovereignty is of growing importance and that a private sector company must develop a strategy to respond to it come from the following four examples.

Decentralisation of Power to Canada's Provinces

The increasing power of the provinces in Canada is leading to a growing decentralisation of economic decision-making. In terms of the costs of doing business Quebec is already, in effect, a separate nation. Quebec uses the French language for business and education, and the provincial government calls the tune in the administration of social services, health services and regulation of the work-place. There is evidence of growing separatist feeling in Western Canada, especially in Alberta. The Atlantic provinces also form a distinctive grouping with common concerns about support for regional development.

Both the Atlantic premiers, and the four Western premiers, have annual meetings to discuss a common economic strategy for their regions. This is supported by a small, but growing, inter-provincial bureaucratic infrastructure, generating data and information from a sub-national point of view.

Ontario, like Quebec, has perfected the technique of a parallel bureaucracy (in its case, parallel to Ottawa). The former Premier of Ontario was fond of remarking that, if it were a separate country, Ontario would be the eleventh largest in the world. It tries to act as if it were one, frequently stepping into areas of federal jurisdiction, including trade and fiscal policy. For example, the province of Ontario fought the Canada–US Free Trade Agreement tooth and nail both during and after the negotiations, over the 1986–8 period. Only recently has Ontario learned to live with free trade.

The provinces as a group also failed to co-operate in 1991 on the introduction of Canada's goods and services tax (GST), one of the most important tax changes in Canada's history. The GST was designed to replace the manufacturers' sales tax, which penalises Canada's exporters and subsidises importers (the latter, of course, are not subject to Canada's manufacturing tax when products are made outside of Canada). The provinces continue to have large public sector deficits; these will likely increase in the future since the provinces are responsive to local lobbies and social interest groups. This will compound the problems of the excessive federal deficit and lead to vicious fighting between federal and provincial ministers as their industrial, educational, social and health programmes are cut.

The failure of the Meech Lake Accord in 1990 and the subsequent impasse over constitutional renewal was another example of the central government's power being eroded by the provinces. In order to accommodate Quebec's requests to sign Canada's constitution the Ottawa government was prepared with Meech Lake to let any one of the provinces have a veto over further changes to the constitution. Provinces already have the power to opt out of responsibility for some aspects of the Charter of Rights and Freedoms, in particular those dealing with language issues. This can occur when a province invokes the 'notwithstanding' clause of the 1982 constitution, as Premier Bourassa did in rejecting a Supreme Court of Canada decision in

1988 requiring bilingual signs in Quebec. The future prospect of Senate reform will also lead to more representation from the regions and less power for the central government, especially in economic decision-making.

The power of the provinces is disturbing for private sector companies and multinational enterprises. Decentralisation of power to the provinces means an increase in the costs of doing business. Corporations must learn to staff offices and acquire information about eleven governments instead of one. They also have to respond to eleven types of regulations and bureaucratic environments. This leads to confusion about standards, inefficient production and ultimately greater corporate expenses. In effect, the private sector is forced to deal with sovereignty at a very disaggregated level.

Canada has always been a federation, with considerable economic power delegated to the provinces. There is ongoing tension between federal and provincial powers over the economy. What is being seen in Canada is that a point is coming when the costs of political decentralisation may become so great that many of the offsetting economic benefits of the federation will be lost. The end result could be close to anarchy; not a good place to do business. In terms of corporate strategy more and more executive time and energy must be invested in understanding the decentralised nature of political and economic power in Canada.

Decentralisation of Economic Power in the United States

The United States also experiences considerable decentralisation in economic decision-making. It is a country in which sub-national units will continue to increase in importance. This issue should not be confused with pluralism. A variety of political opinions and parties is a strength of democracy. The problem comes when the institutional structure of the nation breaks down and business cannot operate in an efficient manner, especially relative to global competitors.

The US constitution was designed to allow Congress to be a broker for regional and special interests. On occasions the Congress works with the Executive branch and a co-ordinated economic and even social policy can be both formulated and implemented. The examples of social reform and government economic activity in the Kennedy–Johnson years can be contrasted with a return to more market-based principles and somewhat reduced role for government in the Reagan years.

However, in many areas affecting the private sector today the overwhelming characteristic of doing business in the United States is the responsiveness of governments to special interest groups and lobbies. The more decentralised the level of government the more responsive is the regulatory activity to the lobbyist. On occasions, businesses themselves can be lobbyists, but there are many other groups, such as environmentalists and social activists who seem to be growing in power. Examples of conflicts in business lobbying occur in the areas of the administration of US trade remedy laws and in the current US debate about the possible regulation of inward foreign direct investment (FDI).

It has been demonstrated by Rugman and Anderson (1987), and by others, that the current administration of US countervail (CVD) and anti-dumping (AD) laws is highly responsive to domestic producer interests and biased against foreign firms. Rugman and Verbeke (1990) demonstrate that US corporations use CVD and AD as a competitive strategy to erect entry barriers against rival firms. Thus, even when the US government was pursuing negotiations for free trade with Canada, individual US corporations still used the CVD and AD laws to help erect entry barriers against Canadian exporters. This was a clear example of the US national interest being offset by selective producer interests. More of the same is in store in the future, although Canadian concerns about the administration of CVD and AD laws have been somewhat answered by the establishment of binational panels under the terms of the Free Trade Agreement (FTA).

The most notorious example of US producer interests offsetting official US trade policy was the 1986 softwood lumber CVD, which led to the Canadian federal government responding by imposing an export tax of 15 per cent on a major Canadian industry. Other examples, over the 1986–8 period of the FTA negotiations, included fresh Atlantic groundfish, potash from Saskatchewan, live swine and pork, and others. Over the 1980–86 period there were over 50 cases of CVD and AD brought by US companies against Canadian exporters, and this barrage of actions did not let up during the negotiations. None of these routine company-led applications of US CVD and AD law was particularly helpful to the US or Canadian governments. In Canada, especially, the FTA was nearly sabotaged by such parochial corporate interests.

While certain Congressional leaders now wish to restrict inward FDI most of the individual US states actively encourage it. Some Americans seem to be concerned with the growing amount of Japanese FDI, which is, in practice, concentrated on the West Coast. Over one quarter of all Japanese FDI in the United States is in Hawaii; another quarter is in California. Many in Congress pushed for protectionist trade bills over the 1981–8 period, leading to the passage of the 1988 trade bill. Its Super 301 provisions are restrictive and protectionist. Members of Congress have urged more screening of Japanese FDI. There is a strong 'Japan-bashing' stance in US trade policy. Yet Tennessee and virtually all other states have officials actively seeking out Japanese FDI in their states; they want the jobs and tax base. Tennessee has attracted Nissan and Bridgestone tyres; state officials there, like their compatriots elsewhere, are falling over themselves endorsing these Japanese-owned firms as good corporate citizens. This potential clash between Washington 'beltway' thinking (which is anti-Japanese) and state-level activity (which is pro-Japanese) parallels Canada's experience with the regulation of FDI.

The United States seems destined in the next ten years to repeat many of the mistakes made in Canada over the last thirty years. Canadians are experts at restricting FDI; it has not been a happy experience. In 1974 the Trudeau government introduced the Foreign Investment Review Agency (FIRA), designed to screen FDI on economic criteria to assess if there was a 'net benefit' to Canada. Yet, over the 1974–85 period FIRA responded to Ottawa's political winds, at times rejecting as much as 30 per cent of applications but at other times (especially 1982–5) approving virtually everything. The administrators at FIRA, and the responsible ministers, abused the economics-based tests of FIRA and made political decisions just as the US International Trade Commission and Commerce Department do today in US trade law cases.

In 1985 FIRA was abolished and a new agency, Investment Canada, was created with the mandate to attract FDI rather than scare it away. Throughout the lifetime of FIRA most provinces, especially those in Atlantic Canada, but also in the West, still wanted FDI for jobs and taxes. The clash between the provinces who favour FDI and the central Canadian economic nationalists who want to scare it off has now led to the federal government giving up many of its powers to regulate FDI by buying into the agenda of the provinces, especially their overwhelming priority about jobs. Perhaps this is some evidence of the triumph of decentralised economic power.

But a paradox emerges. In Canada, the economic nationalists, who have used central government power, are in retreat, while it appears that in the United States economic nationalism is just beginning to take off. If Japan-bashing continues then the US proponents of restrictions on FDI should learn from Canada's unhappy experience with FIRA. In any case, the private sector corporate strategists will need to respond to a large dose of economic nationalism and the downside of sovereignty.

The Revolution in East Europe

The third example of the use of sovereignty and the destruction of centralised economic power and values is in the revolution of 1989 in Central Europe and the collapse of the Soviet Union. The rejection of totalitarian communist regimes by the public in Poland, East Germany, Hungary, Czechoslovakia, Romania and the USSR will have many implications for business. The key point is that all these countries are currently very poor with inefficient economic and financial systems. Some, like Hungary and Czechoslovakia, have the potential to be restructured quickly (perhaps within a five-year period) by West European FDI. Others will take much longer to convert to a market-based system. In the interim they will mainly serve as low-wage producers of standardised products (playing a similar role to that of Mexico within North America).

The economic development of the poor East European nations will probably be through FDI rather than joint ventures. Popular wisdom to the contrary, joint ventures between poor nations and wealthy corporations do not work. The preferable mode of international business is FDI, since the Western firms can then control their proprietary advantages and not risk their dissipation through joint ventures. In the literature on joint ventures in developing countries, it has been found that there exists a great degree of instability and joint venture failure (Beamish, 1988). The multinationals prefer FDI. Countries like India and Mexico, which have restricted FDI, have experienced inefficient economic development and eventually lifted restrictions on FDI. This is the experience relevant for Eastern Europe.

Doing business in Eastern Europe for the next five to ten years will be dominated by the need for economic efficiency. The globalisation concept will dominate concerns about adapting products for sovereignty. It is in the EC nations that sovereignty will be important for corporations. As Harry Johnson said, 'Independence is a luxury good'. In the wealthy Triad powers of Japan, North America and the

European Community, adapting to sovereignty matters. In the Third World, and in Eastern Europe, economic efficiency is what matters.

Japanese Corporate Strategy

In contrast to the growing decentralisation of economic power and decision-making in the Triad blocs of North America and Europe, there is no such problem in Japan. The asymmetry in performance by multinational enterprises from the Triad blocs is largely based on the success of Japanese multinational enterprises relative to their European and North American rivals. A key explanation for the success of Japanese multinational enterprises is that they benefit from a highly centralised home market economy. This has permitted Japan to use levers of industrial policy and strategic trade policy which could not be implemented successfully in the other areas of the Triad.

In a discussion of US versus Japanese corporate strategy and trade policy, Rugman and Verbeke (1987) have demonstrated the critical importance of centralised government policy in order to implement effective corporate strategy. The nature of the Japanese cultural, religious, social and political system is centralised relative to other Triad blocs. As a consequence Japanese multinational enterprises have followed globalisation strategies. After the two OPEC oil cases of the seventies Japanese industry was rapidly transformed out of shipbuilding, heavy engineering and other energy-intensive manufacturing into computer-based manufacturing, consumer electronics, and high value-added services, including banking and financial services. The state and corporations worked together to implement a new industrial strategy in an effective and efficient manner.

Such radical restructuring through industrial policy is unlikely to work in North America and Europe due to the decentralised nature of economic power. Attempts by the United States, or Canada, to implement a new industrial policy will not be successful. Whatever government incentives and subsidies are made available will be appropriated by industries seeking shelter from competitors in the Triad. The decentralised nature of the economic system will be used by companies to erect entry barriers against foreign competitors. This has already occurred in the United States with companies seeking protection from competitors by the use of CVD and AD laws. The US steel, forest products, fish, semiconductor and many other industries have been using short-term legal remedies instead of investing in the development of sustainable, proprietary, firm specific advantages.

What are the implications for corporate strategy of these asymmetrical developments in the Triad? Japanese multinational enterprises can continue to pursue a globalisation strategy, but these multinational enterprises may face difficulties when they need to operate in the decentralised jungles of Europe and North America, since marketing-type skills will become more important than production ones. Over the last decade the multinational enterprises from Europe and North America have often abused the nature of their home country decentralised systems. Sovereignty has hindered efficient corporate development. However, the multinational enterprises from Europe and North America have a potential competitive advantage over Japanese multinational enterprises if they can learn from their past mistakes. Awareness of sovereignty may make European and North American multinational enterprises better equipped in the future to be more nationally responsive than the Japanese multinational enterprises. The Japanese multinational enterprises may become locked into a globalisation only strategy, just as the world begins to demand much more corporate responsiveness to sovereignty.

CONCLUSION

In this chapter we have argued that globalisation forces are blurring the borders of the nation-state, creating the three regional economic blocs now known as the Triad. At the same time that economic integration is occurring, however, there is increasing political fragmentation. As a result the relevant borders for MNEs are now being defined by cultural areas rather than national boundaries.

Globalisation forces are also causing MNEs to lose their home country identity as they move towards integrated production strategies within each Triadic bloc. The Triadic and non-Triadic multinationals will emerge, with the Triadic MNEs distinguished primarily by their differing cultures and social-political- historical roots rather than by their behaviour. For all firms the most important business decision will be the trade-off between thinking global (that is, focusing on economic efficiency) and acting local (that is, being responsive to non-economic issues).

The chapter provided three current examples of the trend towards decentralisation: the shift of power from Canada's federal government to its provinces; the fragmentation of economic power in the United States as the US government becomes more protectionist and responsive to special interest groups; and the revolution and restructuring in Eastern Europe; and contrasted these cases to the centralised home market economy of Japan. The conclusion from these case studies is that sovereignty is of growing importance in the Triad.

6 Big Business and the State[1]

Susan Strange

The first puzzle to be addressed is why it is taking so long for the study of international relations to embrace and incorporate big business into the analysis of the international system. Not only is it 20 years since Vernon's *Sovereignty at Bay* came out in America: it is 20 years or more since, with the blessing of the London School of Economics' International Relations department under Geoffrey Goodwin, that I initiated a small graduate seminar on International Business in the International System.[2] I was not even on the staff at the time, but that acorn grew into a sapling – a regular Master's course with examinations. The only other people at the LSE who were interested in transnational corporations then were Professor Ben Roberts and some colleagues in the Industrial Relations department. Their concerns, however, were narrower and their work more directed at how labour relations with management were affected by the internationalisation of production.

In two decades since then, the LSE's graduate school has probably produced more Masters' dissertations and Doctoral dissertations on subjects related to international business than any other British university. The Business History Unit has become well-established and an interdisciplinary network of lawyers, sociologists, geographers, political scientists and even economists has grown up. Yet in textbooks and regular courses in international relations, the role of transnational corporations (TNCs) is still no more than an addendum, a kind of appendage to the main body of the subject.[3] I have been convinced for some time that this is quite wrong and that we shall never get to the bottom of other puzzles in international relations unless we put the study of international business at the centre, together with states, instead of at the periphery. My question is why international relations still so resembles an intellectual Procrustean bed, too short to accommodate reality, so that the study of international business is either cut-off altogether, or curled up at the bottom of the bed where it safely can be overlooked.

It all goes back to the question of power, and the rather narrowly conceived answer that many people in international relations still have to the questions: What is power in the world system/international political economy? And who has it? They think of power in terms of the ability to create or disrupt order in the system (Waltz, 1979; Bull, 1977). Since order is most often – though not always nor only – disrupted by states, it follows that their prime concern is with the relations between states. It is only when you think of power in terms of the ability to create or destroy, not order but wealth, and to influence the elements of justice and freedom as part of the value-composition of the whole system, that it becomes obvious that big business plays a central, not a peripheral role.[4]

It does so because large enterprises – the oil companies, the manufacturers of capital and consumer goods, the banks, the trading enterprises and those that control transport and communication – all create wealth – and incidentally affect the who-gets-how-much justice and freedom and economic security. Until the mid-twentieth century, many of these enterprises still operated within a framework of national markets, national law and national finance markets. It is only in the last two or three decades that the majority of major enterprises in all these fields have outgrown national markets, national laws and national financial markets and have begun to produce for a global market according to a global corporate strategy. By operating in this way, they cannot help exercising a major influence on the nature of the international political economy and the distribution within it of benefits and costs, or risks and opportunities.

That is why it seems to me that so many writers and teachers in conventional international relations are like the orthodox theologians in Gallileo's time. They are like Flat Earthers who refuse utterly to recognise that the earth is round and revolves around the sun. Similarly, they refuse to see that the relations between states is but one aspect of the international political economy, and that in that international political economy, the producers of wealth – the transnational corporations – play a key role. To do so would upset too much of their received wisdom – not to mention their claim to special expertise in inter-state relations as a defined, discrete branch of social science. Many of the old dogs are not keen to learn new tricks. In short, it is the self-protecting myopia of those who profess international relations which for too long has stunted the growth of international political economy and kept the study of international business as a mere appendage at the periphery, denying it its rightful place at the centre.

Where the first puzzle was an intellectual one, the second puzzle is a normative one. If these TNCs are so powerful in the world market economy of the 1980s, what are governments to do? How should they respond? Firms, after all, are hierarchies, as Oliver Williamson (1975) pointed out. The bosses are in charge, at least for the time being. They are not subject to the popular will and do not have to fight every so often to be re-elected. (Even shareholders nowadays, it is generally agreed, only rarely exercise control over management.) So, if the TNC manager's power to determine what kind of wealth is created, where and by whom it is created and on what terms, is a power exercised more or less independently of the state, how is the national interest, the class interest, the general public interest – however defined – to be secured?

Sanjaya Lall argues that the state has perforce to use whatever powers it has to regulate and restrict the activities of TNCs within its territorial borders. That view is, broadly, shared in the emerging new democracies of Central and Eastern Europe as well as in many developing countries of Africa and Latin America. The state has authority to act by virtue of its role as gatekeeper to the territory. The legitimacy of its power to give or withhold access to its internal market, to its natural resources, to its labour and capital is acknowledged by other states. The only trouble is that, though legitimated, these are all negative powers. The gate can be barred, but when open, it is up to the TNCs, not the state to decide whether they should enter. Therein lies the rub. If there is too much restriction, too rigid regulation of the way they operate once they are inside the gate, then the foreign-owned firm (FOF) will stay away, or leave, or enter only in such a way as to minimise the risk.

Faced with this dilemma, it is true, as Dunning argues (and as the United Nations' Centre on Transnational Corporations reported some while ago), that the governments of developing countries over the past decade have become much more accommodating to the needs of the FOFs.[5] They have more or less given up nationalisation. They have lowered the barriers to entry and relaxed the restrictions on where and how FOFs may operate. Trade barriers have been lowered and the administration of licensing has been simplified and speeded up. By the 1980s, even countries like Myanmar, Thailand and Albania that had hitherto eschewed collaboration with foreign capital and had stuck faithfully to autarky and self-reliance were changing the direction of policy.

Lall and others might argue that they have only done so under the exigencies of indebtedness, and that the change of direction therefore is only a temporary accommodation to the arm-twisting practised by the IMF and World Bank. Caught unawares at the beginning of the 1980s by the U-turn of the Reagan Administration which sent interest rates soaring and with them the burden of servicing loans from foreign banks, the only escape route for debt-burdened lesser developed countries (LDCs) lay through new inward investment by FOFs. Camdessus at the IMF, Conable at the World Bank, their creditors in the Paris Club, all told them so. In other words, if they have eased up towards foreign firms, it is only from necessity, not conviction. As soon as they possibly can, they will tighten up the rules and raise the barriers once again.

I do not think this is so. The reasons for thinking, on the contrary, that the change in attitude of LDC governments is a permanent one are to be found in the structural analysis of change in the international political economy. The key changes in global structure have been in what I have called the 'Production Structure' and the 'Financial Structure' (Strange, 1988). In production – the ways, in brief, that wealth is produced – we have all witnessed the key phenomenon: the accelerating rate of technological change. This change is the speeding up of the process by which new products replace old ones – the word processor for the manual typewriter, the jet engine for the propeller, the cassette and the compact disc for the old 78 rpm records – and equally, by which new processes end new systems of information gathering, storage and dissemination replace and make obsolete the old ones – typesetting in printing, ledgers in accounting, robots in car assembly, containerisation in sea and land transport. The self-evident result is that resource-based, manufacturing and service enterprises have all discovered that this accelerating rate of change does not give them sufficient time to recoup in profits *derived solely from local, national markets* the costs of developing and/or installing new products or new processes. To keep up with their competitors, who may already be transnational corporations, they are obliged to sell on several national markets at once.

This is where a good deal of the literature on the theory of the firm has gone astray. It offers an inside-out explanation, instead of an outside-in one. That is to say, the explanation for the internationalisation of production is not to be found within the firm, but in the context, in the changing political economy within which the firm operates and competes with others in a global market for goods and services. This is why even Vernon had to concede that there were serious limitations to his own product-cycle theory of why firms produced abroad instead of just relying on exports (Vernon, 1971). Part of the reason lay in this accelerating rate of technological change (and, of course, the associated rising costs of capital and of research and development in total production costs relative to land, labour and materials).

But in order to sell in several national markets and to sell with some confidence that trade barriers would not be suddenly and unexpectedly raised against them – TNCs found it prudent (as well as cheaper in many cases) to produce as well as sell locally; thus, the outside-in explanation of the accelerated trend towards the globalisation of production.

The other structural change has been in the international financial system: the integration of capital markets into one worldwide market for savings and credit. Partial and incomplete as it may be, this integration means that the TNCs enjoy far greater possibilities than smaller local concerns of raising money wherever they operate. They do not even have to transfer funds across frontiers and exchanges. They have longer pockets and far, far better market access ertainly in the affluent markets of America, Europe and Japan, and often even in the local markets of their Third World affiliates. So, while the first structural change has driven enterprises, willy-nilly, to compete on the world market, the second has given them very substantial advantages over small, local competitors when they try to do so. The old 'national champions', whether in France or South Africa or Nigeria, have come to be outclassed by the TNCs.

These structural changes are hardly likely to be reversed. The genie of technology cannot be put back in the bottle. And it will be very hard, short of a really catastrophic collapse of the global financial system, to go back to a system of national financial systems linked only by trade and investment flows as they affect exchange rates between national currencies.

With my co-author, John Stopford of the London Business School. I have therefore come to the conclusion that it is structural change that has driven the developing countries into the arms of the TNCs and that the same structural change has driven the TNCs into the arms of developing countries' governments. Since the structural changes we have tried to describe are, broadly speaking, irreversible, the shift in government attitudes to FOFs are unlikely to change even if their difficulties with foreign debt were to be resolved (Stopford and Strange, 1991).

John Stopford and I would both question whether Sanjaya Lall is right to advise the governments of developing countries to persist in saddling multinationals with controls. Our joint research into the experience of recent years of three developing countries (Brazil, Malaysia and Kenya) in dealing with foreign firms suggests that the one that had done least to restrict them has done best, and the one that has done most (Kenya) has done worst. This is not to say that promotion of local firms (the *bumiputras* in Malaysia, for example) is to be avoided, or that protectionist controls that hinder the foreign firms should never be used. It is all a matter of timing, judging carefully the pros and cons. But protectionism is like smoking cigarettes. It is apt to be habit-forming and it does risk damaging your health. This is what Brazil has discovered with its Law of Similars that kept IBM out of the local market and protected local firms and a few foreign associates from competition. For Brazilian business, the computers they could buy legally became unduly costly and were two years behind the state of the art in the world market.

This is why we believe that the Central European politicians who are wondering how to respond to Western and Japanese TNCs would do well to make careful studies of the recent experience of the more successful developing countries in terms of economic development. They might conclude, as we do, that the game of diplomacy these days is triangular; just as important as the bargaining processes between governments are the bargaining between governments and enterprises, and that between enterprises. Central Europe's best brains therefore ought not to be directed to the Foreign Ministry, but to the ministries in charge of trade and investment and industrial policy; and also perhaps to the top management of those local enterprises that will have to negotiate (for new capital, for new technology and for market access) with the managers of foreign firms with whom they contemplate alliance, whether temporary or permanent, general or specific.

The lessons for international business are not less important. The enterprises, too, have to learn diplomacy. Bull-headed disregard for the political constraints upon governments or for the social concerns which are often the main source of political legitimacy will do a company no good in negotiations with a host government. Considerations of cost and short-term profitability can no longer always be paramount in corporate strategy. In short, those in the future with Master's of Business Administration degrees should have some training in international history and international relations. Just as students of international relations, as was implicitly argued earlier, really need to know and understand the processes and the problems of international business.[6]

Notes

This article is reprinted from *Millennium*, vol. 20, no. 2 (Summer, 1991).

1. This title is borrowed from Raymond Vernon (ed.), *Big Business and the State: Changing Relations in Western Europe* (London: Macmillan, 1974).
2. Acknowledgements to the Ford Foundation which, in the early 1970s, funded a research project at Chatham House in London on transnational relations. I was the director and my interest in the role of international business was nourished by collaboration with colleagues Andrew Schonfield, Marcello de Cecco and Louis Turner as well as by others who came to study group meetings in St James's Square.
3. I prefer the more accurate UN usage of 'Transnational Corporations', even though 'multinationals' is a shorthand everyone understands. But it is, after all, a misnomer: the enterprises are not truly multinational, though their markets are.
4. For a discussion of how and why social systems, including the world system, should be analysed in terms of the 'mix' as well as the distribution of these four basic values, see the prologue and Part 1 of Susan Strange (1988).
5. UNCTC, *Transnational Corporations in World Development: Trends and Prospects* (1988). This was the third such report and its contents were the more surprising for coming from a body set up at the insistence of the Group of 77 as a kind of critical watchdog for LDCs over the behaviour of TNCs.
6. For the arguments for this synthesis as the next stage in the development of research and teaching in international political economy, see Strange (1991).

7 TNCs in the Third World: Stability or Discontinuity?

Raphael Kaplinsky

INTRODUCTION

In 1976, there were approximately 11 000 transnational corporations (TNCs), with about 82 600 foreign affiliates. Of these, the largest 371 accounted for two-thirds of all TNC sales. There is no unambiguous measure of the contribution of TNCs to global production, but an indication of their importance can be gauged from the following observations: in 1980, the sales of the largest 350 TNCs were equivalent to 28 per cent of the gross domestic product of all non-communist economies; their employment of 25 million people accounted for one-quarter of all manufacturing employment in these economies; their liquid financial assets exceeded (by a factor of more than three times) total global assets of gold and foreign exchange; and by the early 1980s, these 350 largest TNCs contributed approximately one-third of global industrial output and their intra-firm trade accounted for more than 40 per cent of total external trade in a number of the world's largest economies.

Economic historians refer to the 1945–73 period which had unprecedented growth, as 'the Golden Age'. It was a period in which output growth occurred at more than twice the rate of any equivalent historical epoch and one in which global trade grew at more than twice the rate of output. The growing global integration of production in the post-war period was reflected, and indeed partly caused by, the operations of these TNCs. 'World firms' produced 'world products' (often semi-manufactured components) in 'world plants', to be shipped around the world for final assembly. For example, in the mid-1980s, Apple Corporation could boast that each of its computers had 'travelled' two million miles before it reached the final customer.

The role of the individual developing countries in this global extension of production by TNCs was far from homogeneous. First, and this was not unique to the developing world, most TNC production was market oriented, largely producing to meet local needs. This has been estimated to account for some two-thirds of total foreign direct investment (FDI). Second, however, there were a limited number of less developed countries (LDCs) in which TNCs located production for world markets – Mexico, Singapore, South Korea and Malaysia were especially prominent. Third, there were key sectors in which TNCs pursued a path of global integration through production in the Third World, notably in garments, shoes, electronics and toys. Fourth, TNC participation in this international division of labour was not confined to a direct role in production; they also became increasingly important as buyers of the output of locally-owned firms and as organisers of sub-contracting (a sort of 'international putting-out system').

Those developing countries in which TNCs located production for export generally achieved significant rates of economic growth. Their relatively low wage rates were complemented by long working hours and lack of labour militancy, thus allowing for the effective utilisation of fixed capital. This meant that these countries rapidly became the lowest-cost producers. This process of export-oriented FDI has come to be called the New International Division of Labour (NIDL), one in which:

> The development and refinement of technology and job organization makes it possible to decompose complex production processes into elementary units such that even unskilled labour can be easily trained in quite a short period of time to carry out these rudimentary operations ... Usually vertically integrated into transnational enterprises world market factories produce, assemble or finish components, intermediate products or final products in processes which allow for the profitable utilization of the labour-force available at the respective sites ... to produce for the world market (Frobel *et al.*, 1980).

The profound balance of payments and debt problems of much of the Third World during the 1980s proved to be fertile ground for the seeds of NIDL-type industrial strategies. Surely their comparative advantage of low wages and non-militant labour forces could become the basis for a path of export-led growth in which the global corporations produced at lowest cost for global markets? Indeed, fostered by multilateral aid agency preoccupations with recovering the ground of comparative advantage, many LDCs have reoriented their development paths to achieve these goals. Debt-equity swaps have been promoted to encourage TNC entry, 'anti-export biases' have been removed from policies, export processing zones have proliferated and expectations have been raised that export-oriented growth through TNC production is an attainable goal of policy.

But, at the same time that this policy reorientation was occurring, the very basis of global competition in manufacturing was changing. The principles of optimum location (which had favoured the site of least cost) and scale (which had favoured large-scale production) during the post-war boom had begun to change. It is no longer self-evident that past success with NIDL-type strategies, especially those involving FDI, are likely to bear fruit in the coming years.

The discussion which follows addresses these issues, but only in cursory form.[1] Because of space limitations, the treatment of these complex issues will be confined to the general level (although there are important sectoral variations) and will refer only to the role of FDI in the Third World in the manufacturing sector. Ancillary developments in minerals, agriculture and services sectors are equally worthy of attention, but are not treated here.

In pursuit of this discussion on changing determinants of global location and the role played by TNCs in the Third World, it is necessary to consider briefly the following issues: the transformation in the ground rules of competitiveness in manufacturing; changing economic determinants of optimum location; unevenness in the world economy, the changing political determinants of location and changing parameters of scale economies. Once this ground has been covered it is possible to return to the question of the role of TNCs in the Third World.

FROM FORDISM TO POST-FORDISM: THE CHANGING DETERMINANTS OF INTERNATIONAL COMPETITIVENESS[2]

The post-war boom was fuelled by the global expansion of the system of mass production. In this era, price competitiveness was dominant and, following decades of improvement in organisation and technology, was broadly achieved by adopting the following corporate strategic parameters. First, products were standardised in order to minimise change over costs in production. Second, the division of labour was pursued (separating conception from execution), work was organised in a hierarchical manner, and clear distinctions were drawn between high- and low-skilled tasks. Third, special-purpose automation developed to support this production organisation. Fourth, inter-firm relations were arm's length and characterised by distance and conflict. And, finally, lowest cost production was achieved at ever higher levels of scale.

Two other features of this mass production paradigm are relevant to our discussion. First, 'efficiency' was achieved by a combination of embodied and organisational technologies, which Perez has referred to as a 'socio-technical system' (Perez, 1985). These social determinants of competitiveness were relevant at both the micro plant level and in the wider sphere of social organisation such as education and the welfare state.[3] Second, the NIDL and Third World export manufacturing can be seen as clear expressions of this paradigm. In those sectors where unskilled labour was a major determinant of cost, production was shipped out to low wage economies that had a comparative advantage in labour intensive production. This was achieved either directly within the production control of TNCs or via relations of sub-contracting.

Toward the end of the 1960s, this pattern of accumulation began to falter and productivity growth to slow in those firms and economies that persisted in pursuing this strategic orientation of mass production. At the same time, a new pattern of production was emerging, which has variously been referred to as 'post-Fordism', 'flexible specialisation', 'systemofacture' and 'the New Competition'. Within this new paradigm, the basis of global competition has changed from price to product innovation. This is not, of course, to say that price is unimportant in post-Fordism, but rather that the maxima and constraints in the objective functions have changed from one in which price-competitiveness is maximised (constrained by minimum levels of product innovation) to one in which product innovation is maximised (constrained by minimum levels of price-competitiveness).

The maximisation of product innovation and quality required a different type of socio-technical system. Product flexibility (which is a natural concomitant of product innovation), required work flexibility; work flexibility required a multikilled labour force; product flexibility required the utilisation of flexible automation (increasingly controlled electronically); and rapid innovation, meant that formerly distant inter-firm relations had to give way to much closer integration of production schedules and product development (known as 'simultaneous engineering').

As will become clear when we discuss the implications for the Third World, it is important to note that there are alternative paths to post-Fordist efficiency. In Japan and northern Germany, flexibility is achieved within large firms which organise relationships between different affiliates. By contrast, in central Italy (the so-called 'Third Italy') and even parts of Japan, the new flexibility is achieved through the development of innovative networking relationships between small firms.[4] This process is most apparent in Italy. Italy has become the world's largest net exporter in many sectors through production by small firms. For example, in garments this has been achieved through an average firm-size of 5.3 employees; in shoes, average firm size is 17 employees; and in furniture, it is 5.7. Thus, there is no unique path to post-Fordist competitiveness, and it is becoming increasingly evident that each firm and country will necessarily need to fashion its own individual response to these changing parameters of competition.

CHANGING ECONOMIC DETERMINANTS OF LOCATION

A number of features of this post-Fordist production system are relevant to the optimum location of production and hence to the operations of TNCs in the Third World. First, the adoption of more flexible product mixes has necessitated the introduction of just-in-time (JIT) inventory systems. In Fordism, large levels of stock were available just-in-case there were any interruptions to continuous production, including delivery disruptions by suppliers. In post-Fordism, these high levels of stock are dysfunctional, and it is common for suppliers to deliver directly to the production line (rather than to warehouses), in some cases only a few hours before the components are installed in the final product. Clearly, in this pattern of inter-firm relations, proximity and reliability of supply are of the essence. Both factors mitigate against the principles of geographically spread production inherent in the NIDL.

Second, greater product flexibility has allowed manufacturers to become much more sensitively attuned to the final market and, consequently, has led consumers to become much more conscious of design and innovation. For example, it has been estimated that approximately one-quarter of the cost of garments in Fordist production was accounted for by large inventories (entailing working capital costs) and insensitivity to final markets (requiting end-of-season sales or shortages of designed products). Thus, there is an increasing premium in locating production near (in the temporal sense) final markets, thereby militating against the export of products with a high transport-to-value ratio in distant developing countries since these require time-consuming shipping, rather than allowing for rapid air transport. It is partly for this reason that much export processing zone (EPZ) production in the garments industry has shifted to the Caribbean.

A third factor militating against the NIDL in post-Fordist manufacturing is the requirement for 'simultaneous engineering' to speed up product development. For example, in the auto sector, the old pattern of arm's length inter-firm relations was associated with product cycles of ten years; the Japanese have reduced this to less than three years and have done so by close integration of development and design between a large range of firms in the production chain. Whilst to some extent the new information technologies allow for this to occur through geographical separation, they are only a mitigating factor: there is no substitute for proximity.

Fourth, as the Japanese have shown, rapid product innovation requires a process of continuous improvement (*kaizen*), by a series of incremental changes in product and process. This can only be achieved by a reversal of the historic separation of conception and execution which was such a central feature of the 'production politics' of Fordism. Coupled with the transition from single-tasking and single-skilling to multi-tasking and multi-skilling, mentioned above, this has led to an altered perspective on the role of labour in production. No longer is labour to be seen as a cost of production which has to be minimised (the essential premise of the NIDL), but rather as a central resource whose potential has to be maximised. Given the comparative advantage of the industrialised countries in skilled human resources, this undermines one of the central elements of Third World comparative advantage in manufacturing (and indeed suggests itself as an alternative explanation of the Asian NIC's past export-led growth).

Lastly, whilst it is evident that there will always be *relatively* labour intensive industries (even though the inter-industry ranking on this score may vary), over the decades there has been a continuous process whereby the labour content in production shrinks. The introduction of electronics-based flexible technologies allows for a further twist to this historic tendency towards automation and whilst, in itself, this is not enough to switch production from low wage to high wage economies, it does mean that the costs of this switch may be significantly reduced.

For all these reasons, the historic production logic of the NIDL – minimising production costs in many sectors by locating the production of standardised 'world products' in low-wage 'world factories' – alters in the transition from Fordism to post-Fordism. Proximity to suppliers, as we have seen, is one important element of this, but in itself it is not enough to suggest that production for world markets will move away from developing countries. This is because clusters of production may be located in low wage developing countries so that final products, rather than semi-manufactures, are shipped to external consumers. However, this potential clustering of post-Fordist production in the Third World may be undermined by the changing political determinants of location.

CHANGING POLITICAL DETERMINANTS OF LOCATION

The boom of the post-war global economy occurred in tandem with the expansion of world trade which, as we have seen, grew twice as fast as global output. This pattern of trade growth was furthered through a series of successive trade liberalisation agreements fostered through the General Agreement on Tariffs and Trade (GATT). By the mid-1970s, tariffs were systematically reduced in most of the OECD economies to insignificant levels (a process occurring in many LDCs in the early 1990s). But it was precisely at this time that the uneven growth rates among the major OECD economies was becoming most apparent, and the Fordist economies (such as the US and the UK) were experiencing structural imbalances in their external trade with the more innovative industrialised economies. Simultaneously, the OECD economies as a whole were finding it difficult to compete with the NICs in those sectors where automation was then impractical, especially garments and the assembly sectors.

Faced with this structural trade deficit, the OECD economies had limited options for correcting their imbalances. Their commitment to tariff reductions meant that price protection was infeasible, and devaluation of their currencies provided little respite given demand and supply elasticities, the inflationary consequences of import-intensive production and the size of individual economies in global trade (which would merely spur a process of competitive devaluations).

The alternative response of these economies was the erection of various forms of non-tariff barriers. Japan had long utilised this strategy, and indeed had been a major victim itself during the 1950s and 1960s as the Multi-Fibre Agreement was erected to limit its penetration of European and American markets. Gradually, as the 1980s progressed, world trade came to be circumscribed by a series of 'orderly marketing agreements' and 'voluntary export restraints'. These meant that if firms wished to service a particular final market, they would have to assemble there. Given the locational implications of post-Fordist production, assembling in final markets dictated that suppliers would also produce there.

This new pattern of global location is increasingly familiar. Europe now has induced local assembly by foreign TNCs in automobiles, computers, semiconductors, TVs and VCRs, machine tools, printers and in other sectors. As a consequence of the optimality of proximity (and when this is not the case, through political attacks on 'screwdriver assembly plants'), the suppliers have followed close behind. In North America, similar events have been acted out in these and other sectors. Thus, it is that the confluence between the changing economic and political determinants of location have begun to undermine the global integration of production through the further extension of the NIDL in the Third World. Comparatively, the advantage of low wages is no longer as important as it used to be.

CHANGES IN THE DETERMINANTS OF SCALE[5]

Price competitiveness in Fordism was accompanied by the pursuit of scale economies. This was reflected in three dimensions – in product-, plant- and firm-size. As we have seen, mass production involved the standardisation of the final product, Henry Ford's black Model T automobile being the classic example. But this was not confined to automobiles, and in a wide range of sectors, interchangeability of components was allied to ever larger runs of particular products. (Perhaps one of the more extreme cases in the Third World has been India's concentration on the production of a single auto design of the 1950s, as well as in similar cases in Poland and other Eastern European economies.) Associated with this expansion of product scale was the sustained growth of factory size. It became a rule of thumb that the larger the plant, the lower the unit costs of production. Further, as we have seen, mass production was accompanied at a global level by the concentration of ownership, with 350 very large corporations dominating global production.

Because these three dimensions of scale – product, plant and firm – increased in tandem, it became common to talk of the growing dominance of economies of scale in production. This was said to militate against domestic production in much of the Third World and to account for the exhaustion of the 'easy stage of import substituting industrialisation'. Yet, as post-Fordist production strategies have emerged and begun to dominate global competitiveness, the conflation of these three dimensions of scale – and the attractiveness of the 'large' – has increasingly been questioned. The changes are evident in respect to all three dimensions of scale and not in uniform directions.

Production strategies are changing to promote flexibility of output so that a single plant is able to produce a much wider range of products. This has meant that the average product run in most sectors – and, concomitantly, the average vintage of products – has fallen significantly. This tendency has been especially, but not uniquely, marked in Japan as well as across a wide range of sectors (Bessant, 1991). (It is similarly evident in the aforementioned case of the Indian and eastern European automobile industry where the 1950s design is increasingly seen to be inefficient, and where a number of new products are being launched.) This undermining of product scale economies is also associated with an enhanced ability to tailor products to a much wider set of customer specifications, providing a capability for what might be termed 'product appropriateness' in a wide range of markets, including developing economies.

In many sectors, plant size is also falling, partly as a consequence of new production philosophies, partly as a consequence of new flexible work practices, and partly as a consequence of the availability of flexible automation technologies. It also partly results from the descaling of product runs since a single factory can produce a range of different items. This ultimately undermines plant scale in many individual product areas. In the automobile industry, for example, not only is the optimal average plant size falling, but since the new plants can produce a variety of types of cars, the effective descaling of production is even more significant. In electronics, the plant size (in terms of number of employees) is falling at the same time as output flexibility is increasing. Modal plant size (number of employees) in Malaysia, for example, is said to have fallen by a factor of 10 over the past 15 years. In steel, chemicals and electricity generation, smaller plant sizes (measured in output as well as number of employees) are increasingly common. Of course this is not true for all sectors (especially in the chemical process sector where the inherent scaling efficiency, the so-called '0.6 rule', continues), but there is no question that it does influence a significant, if not the major, segment of modern manufacturing.

Thus, the scaling factors in product and plant, which influenced increased optimal plant size for many decades, can now be seen to be in reverse. However, the same cannot be said for those factors which help to determine firm size and hence the extension of TNC dominance in the world economy. Firm scale is affected by indirect costs of production, whereas plant scale is determined by direct costs of production. This means that when research and development, design, marketing, organisational and other indirect inputs are large, unit costs diminish if these indirect expenditures can be offset against a large volume of sales. This may occur through production in a limited number of very large factories or a very large number of small factories. From the firm's point of view it does not matter which pattern of production is involved as long as it is able to attain effective control over the production process and the appropriation of technological rents and profits. The growing knowledge and design intensity of production means that the relative importance of these indirect costs has continued to increase, thereby promoting the growth of large firms, albeit with more diversified and rapidly changing product portfolios and production in smaller plants. In this sense, it can be argued that, if anything, the historic dominance of TNCs is likely to grow even further. However, the advantages of the intra-firm organisation of these activities ('lowering transaction costs') are often offset by the bureaucracy of large firms as contrasted with the greater flexibility of small firms. Thus, there is a small firm alternative to the large firm logic of post-Fordist production. Moreover, there is a further organisational option to either of these, that involving technological collaboration between medium and large firms as a way of spreading indirect production costs.

IMPLICATIONS FOR THE ROLE OF FDI IN THE THIRD WORLD

Although research in this area is still in an embryonic stage, it would appear that the new paradigm of production is not merely of indirect relevance to developing countries. In other words, due to the altered pattern of international trade and behaviour by TNCs, Third World policy-makers need to be cognisant of the significance of these changes in production efficiency.

There are four respects in which these events have direct relevance to manufacturing in developing countries. First, as we have seen, post-Fordist production is inherently descaling at the plant level in many sectors. This opens new possibilities for renewed import-substituting industrialisation. Second, it is increasingly possible to fashion production to take account of product specialisation. This ability to 'niche' output to the specific conditions of individual markets, without sacrificing quality and price, opens the prospect of developing appropriate products for developing country markets. Third, since the primary changes required in the transition to post-Fordist production are of an organisational nature, they are neither capital nor foreign exchange intensive; they are, however, often human resource intensive, and this may create problems for parts of the Third World (especially, sub-Saharan Africa). Finally and paradoxically, post-Fordist production is often low cost production. The irony of the mass production framework – especially in the developing country context – as that it aimed to sacrifice product innovation in order to achieve low cost production, and yet it achieved neither. By contrast, post-Fordist production strives for product quality and innovation, and in doing so, simultaneously achieves low cost production.

Given the existence of these factors, which suggest the direct and indirect impact of post-Fordist production on developing countries, it is of interest to examine how this might affect the operations of TNCs in the Third World. A number of tentative conclusions are revealed by the earlier discussion. To begin with, the power of the Third Italy is that it is suggestive of alternative organisational forms to TNC dominance. This is especially relevant to smaller developing countries, and at least two of them – Cyprus and Jamaica – have specifically modelled their industrial strategies in the image of this form of small firm collaboration. There is, however, little evidence that this co-operation extends to inter-Third World co-operation, except in a few cases between TNCs. The pioneering joint venture between Ford and Volkswagen in Brazil and Argentina are examples of this.

Most clearly, though, it suggests that TNCs are unlikely to utilise developing country production platforms for the world market to the same extent as during the past two decades, since both the new economics and politics of production lead to the optimum location being at the point of the final market. One obvious exception to this, however, is where the changing determinants of global market access specifically promote location in developing countries. This has been the major factor explaining the growth of Third World transnationals that have located in other developing economies in order to obtain access to quotas in final developed country markets. However, for reasons considered earlier, it is unlikely that this will continue to be a major factor driving FDI in the Third World. Another exception to this is where the proximity of individual developing countries to large markets, such as Mexico and the Caribbean, favours them relative to more distant production sites.

The down-sizing of optimal production and product scale has important implications for renewing the dynamic of import-substituting industrialisation. Since the major objective of FDI in the past – and even more so in the future – has been to serve local markets, this suggests a new impetus for market-oriented FDI. Associated with this, in those sectors in which scale economies continue to be too large for local markets despite down-scaling, the growing importance of proximity suggests greater intra-regional Third World trade. Thus, instead of Brazil becoming a major exporter of automobile components and/or cars to the US and Europe (as it might have hoped in the NIDL), there will be growing intra-regional production integration and trade. There is no reason why TNCs should not be at least as effective in this regional integration as are local firms.

It may well also be the case that inter-regional South–South trade is favoured in post-Fordism. This is because the growing ability to 'niche' products to specific needs is suggestive of product portfolios appropriate to developing country consumers and operating conditions. Once again, there is every expectation that TNCs will be at least as efficient in capturing these external economies as are locally-owned firms.

Finally, there are inevitably important regional differences. Sub-Saharan African manufacturing is so debilitated that with the exception of a post-apartheid South Africa, there is little likelihood of export-oriented manufacturing by TNCs, whether in the Fordist or post-Fordist mode. By contrast, the growing importance of proximity is especially evident in the region represented by the Association of Southeast Asian Nations (ASEAN) where TNCs went originally in the search for cheap labour and have stayed because of the quality of human resources and the closeness to other suppliers. These production platforms are becoming major exporters because of their technological attributes rather than their cheap labour. For example, two nominally developed country TNC computer disk drive manufacturers – Seagate of the US and Rodime of the UK have effectively closed their factory operations in their home bases and have confined their production to Singapore. In Latin America, some TNCs are already beginning the process of regional integration, predominantly to serve local markets. The major exceptions to these trends are probably those developing economies in closer proximity to final markets, especially when they possess higher quality labour. Thus the potential of Mexico and the Caribbean (close to the US), North Africa (close to Europe) and the ASEAN economies (close to Japan and having growing demand in their own right) are probably likely to be relatively favoured by what remains of export-oriented FDI in the transition to post-Fordist production.

CONCLUSIONS

We have painted a picture with a very broad brush, since the canvas is large and there has been little opportunity to paint in detail. Our concern has been to identify the major trends which are emerging and to contrast these with what has occurred in the post-war period. This is not, of course, to deny the complexity and diversity of these trends. There will inevitably remain important areas of TNC involvement in export-oriented production in the Third World and there will be sectors in which this is especially important. Nevertheless there are strong grounds to suspect a significant change in the nature of TNC involvement in many LDCs.

If this is considered to be too bold, two final considerations may be borne in mind. First, there is no inevitability about the continued rise in the trade component of global manufacturing value added, and, in fact, the ratio of merchandise trade to GDP fell in all the Group of Seven countries between 1912 and 1960 (for example, from 11 to 7.9 per cent for the US, 28.5 to 18.8 per cent for Japan and 43.5 to 30.4 per cent for the UK). And, second, a continued disparity in the rate of trade and output growth (as occurred in the post-war period) faces inherent limitations, as do all exponential trends. *Reductio ad absurdum*, if past trends are sustained, no production will occur at the site of the final market. Carried to this extreme, the argument is clearly absurd, but the substantive conclusion remains – there are inevitable limits to the global integration of production.

Notes

Reprinted from *Millennium*, vol. 20, no. 2, Summer, 1991.

1. For more extended discussion, backed by a case study of the automobile sector, see Hoffman and Kaplinsky (1988).
2. More detailed treatment of these issues can be found in Best (1990).
3. For a brief discussion of the implications for the educational system most appropriate to the Caribbean mass production, see *IDS Bulletin* (vol. 20, no. 1, 1979). For an extended discussion of the macro environment most appropriate to this system of mass production, see Piore and Sabel (1984).
4. See Best (1990) for Italy.
5. For a discussion of these changing determinants of scale, see Kaplinsky (1990).

8 Multinational Enterprises and Developing Countries: Some Issues for Research in the 1990s

Sanjaya Lall

The heat of the debate surrounding the role of Multinational Enterprises (MNEs) in developing countries has subsided considerably in recent years. The closing years of the 1980s have, in fact, witnessed a general warming of attitudes to foreign direct investments, not just in the development literature, but also on the part of the national governments that were traditionally strongly hostile to multinationals. There are many explanations for this change: a 'maturing' of the theory of international production, with a better appreciation of the nature and advantages of MNEs; the accumulation of experience of industrialisation in the developing world, with some of the exceptionally successful countries drawing heavily on foreign investors, and with many regimes restrictive to foreign investments faring poorly; the growing capability of many developing countries to negotiate with MNEs, and, for the more advanced ones, to absorb the leading edge technologies possessed by them; the onset of the debt crisis, with the sharp fall in flows of commercial lending to developing countries; and the speeding up of the process of technological change, with a resulting need of most countries to gain speedy access to modern technologies, services and information networks.

All these developments have coincided with a decline in ideological underpinnings of the more extreme criticisms of MNEs. As radical and 'dependency' analyses have grown unfashionable, and strategic shifts in most formerly socialist economies have gathered pace, there has been a widespread move to greater belief in market efficiency. This move has sometimes been carried to excessive lengths, and possible deficiencies of free markets (what economists term 'market failures') have been glossed over. In the context of MNEs, this has meant, to some analysts, a belief in the absolute virtues of free capital flows, with any interventions regarded as necessarily harmful. Many long-standing concerns about MNE operations have been forgotten by policy-makers, some legitimately but others not: not only are issues of sovereignty being relegated to the background, the economic tools being applied are biased by ideological concerns.

The 1990s should witness two trends. First, there is likely to be a continuation of a shift away from excessive interventions in interna-tional capital flows by developing country governments. More countries will seek to emulate the success of the newly industrialising countries (NICs) of East Asia by becoming more outward oriented and open to foreign technology and direct investment flows. A branch of research will support this liberalising tendency. Second, there is, on the other hand, likely to be a reaction to the excessive free market propositions currently in vogue. It will be realised that market failures are widespread in developing countries, and that they may be costly if left untreated. The present disillusionment with the ability of govern-ments to intervene is likely to diminish, as the forms and implementa-tion of rules, regulations and direct interventions improve.

As far as MNEs are concerned, these trends are likely to converge to a more balanced agenda for research and policy formulation. Greater liberalisation of MNE activity may then be accompanied by more efficient controls, driven not by ideological or nationalistic concerns (as in the past), but by economic considerations of market failures and the need to remedy these efficiently.

Issues of market failure in development are complex and contro-versial. Market failures occur when the idealised conditions of perfect competition are not met because of missing or fragmented markets, high transactions costs, lack of information and foresight, economies of scale, risk and uncertainty and so on. While no real life markets meet the stringent conditions of theory and not all market failures are of practical (development) concern, a number of failures have been identified that need remedial action. For instance, capital markets function inefficiently in developing countries; private education markets are unlikely to meet social needs; technology markets often fail; small farmers or firms are discriminated against in several ways; investments in capability development (see below) are usually sub-optimal because of risk, dynamic learning phenomena and lack of information. The existing MNE literature treats the existence of the MNE itself as a response to market failure: in the creation, diffusion and exploitation of the 'ownership advantages' that are necessary for foreign direct investment to take place.[1] The MNE exists because it is economical for a firm to 'internalise' deficient markets in the presence of high transactions costs, especially for intangible assets (e.g., technology, skills, brand names and the like), across national boundaries. However, the impact of such internalised markets on economic agents in developing countries is far from clear. MNE entry may, in the highly fragmented, inefficient or missing markets for factors, knowledge, skills and institutions in a developing country, boost the efficient development of some markets while retarding others.

The current literature tends to emphasise the beneficial impact of MNE transfer of capital, technology, skills and marketing, both directly (within foreign affiliates) and indirectly (by spillovers to competitors, suppliers or customers).[2] There is no doubt that major benefits of this type do exist. MNEs are among the world's most powerful and effective agents for the transfer of productive factors, and they may well have desirable 'externalities'. Many of the earlier concerns of critics regarding dependency, exploitation, inappropriate technology transfer or excessive product differentiation, have turned out to be exaggerated or unfounded. Nevertheless, some issues of policy concern do remain, mainly because the powerful internalised markets of MNEs can distort or retard the development of similar markets in host developing countries.

The problem may be illustrated with reference to *technology*. Technology transfer is, in the eyes of developing countries, perhaps the single most important contribution of MNEs. Whether the technology provided by the MNE is 'appropriate' to factor endowments of host countries is not a subject which has (or should have) greatly exercised policy-makers, though it has attracted a disproportionate share of research in this area. The more important set of questions, of how well the transferred technology is absorbed, diffused and built upon in the host country, has drawn relatively little attention. Yet it is this question which, in my view, is critical in the context of technology: What is the contribution that MNEs make to the *development of technological capabilities* in the host country? Issues of market failure, internationalisation and intervention arise here in forms often neglected in the past.

A large and growing body of recent research shows that technological development plays as vital a role in the industrial success of developing countries as it does in developed countries. Though developing countries are not on the frontiers of innovation (and some are not even able to effectively utilise modern technologies), in order to grow they need to develop new skills, knowledge, institutions and organisational structures to master the technologies they import. This entails a process of learning, with risk, uncertainty and cost, and with significant scope for interventions and supportive policies. Different countries display differing degrees of development of their capabilities to cope with modern technologies, depending on their initial endowments and effectiveness of interventions. The NICs of East Asia succeeded largely because they overcame market failures in technological development by providing incentives (i.e., by giving selective infant industry protection), developing skills (i.e., by investing massively in education, especially technical training) and promoting technological effort (i.e., by subsidies, protection and institutional support), all within the context of export orientation (Lall, 1990; 1992). Other developing countries failed by comparison, partly because of external shocks or macroeconomic mismanagement, and partly because of the wrong choice of trade strategies, excessive or misplaced intervention and inadequate support for capability development.

The role played by MNEs in the technological development of host countries is somewhat ambiguous. To the extent that technological development· consists of mastering the 'know-how' (operational procedures) of a given technology, MNEs may be generally presumed to have a positive effect. They transmit state-of-the-art knowledge, and provide the skills and equipment to make it operational. Even if foreign personnel are needed in initial stages, it is in the MNE's economic interest to develop cheaper skills in the host country to take over all local tasks. It is also in its interest to make the adaptations needed to make the technology function efficiently. And, finally, it is to its own benefit to continually update the affiliate's technology as local circumstances dictate, providing it with the fruits of innovations created in developed countries. Moreover, a foreign presence tends to stimulate local competitors to perform more efficiently. Thus, the 'ownership advantage' of MNEs with respect to technology seems to offer significant benefits to countries that wish to apply that technology to production.

Nevertheless, to the extent that technological development involves the growth of deeper indigenous research and innovation ('know-why') capabilities, the benefits of MNE presence are less evident. The very fact that transnational corporations locate their innovation in developed countries (and their research and development activities in various centres there increasingly feed into each other), and internalise technology markets, means that affiliates in developing countries can import all their 'know-why' and need to conduct little research and development themselves, beyond that needed for adaptive activity.

Not all developing countries can sustain efficient innovative activity, but for the growing number that can, a strong foreign presence may inhibit the development of the indigenous technological base (beyond that needed for adaptive research). This may happen not just in affiliates but, by raising the cost and risk of local innovative activity, also in competing local firms (a typical market failure resulting from poorly functioning capital and information markets). The argument may apply also to developed countries: where the host country has established technological strengths, may draw upon it and add to it by setting up local research and development; but where local technology or entrepreneurship are weak, MNEs may contribute little to its development and may even harm it (Cantwell, 1989). In addition, the impact of a strong MNE presence, with established links with science and technology institutions in advanced home countries, may not contribute to infrastructural development in less advanced host countries. A case thus may exist for *promoting local technological capabilities by supporting national firms and institutions, and restricting foreign entry, at certain stages of development.*

An evaluation of this kind can only be based on comparing countries that have pursued different policies towards MNEs and technological development. Several country 'types' may be distinguished. Korea and Taiwan (and Japan before them) are clear examples of coherent and successful technological strategies based on restricting MNE entry and developing local 'know-why' (Wade, 1990; Lall and Kell, 1991). Large Latin American countries, like Brazil, that have relied heavily on MNEs in certain sectors and excluded them in others, have not followed these coherent strategies for the industrial sector as a whole. Their technological development seems to have been most rapid in activities where MNEs have been restricted and sufficient skills and institutional support created, but the overall inward orientation of the economies and inadequate skill and institutional development have held back a broadening of the technological base. Singapore has depended most heavily on MNEs, but has intervened actively in the entry process and by improving domestic skills, to induce an upgrading of the industrial structure.

Singapore has displayed no ambitions to build up an indigenous technological base, and its indigenous enterprise is the weakest of the four NICs: the consequence of its strategy has been a dynamic and efficient industrial structure but little indigenous 'know-why'. This may have been a good strategy for a very small economy, but is unlikely to work as well in larger economies.

The lessons of this experience seem to be that a strategy based on restricting foreign entry may be highly productive *if combined with a number of other market-strengthening measures* (export orientation, skill creation, institution building, promotion of large firms and so on). In the absence of such measures, however, keeping MNEs out may be damaging: it would do little for domestic capabilities, and would deprive the economy of the benefit of know-how upgrading and competition that MNE presence involves.

This example shows the sort of enquiry that may be fruitfully undertaken in the future with respect to MNEs. This approach eschews the ideological preconceptions of those opposed to or supportive of MNEs, and focuses instead on pressing issues of capability development in environments where markets do not function efficiently. It departs from current orthodoxy in examining the efficiency of the free markets (instead of taking it for granted), and in allowing some scope for efficient government intervention (instead of assuming all governments are incompetent). It reintroduces issues of political economy rather than making extreme and naive assumptions about governments and politics.[3] It seeks to draw the real lessons from the success of the NICs, rather than starting from the premise that the best policy with regard to MNEs is to 'get prices right' and intervene as little as possible.

In general terms, the subject of MNEs in development is perhaps less exciting than it once was. Recent development experience, a disillusionment with past interventionist policies, growing government sophistication and adverse international economic circumstances, have combined to produce a much more favourable, and less controversial, environment for direct investment flows. The 'maturing' of the literature on MNEs in development reflects this shift. This maturity is to be welcomed, since many of the heated debates of the past turned out to be arid and irrelevant. It does not, however, signify that all issues have been resolved. This chapter suggests that this is not the case: many basic questions do remain. Many of the insights on such issues offered by Raymond Vernon in his classic, *Sovereignty at Bay*, retain validity and deserve probing in the future.

Notes

Reprinted from *Millennium* (vol. 20, no. 2, Summer, 1991). I am grateful to Lorraine Eden for perceptive and helpful comments on an earlier draft.

1. For a succinct and comprehensive review of the theory of interregional investment, see Dunning (1988).
2. A good example is the United Nations Centre of Transnational Corporations, *Transnational Corporations in World Development* (1988).
3. For a critique of such assumptions, see Schapiro and Taylor (1990).

9 The Competitiveness of Countries and their Multinational Firms

Magnus Blomström and
Robert E. Lipsey

INTRODUCTION

Analyses of international competitiveness and comparative advantage focus on the characteristics and behaviour of countries. They generally assign the responsibility for changes in countries' competitiveness to macroeconomic developments and for changes in comparative advantage to changes in factor abundance and factor prices, to industry productivity developments, or to economies of scale in production. There is also another strand of literature that attributes changes in competitiveness to more 'structural' developments, in the sense that they are more deeply imbedded and long term, and not subject to manipulation by macroeconomic policy. These include changes in the aggregate productivity of the country, its workers, and its firms relative to those of its competitors. Recent discussions of US trade problems have emphasised factors of the second type, in particular worker skills or motivation, or the innovativeness, inventiveness, management abilities, and technological capabilities of US firms, all or some of which have supposedly declined.

These characteristics of firms are given a different role in the literature on the multinational corporation (MNC). These are the elements of the competitiveness of individual firms that, if possessed in sufficient quantity, enable firms to produce outside their own countries in competition with local firms that presumably have the advantage of knowledge of local markets and the favour of local consumers and governments. Thus, these elements of competitiveness and comparative advantage are treated in the literature on multinationals as belonging to firms rather than countries, and as being transferable from country to country within the firm. The more geographically transferable these attributes are, and less transferable they are between

129

firms, the less they can be the basis for national competitiveness and comparative advantage, but the more they can explain the competitiveness and comparative advantage of firms in their worldwide activities.

In a series of papers, we have emphasised the distinction between the competitiveness of countries, as geographical entities, and that of firms that may have headquarters in a country, but can produce in many countries (Lipsey and Kravis, 1985; 1987; Blomström *et al.*, 1988; Blomström and Lipsey, 1989; Blomstöm, 1990a, Kravis and Lipsey, 1992). We focus on the implications of the increase in the internationalisation of firms for the way we think about competitiveness and comparative advantage. The basis for the comparative advantage of a country is the set of resources located within it and immobile across national borders. Immobile factors of production, such as climate, land, and other national resources, and possibly labour (although there has been considerable mobility of that factor), are clearly bases for the comparative advantage of countries. To the extent that a resource moves freely and at a low cost from one country to another, it cannot be the basis for a country's comparative advantage or competitiveness. Thus, there are factors that determine the geographical location of production and factors that determine the ownership of production. To the extent that a factor has both geographically mobile and immobile elements, it may affect both location and ownership.

If, for instance, there were only two countries, the United States and Japan, and free entry for each country's firms into the other country, the combination of US country and US company comparative advantage would result in home production by US firms, while the combination of Japanese country and company comparative advantage would result in home production by Japanese firms. The combination of US company comparative advantage with a location advantage for Japan as a country would result in production in Japan by US-owned companies, while the combination of Japanese company comparative advantage with location advantage for the United States would result in production in the US by Japanese firms. The location advantage might rest on factor abundance or factor prices, on access to that country's market, or on closeness to other markets.

There are various ways we could compare a country's competitiveness and comparative advantage and those of its firms, with those of the world as a whole or of particular countries. We could compare, for instance, the US and US firms with others by examining shares in world production or exports, shares as exporters to particular markets, or shares as producers in or exporters from individual country markets. In the comparison of shares in individual markets, we would be holding constant the consuming market, and in the comparison of exports from particular countries we would be holding constant the characteristics of the country of production.

We have studied mainly competition on the world market and we have measured competitiveness and comparative advantage by exports rather than by production. The main advantage of using exports rather than production for this purpose is that exports are somewhat more footloose. A country inclined towards protecting its producers has more power to determine which producers supply its home market than which supply export markets. For this reason, shares in export markets may represent the underlying advantages of countries or firms to a greater degree than do shares in domestic markets.

That is not to say that export markets are unaffected by government interventions or other non-economic factors. It is more that the effects of export promoting or obstructing policies are circumscribed. Obstructing policies are limited by the ability of companies to move their export production to other locations if a country's policies impose too heavy costs on them. Promotion policies are limited by the watchfulness of other countries over their own home and export markets.

Ideally, one should study a variety of measures of firms' competitiveness. A drawback of the export measure is that it ignores differences in the ability of products to be traded. For instance, the skills of US food companies in advertising and promotion that enable them to operate in many countries are probably undervalued by this measure because the products are traded very little. The strengths of these US firms might therefore be reflected mainly in their shares in consumption relative to local producers. Production, consumption, or employment shares might reflect some of these advantages better than exports. However, they have drawbacks of their own, including greater difficulty in assembling comparable data and the greater susceptibility of production for a host country market to manipulation by government interventions.

In this chapter we first set out measures of the international competitiveness of the United States, Japan, and Sweden in manufacturing as a whole, and compare them with the corresponding measures for each country's MNCs. We then divide the exports into high-, medium-, and low-technology products and, for the United States, compare its export performance with that of its multinationals in these three technology categories, and offer some explanations of the export shares of several countries and their MNCs. The concluding section discusses some implications of our findings.

THE EXPORT SHARES OF THE UNITED STATES, JAPAN, AND SWEDEN AND THEIR MNCs

From the mid-1960s to the mid-1980s, the United States and Sweden performed very differently from Japan in world export markets. The US and Sweden lost significant portions of their shares of world markets for manufactured goods, while the Japanese share increased (see Table 9.1).[1] The US share dropped from 17 per cent in the mid-1960s to 12 per cent in 1986, after the period of high exchange values for the dollar, and then recovered a little in 1988 and 1989, after the sharp devaluation of the US dollar. Sweden suffered a persistent long-term decline in competitiveness, losing over 20 per cent of its share in

Table 9.1   Shares (%) of the US, Japan, Sweden and their MNCs* in world[†] exports of manufactures, selected years, 1966–89

	1965	1966	1977	1985	1986	1988	1989
US	17.2	17.1	13.2	13.4	11.7	12.2	12.8
Japan	6.9	7.2	11.1	13.7	13.7	12.3	11.8
Sweden	3.0	2.9	2.5	2.2	2.3	NA	NA
US MNCs	NA	17.3	17.5	18.3	16.7	16.1	16.1
Japanese MNCs	NA	NA	8.6	NA	12.2	12.4	NA
Swedish MNCs	1.6	NA	1.8‡	NA	1.8	NA	NA

* Parents and majority-owned affiliates.
† Market economy.
‡ 1978.

Source: Country trade data from UN trade tapes through 1986, extrapolated to 1989 by short-cut method, using data from *United Nations Yearbook of International Trade Statistics and Commodity Trade Statistics*, various issues. Multinationals trade data are from US Department of Commerce (1975), (1981), (1988), (1991), and (1992), Blomström and Lipsey (1989), Lipsey and Kravis (1987), MITI (1980) and (1989), and Ramstetter (1991).

world exports of manufactured goods between 1965 and 1986. Japan doubled its share during the same period, but lost ground after 1986, as the exchange value of the Yen rose.

The multinationals' shares of world exports behaved very differently from those of their home countries. Sweden was the most extreme case: Swedish MNCs increased their share of world exports over the same 21 years as the share of Sweden itself fell by over 20 per cent. The share of the US-owned firms also showed a slight upward trend until 1985, while the United States as a country lost more than 20 per cent of its share. The Japanese multinationals' export share grew faster than that of Japan between 1977 and 1986, and then continued to increase after that, while the share of Japan began to fall.

There could be two main reasons why a country's multinationals show very different trends in exports from those of the country itself. One is that firms may shift into or out of the status of multinationality, which is defined as owning affiliates in foreign countries. The other is that firms that are already multinational change the location of their production. We have demonstrated elsewhere that the former reason is not dominant for the United States and Sweden (Blomström and Lipsey, 1989). Both countries have fairly complete surveys of their multinationals. The set of US multinationals did not grow significantly and the Swedish trends are observable for a fixed set of the major firms. In the case of Japan, however, we cannot be so sure, because the coverage of the MITI surveys, on which our estimates are based, is incomplete to an unknown, but changing, extent. However, during the 1980s, and especially since the rise of the Yen, there has been a great deal of anecdotal evidence of shifts in production to lower cost areas and strong quantitative evidence for such a shift to the United States from the US inward direct investment surveys.

What we consider to be the main explanation for the difference in export performance between multinational firms and their home countries is that these firms have the flexibility to shift production from high-cost to low-cost countries, as there are changes in the competitiveness of different places for the production of specific goods and services. US multinationals held on to their shares of world export markets by shifting their source of supply of exports from their home operations to their overseas facilities, which supplied less than 40 per cent of their firms' exports in 1966 and over half in the late 1980s (Table 9.2). While the US parent operations' share of world manufactured exports fell almost as much proportionately as that of the United States as a country, the foreign affiliates' share was 35 per cent

Table 9.2   Share (%) of majority-owned affiliates in exports of US, Japanese and Swedish multinationals

Year	US	Japan	Sweden
1965	NA	NA	10.4
1966	38.1	NA	NA
1977	47.6	6.7	NA
1985	48.6	NA	NA
1986	51.3	8.9	24.3
1988	52.5	11.7	NA
1989	50.2	NA	NA

Source: See Table 9.1.

higher in 1988 than it had been 20 years earlier. Thus, it was the expansion of foreign affiliates' exports that sustained the share of US multinationals in world exports of manufactured goods.

Swedish MNCs were able to stay competitive by moving export production from Sweden to their affiliates abroad. This was particularly the case during the 1970s, when increasing costs made Sweden less attractive as a production location for exports. There was a large shift towards exporting from foreign affiliates among Swedish multinationals, and by 1986, 25 per cent of their exports took place from abroad, a much larger increase than for US firms, but starting from a much lower affiliate share in the MNCs' exports. This was twice as much as 20 years earlier.

The Japanese story is a little different. Until the mid-1980s, exports from Japan were growing so rapidly that there was little incentive for Japanese multinationals to move their export facilities abroad, although such a shift did begin, at a low level. After the sharp appreciation of the Yen, the Japanese MNCs, following the same pattern as US and Swedish firms, continued to relocate their export production to their foreign affiliates.

Thus, the overall record of the years since the mid-1960s is one of a declining share for the United States and Sweden in world exports of manufactures, while US and Swedish multinational firms, exporting from both their home countries and from their overseas operations, kept their shares or even increased them. The Japanese export share, after a 20-year increase, fell after 1986, but Japanese multinationals continued to expand their shares.

EXPORT SHARE TRENDS AND TECHNOLOGICAL INTENSITIES

Changes in aggregate export shares could reflect pattern of demand rather than gains or losses in particular types of product. For example, trade in manufacturing for the world as a whole has been shifting out of low-technology goods into high-technology products (see Table 9.3). Moreover, much of the current discussion of the American trade position focuses not on the overall share, but on whether the United States has lost or is losing its technological leadership.

Of the three technology categories, the high technology one is the sector in which the United States has had its largest share for 25 years, and the low-technology sector is where it has had the lowest shares (Table 9.4). There were some notable changes in US shares between the

Table 9.3   Distribution of world* exports of manufactured goods, by technology class†

Year	Low technology	Medium technology	High technology	Total
1966	48.4	37.2	14.4	100.0
1977	40.9	40.1	19.0	100.0
1982	39.3	40.2	20.5	100.0
1985	36.0	40.2	23.8	100.0
1986	25.7	40.4	23.9	100.0

* Market economy.
† Defining technology level by the R&D intensity of the industries from which exports originate.
Source: NBER reclassification of data in UN trade tapes.

Table 9.4   Shares (%) of the United States in world exports* of three technology classes of products, selected years, 1966–86

	1966	1977	1982	1985	1986
High technology	23.9	18.8	22.0	20.8	18.7
Medium technology	20.9	15.6	15.9	14.3	11.8
Low technology	11.5	8.3	9.1	7.5	7.0

*Market economy
Source: NBER classification of export data from UN trade tapes.

mid-1960s and mid-1980s, some of which represent mainly changes in overall US competitiveness, while others represent shifts in comparative advantage in exports.

The US comparative advantages across these technology groups are shown in Table 9.5 by the ratios of shares in each technology class to US shares in total exports of manufactures. There were clear trends in comparative advantage toward high-technology and away from medium-technology exports. The United States had a comparative advantage relative to the world as a whole in both groups initially, but lost it in the medium-technology group by 1986. The US comparative disadvantage in low-technology exports in 1985 was the largest in the 20 years, but it was reduced in 1986. However, if there was any trend, it was for that disadvantage to increase.

Table 9.5 Comparative advantage* of the United States by three technology classes of products, selected years, 1966–86

	1966	1977	1982	1985	1986
High technology	1.40	1.42	1.51	1.55	1.60
Medium technology	1.22	1.18	1.09	1.07	1.01
Low technology	0.67	0.63	0.62	0.56	0.60

*Share in technology group relative to share in all manufactures.
Source: UN trade tapes and previous table.

The shares of US multinationals in world exports were consistently much higher than those of the United States for the high- and medium-technology groups (see Table 9.6). The implication is that while technology is an element of US competitiveness, it is even more important for the competitiveness of US multinationals. The same pattern of shares across technology groups is visible in 1977, and in 1985 and 1986.

The changes in competitiveness from 1977 to 1982, and from 1982 to 1985 and 1986, although they provide only a few observations, seem consistent with the speculation that exchange rates influence US trade shares more than they affect US multinational firm shares (see Table 9.7). We might think of the earlier period changes in trade shares as being influenced by the low level of the exchange value of the US dollar reached around 1980, and the latter period as influenced by the

Table 9.6 Shares (%) of US multinationals in world* exports of three technology classes of products, selected years, 1977–86

| | US multinationals, by industry of parent | | | |
	1977	1982	1985	1986
High technology	28.8	33.3	(32.6)	(29.7)†
Medium technology	26.5	24.1	(24.7)†	(22.5)†
Low technology	8.3	8.1	(8.3)†	(7.6)†

*Market economy.
†Extrapolated from 1982 on the basis of the data by industry of affiliate.
Source: UN trade tapes and US Department of Commerce (1981), (1985), (1988) and (1989).

subsequent rise of the value of the dollar. The changes in the share of total manufactured exports that we might attribute to exchange rate movements were much larger for the United States than for US multinationals. That is especially clear for the period of the rising value of the US dollar: from 1982 to 1985, the multinationals' share rose while that of the United States declined. From 1977 to 1982, when

Table 9.7 Percentage change in shares of the US and US multinationals in world* exports of three technology classes of products

	1977–82	1982–5	1982–6
All manufacturing			
US	+11	−9	−20
US multinationals	+1	+4	−5
High technology			
US	+17	−5	−15
US multinationals	+16	−2	−11
Medium technology			
US	+2	−10	−26
US multinationals	−9	+2	−7
Low technology			
US	+10	−18	−23
US multinationals	−2	+3	−6

*Market economy.
Source: See Table 9.6.

the exchange value of the dollar fell to low levels, the US share gained much more than did the share of the US multinationals.

Another contrast is by the technology levels of products: the decline in the US share of medium-technology products from 1982 to 1985 was much larger than that for high-technology products, and the decline for low-technology products much larger than for medium-technology products. The differences could reflect differences in trend, but they might also represent a lower sensitivity to exchange rate changes – that is, a lower price elasticity of demand – for the higher-technology products.

The contrast between the change in shares of the United States and that of US multinationals was also much greater in the medium- and low-technology groups than in high-technology exports. High-technology exports by US multinationals may be more dependent than medium- or low-technology exports on events specific to the US economy, such as changes in US exchange rates or other macroeconomic developments. That may be because high-technology exports are more likely to originate in the parent company or because there is less possibility of switching such exports from parents to affiliates.

We can also translate the export shares of the United States and its multinationals into a comparative advantage framework by comparing the export shares in each technology group to overall manufactured export shares (Table 9.8). Relative to the United States as a country,

Table 9.8   Comparative advantage[*] of the US and US multinationals by three technology classes of products selected years, 1977–86

	1977	1982	1985	1986
High technology				
US	1.42	1.51	1.55	1.60
US multinationals	1.65	1.89	(1.78)†	(1.78)†
Medium technology				
US	1.18	1.09	1.07	1.01
US multinationals	1.51	1.37	(1.35)†	(1.35)†
Low technology				
US	0.63	0.62	0.56	0.60
US multinationals	0.47	0.46	(0.45)†	(0.46)†

[*]Share in technology group relative to share in all manufactures.
†Extrapolated from 1982 using data by industry of affiliate.
Source: See Table 9.6.

US multinationals had strong comparative advantages in high-technology and especially medium-technology exports and a comparative disadvantage in low-technology exports. However, the shift toward comparative advantage in high-technology exports was stronger for the United States as a whole than for US multinationals.

EXPLAINING THE COMPETITIVENESS OF THE US AND OF US MULTINATIONAL FIRMS

The differences in the behaviour of the shares in world manufactured exports between the United States as a location and US-controlled firms in all locations suggest that the competitiveness of US multinationals rests on different factors from that of the United States, or on the same factors, but to different degrees. In a set of regressions described elsewhere (Kravis and Lipsey, 1992) we attempted to explain differences among industries in the competitiveness of the US and of US multinational firms.

The competitiveness of US multinationals rests on firm-specific assets not available to other US firms or to other firms in the countries in which the multinationals produce, but exploitable by the multinationals anywhere in the world. The competitiveness of countries rests on factor endowments and macroeconomic policies. We therefore used in our analysis industry characteristics that represent the prevalence of firm-specific assets in an industry (R&D intensity and advertising intensity) and characteristics that reflect factor proportions (physical capital intensity, human capital intensity, and labour intensity). Since we were dealing with differences among industries rather than among firms within industries, the determinants of competitiveness we used were industry, rather than firm characteristics. That is, if we find, for example, that high R&D intensity is associated with high world export shares for US multinationals, that result means that US multinationals will be competitive in an industry in which R&D intensity is high.

The results of that analysis were that R&D intensity was positively related to the competitiveness of both the United States and US multinationals, but more to that of the multinationals. Advertising intensity contributed to the export shares of US multinationals, but was a negative influence on those of the United States. Human capital intensity contributed to both the US and US multinationals' competitiveness, and labour intensity was an unfavourable influence on shares for both.

A crude experiment using US industry characteristics to explain Japanese, EC, and NIC (newly industrialising country) exports suggested that the sources of US and Japanese comparative advantage are similar. Those for the EC and the NICs are quite different, neither including R&D intensity and the latter strongly dependent on high labour intensity.

Parent and affiliate export shares may respond to different factors, since the parent exports are the outcome of a combination of own-firm and home country characteristics, while the affiliates' exports are the result of a combination of the same own-firm characteristics and various host country characteristics. In the case of the United States, R&D intensity showed some tendency towards encouraging parent (home) production for export, while high advertising intensity was associated with affiliate production.

CONCLUDING REMARKS

We have shown here that the competitiveness of a country's firms can behave differently from that of the country itself. That is the case with respect to long-term trends, short-term responses to changes in exchange rates, and even the underlying determinants of competitiveness.

With respect to trends, large declines in shares of world exports on the part of the United States and Sweden can be contrasted with the stability or increase in shares for US and Swedish multinationals. The short-term responses to exchange rate developments indicated that the trade shares of the multinationals, especially in the medium-technology and low-technology industries, were less affected by exchange rate developments than were the shares of their home countries. And finally, factors that are geographically mobile but tend to be firm-specific, such as R&D and advertising, were more important for the competitiveness of the multinationals than for that of their home countries.

All of these differences are related to the flexibility of multinational firms in allocating their production for export. They do seem to be able to shift some part of their production from one geographical location to another to avoid, or take advantage of, some of the effects of host countries' and home countries' policies or economic conditions. The short-term responses are more surprising than the long-term ones, since the economic conditions are mostly unpredictable and productive capacity cannot quickly be altered or moved from place to place. The implication would seem to be that there is some slack in companies' worldwide operations that may be built in to increase flexibility.

One implication of these findings for policy-making is that the balance of power has shifted away from governments. The more flexible multinationals are, the less free governments are to impose unfavourable conditions on them, either their own or foreign firms, and the more likely it is that governments will compete for the establishment of production facilities by multinationals. Another implication is that measures to increase a country's competitiveness must take into account the distinction between country-specific and firm-specific factors. Subsidisation of R&D, for example, may promote the competitiveness of a country's firms in high technology industries, but have little effect on the country as a geographical unit, if it is not a good location for high-technology production for lack of skilled labour, infrastructure, or other factors. The effect of such a subsidy might be to raise the share of the country's firms in production overseas, but not at home. Similarly, if a country's firms have no comparative advantage in labour-intensive production, a subsidy to labour input may promote local production, but the production may tend to be carried out by foreign firms that have firm-specific advantages in such production. They might be, for instance, firms from more labour-abundant countries.

In general, we conclude that the dichotomy between firm-specific and country-specific factors needs to be incorporated more widely into both economic theorising and economic policy making.

Note

1. The export data are based on UN trade tapes, converted from the SITC classification to an industry classification to match the data on multi-nationals. The methods are described in Blomström *et al.* (1988). The data on US multinationals are from the surveys carried out by the US Department of Commerce. These are presumably quite complete censuses of United States firms operating abroad. Swedish MNC data are from Blomström and Lipsey (1989) and originates from the surveys of IUI of Stockholm. In general, the Swedish and US surveys are comparable. The data on Japanese MNCs are from the MITI surveys, which are not complete censuses. The proportions of firms reporting varies from one survey to another and we have not adjusted for coverage.

10 No Entry: Sectoral Controls on Incoming Direct Investment in the Developed Countries

Robert T. Kudrle

'If you don't want Japan to buy it, don't sell it.' – Akio Morita

Michael Crichton chose this bit of cautionary advice to end his best-selling novel about Japanese business perfidy in the United States.[1] Not since *The Jungle* or perhaps *Uncle Tom's Cabin* has a political polemic been as skillfully woven into so gripping a tale. A central Crichton theme, that too much of the American economy has fallen into the hands of foreigners, played to an audience already sceptical about incoming foreign direct investment (IFDI). A 1989 poll found 78 per cent of Americans favouring greater legal restriction of foreign investment in American business and real estate. Ironically, these are the same Americans whose leaders for the previous several decades had counselled Europe and the Third World that their fears of foreign investment penetration reflected little more than baseless superstition.

The rest of the world seemed to be taking the long-standing American advice most seriously just as the US began to doubt its own wisdom: Canada unilaterally abandoned most of its IFDI controls even before the Free Trade Agreement with the United States that reduced them still further; Mexico emerged as only the best known of a raft of Third World countries seeking IFDI as never before, and 'EC 1992' promises the final removal of remaining investment controls within the twelve-nation community.[2]

Despite the unprecedented openness to IFDI in much of the world and a continuing liberal policy by the United States, all nations prohibit or explicitly control IFDI in certain sectors of the economy (Wallace, 1982). Raymond Vernon argued in *Sovereignty at Bay* that

Most countries ... including the United States have no hesitation in deciding that it was worth any price to keep foreign-controlled interests out of certain sensitive national industries. Accordingly, practically every country limits the right foreign-owned subsidiaries to participate in industries such as ordnance and aircraft, public broadcasting, coastwise shipping, banking, and minerals exploitation on public lands (Vernon, 1971, pp. 241–2).

While the generalisation remains broadly correct, the blockage of those sectors has softened greatly in some circumstances, and the variety of motivation for restriction has remained an under-explored topic.

Several questions will guide our investigation. What are the commonalities and differences among the developed countries in their restricted sectors? What are the characteristics of those sectors most commonly restricted? What are likely future developments in international co-operation?

The subject of reserved sectors deserves careful consideration. In their comprehensive study of the American situation, Graham and Krugman consider and dismiss many arguments against IFDI but make no case for opening up protected sectors. 'We claim no expertise in determining which specific sectors, if any, the national interest requires be performed by domestically controlled firms' (Graham and Krugman, 1991, p. 111).[3]

This chapter's focus on closed or explicitly controlled sectors precludes several other equally important subjects having to do with effective access for foreign direct investors. Many commentators divide such access for foreigners into two major parts: right of establishment and national treatment. Foreigners may be nominally allowed into a sector only to find that a myriad of practices combine to make their commercial life unsatisfactory. In particular, although it may allow entry, the host government can subsequently fail to give the foreigners the same fiscal support as afforded its domestically-owned competitors, it may treat the foreigner differently in its own procurement practices, or it may apply other laws or regulations in a way prejudicial to the foreigner's interest (Hoekman, 1991).

Even at the entry stage, nominal openness has a differing meaning among countries. The most common form of entry into many markets by foreign firms involves the acquisition of an existing firm in the entrant's industry. Until at least very recently, the Japanese economy has effectively denied this option, however, because of the extreme difficulty all firms – foreign and domestic – have had in acquiring existing firms. Some European countries, including Holland and Switzerland, have legislation that makes entry through a hostile takeover very difficult (although only a few per cent of all takeovers are hostile in the US and Britain) (Nicolaides, 1991, p. 132). And countries differ in their degree of general foreign investment screening. Many countries, including the United States, have legislation prescribing screening of IFDI where a specific act of entry or expansion – typically by acquisition – could have deleterious impact on the national interest. Such issues are handled in Britain as part of the general activities of the Monopolies Commission, and, at least in theory, need not be aimed unduly at foreigners, while in the United States the Exon-Florio Amendment to the Trade and Competitiveness Act of 1988 authorises the President to disallow foreign entry on grounds of 'national security'.[4] As in most other countries such screening authority overlays specific sectoral prohibitions.[5]

This discussion cannot examine all forms of differential treatment of foreign investors. At the same time, it must consider some trade issues that are closely connected with investment in controlled sectors, while ignoring trade in services more generally. IFDI freedom and service provision in the purchasing country can be closely linked, but they are clearly distinct. For example, a foreign management firm might operate a public utility that it could not legally own, while issues such as foreign resource ownership are completely independent of service provision.

Finally, this study will confine its attention to the industrialised democracies of the Organisation for Economic Co-operation and Development (OECD). This allows us to isolate the sectors protected by countries whose general posture towards IFDI is broadly accepting. In fact, the OECD has a long history of encouraging direct investment, and has conducted much of the research upon which this investigation is based (Bergsten and Graham, 1991, pp. 24–8). The OECD countries account for approximately two-thirds of world trade and about 80 per cent of foreign direct investment (Bergsten and Graham, 1991, p. 24).

THE CONTROLLED SECTORS: AN OVERVIEW

Pursuant to its activity in support of liberalisation of capital movements, the OECD has intermittently compiled data on IFDI restrictions. Although most countries continue to oblige all foreign investors to gain formal approval for their activities, such approval is typically *pro forma* and in many cases little more than a means of keeping track of new IFDI.[6]

The OECD stresses three categories of genuine restriction: general authorisation and regulation, controls and impediments by sector, and preemption by state authorised or operated monopoly that controls or excludes entry by both domestic and foreign firms.[7] The last two categories vary considerably among countries and provide the focus for our attention. Table 10.1 reproduces the results of the most recent survey based on information from the mid-1980s. While generally accurate, changes have since taken place in many countries; most of them have apparently been liberalisations. The situation in the EC is particularly fluid. The Single European Act does not officially deal with direct investment but apparently depends on intra-European complaints about prejudicial treatment from fellow community members to flush out remaining discrimination (Kline and Wallace, 1991, pp. 40–1).[14] The only remaining barrier to establishment for community members within one another's territory should be some element of government-sanctioned monopoly – which, if it is private, should be justified by incumbency rather than nationality.

Table 10.1, on the following pages, codes restrictions into three major categories, but our concern will focus on the distinction between R (restrictions) and I (impediments) on the one hand and sectors imbued with elements of officially recognised M (monopoly) on the other.

Although the data can be variously organised, six clusters will prove useful for subsequent analytic purposes: (1) banking, other financial services, and insurance (Sectors 1, 2, 4); (2) broadcasting (Sector 6); (3) post and telecommunications (Sector 7); (4) other public utilities and energy production (Sectors 21–22); (5) transportation (land, sea, and air) (Sectors ll–13); and (6) land and natural resources (Sectors 1417, 19). These categories exhaust most of the OECD sectors from 1 to 22. The remaining sectors in that group and all sectors from 23–35 are either restricted by only a few countries, cover only a miniscule part of the economy, or both.[8]

The sectors in Table 10.1 have been slightly reorganised in Table 10.2 to give an overview that maintains the original sectors while also highlighting the clusters just described. To give some sense for the orders of magnitude of the sectors with restrictions, Table 10.3 presents data on the shares of US GDP accounted for by those sectors in 1989. Ignoring variations in the relative size of the restricted sectors among

Table 10.1 Position of member countries regarding sectoral controls and impediments to inward direct investment

Sectors Countries	1	2	3	4	5	6	7	8	9	10	11	12	13	14	15	16	17	18	19	20	21	21	22	23	24	25	26	27	28	29	30	31	32	33	34	35
Australia	RI	R			RI	R	M				MR	MR	R	R	R	R	R	R	R	M	M	M				MR						M				
Austria	RI	I	R	I	RI	N	M			I	I	R	R	R	R	R	R	R	R	M	R	M				M	R				M	M				
Belgium						M	M			M	M	M	MR								M	M														
Canada	RI	R		MR	R	R	M					R	R			R	R	R			M	M									R					
Denmark				RI																			23													
Finland	RI	RI		MR	MR	MR	M	M	M	M	MR	R	R	R	R	R	R	R	R	MRI	RI	R	R	R	R	M										
France	RI	RI	R	RI	I	MR	M	RI	R	MR	MR	R	R			MRI	MRI	RI		MRI	M	RI	M			RI	R	R	RI	I		M				M
Germany	I									M	MRI	R				I					M															
Greece	RI			I		M	M			M	M	M	MI		I	I				M	M						M		M							
Ireland	RI	I		RI	M	M	M			M	R	R	RI			I		R		M	M															
Italy	RI			RI	MR	MR	M			M	R	R	RI	I	I	R	R	R		M	M					M										
Japan	I	I	I		I		NI			I	I	I	I	R		R	R		R																	
Luxembourg				MI		M															MM															
Netherlands	RI	I			M	M				M	R	R	R		R	R	M				MM	M	I													
New Zealand	RI	R		MR	M	M	R	M		M	R	R	R	MR	R	R					M															
Norway	RI	R		RI	MR	M	M			M	M	R	MR	R	R	R		M		R	R	M	M		R	M				M		M				
Portugal	R			RI	M	M	R	R		M	M	M	MR		R	R	M			R	M	M				R									M	I
Spain		I		MI	MR	M	M			M	M	R	R				M			M	I	I				M					M		M			
Sweden	R	R		I	M	M			M	M	M	R	R		R	R				I		I	I			M			M		M		M			
Switzerland	RI	I		RI	N	N		R		M	MI	MI	MI		R	M	M			I	I	M				M			M		M					
Turkey	RI	I			M	M			R	M	M	M	M		R	R	R			I	M	M				M			M		M					
United Kingdom	I	I	I	I	MR	M				M	R	R	R	R	R	R	M				M											M				
United States	I	I		I	MRMR	MR	M		R	R	R	R	R	R	R	R	R	R	R	R	R	R														

Key to Table 10.1

Banking	1
Other financial services (including stockbroking)	2
Auditing	3
Insurance	4
Press, publishing, printing	5
Broadcasting (radio, television, cable)	6
Post, telephone, telecommunication	7
Audiovisual works, film distribution	8
Health and social security	9
Employment agencies and services	10
Land transport (includes railways, buses, road construction and maintenance)	11
Air transport (includes airport construction and operation in some cases)	12
Maritime transportation (includes of alcoholic beverages shipping, ship brokerage, forwarding, inland waterways, operation of seaports, cabotage, offshore supply, salvaging and dredging, ownership of fishing vessels)	13
Fishing	14
Real estate	15
Mining, minerals	16
Petroleum	17
Agriculture, agricultural products	18
Forestry	19
Nuclear industries	20
Exploitation of water resources, water power	21
Overall energy production and public utilities (including water, gas, electricity)	22
Armaments, explosives, gunpowder	23
Security guard and private detective services	24
Tourism, travel services	25
Gaming, casinos, lottos, lotteries etc.	26
Jurisprudence, legal profession	27
Teaching, education	28
Merchants and craftsmen	29
Import, export and distribution of alcoholic beverages	30
Tobacco, matches	31
Salt	32
Pharmaceuticals, medicines, narcotics	33
Steel	34
Public works and services	3

Notes to Table 10.1

R = Sectors in which some or all activities are subject to controls or impediments to inward direct investment that are regarded as restrictions in the sense of the Code of Liberalisation of Capital Movements.

I = Sectors in which some or all activities are restricted by other impediments.

M = Sectors in which some or all activities are closed to investment due to public, private or mixed monopolies.

This table shows on a country-by-country basis those sectors which, to a greater or lesser degree, are restricted to foreign investment either because of *obstacles* which apply specifically or more severely to non-resident investors, or because of the presence of public, private or mixed *monopolies*. Where obstacles are considered as restrictions in the sense of the Code they are marked with an R. In other cases, an I (for impediments) is used. Monopolies are indicated with an M. As a result of space limitations, some sectors include a number of specific activities (see for example maritime transportation); the presence of an obstacle or monopoly in any activity of a specific sector may be restricted in the sense of the Code as this table is concerned, in a mark being entered against the entire sector. In some instances, an activity of a specific sector may be restricted in the sense of the Code and R appears in the column, while in another activity of the same subject a monopoly may exist, which is reflected by an M. Thus, for the same sector, two letters may appear. Detailed information is not available from Iceland which maintains a general derogation from the obligations of the Code of Liberalisation of Capital Movements.

Source: OECD, *Controls and Impediments Affecting Inward Direct Investment in OECD Member Counties* (Paris: Organisation for Economic Cooperation and Development, 1987).

Table 10.2   Summary of controls on IFDI by sector – 1986

Cluster	Sectors	Name	R^*	M^*	Total
1	1	Banking	18	0	18
1	2	Other financial services	14	0	14
1	4	Insurance	13	5	18
2	6	Broadcasting	3	17	20
3	7	Post, telephone and telecommunications	1	21	22
4	21	Exploitation of water resources and power	6	2	8
4	22	Energy production and utilities	3	12	15
5	11	Land transport	2	17	19
5	12	Air transport	12	9	21
5	13	Maritime transportation	14	4	18
6	14	Fishing	4	1	5
6	15	Real estate	11	0	11
6	16	Mining, minerals	11	1	12
6	17	Petroleum	7	5	12
6	19	Forestry	3	0	3
	3	Auditing	2	0	2
	5	Press, publishing, and printing	3	0	3
	8	Audiovisual works and film distribution	3	1	4
	9	Health and social security	1	1	2
	10	Employment agencies and services	1	3	4
	18 ·	Agricultural products	3	1	4
	20	Nuclear industries	2	3	5
	23	Armaments, explosives and gunpowder	4	4	8
	24	Security guard and private detective	1	0	1
	25	Tourism, travel services	4	0	4
	26	Gaming, casinos, lottos, lotteries	2	9	11
	27	Jurisprudence, legal profession	2	0	2
	28	Teaching, education	1	0	1
	29	Merchants and craftsmen	1	0	1
	30	Import, export & distribution of alcohol	1	5	6
	31	Tobacco, matches	0	5	5
	32	Salt	1	2	2
	33	Pharmaceuticals, medicines, narcotics	0	2	2
	34	Steel	0	1	1
	35	Public works and services (construction)	1	1	2

Notes: $R^* = R + I + RI$, $M^* = M + MR + MI + MRI$.

Source: Table 10.1.

Table 10.3   Relative size of selected sector clusters–US, 1989

Cluster	Name	% of US GDP
1	Banking, other financial services, and insurance[*]	5.61
2	Broadcasting	0.32
3	Post and telecommunications	2.27
4	Other public utilities and energy production	3.36
5	Transportation	2.95
6	Land and natural resources	13.97

[*]Insurance figure based on Canadian data to avoid counting private health insurance.

Source: Table 10.1 and National Income Accounts of the United States and Canada.

countries can be defended by emphasising the specious precision that would be gained thereby. The sectors are not always completely blocked by a country just because it has restrictions – sectoral reciprocity may be the principal condition, and it may already have been granted by major trading partners. More frequently, only part of a sector is denied foreign participation, a foreigner's equity role is restricted, or discretion is given to some national authority to control entry. Any kind of meaningful aggregation becomes impossible.

Keeping in mind that the data are several years old, Table 10.4 none the less provides some initial indication of the extent of liberal policies towards IFDI by country. At the signing of the Single European Act in 1986, France clearly had a far more extensive set of measures to deal with IFDI than did her Community partners. Germany and Britain, in particular, stand in sharp contrast. Indeed, using this admittedly crude set of indicators, those countries appear to be more liberal than the United States.

Looking only at restrictions not linked to monopoly, Canada and Australia with their long-standing apprehension about domination by Britain and the United States, corporatist Austria and Finland, and traditionally inhospitable Japan stand at the top. Since these data were gathered considerable liberalisation has taken place, quite independent of the EC. Australia, Canada, and Japan have all considerably softened their posture towards IFDI.

Table 10.4 Summary of controls on IFDI by country – 1986

Countries	R^*	M^*	Total
Australia	11	6	17
Austria	12	6	18
Belgium	1	6	7
Canada	9	3	12
Denmark	2	0	2
Finland	12	8	20
France	14	11	25
Germany	2	5	7
Greece	4	8	12
Ireland	6	3	19
Italy	7	6	13
Japan	10	3	13
Luxembourg	0	4	4
Netherlands	5	4	9
New Zealand	4	5	9
Norway	9	9	18
Portugal	5	8	13
Spain	4	7	11
Sweden	7	7	14
Switzerland	7	8	15
Turkey	7	9	16
UK	5	4	9
US	11	2	13

Notes: $R^* = R+I+RI$, $M^* = M+MR+MI+MRI$.
Source: Table 10.1.

THINKING ABOUT THE RESTRICTED SECTORS: NATIONAL INTERESTS AND VESTED INTERESTS

Many writers have attempted to summarise the motivation for sector restrictions. Nearly all emphasise the relation of restrictions to national security (US Department of Treasury, 1988, p. 4; Tanzi and Coelho, 1991, p. 157; Services of the Commission of the European Community, 1991, p. 8). McCulloch adds infant industry protection (McCulloch,

1990, p. 342), while Bergsten and Graham further suggest 'control of national patrimony, and various shades of mercantilism' (Bergsten and Graham, 1991, p. 52).

Although the work here is preliminary, my contention is that the overwhelming part of the protected sectors, whatever their historical link to national security, now have no necessary connection with security at all. Each of the six major clusters of heavily protected sectors has a somewhat different central justification that doubtless differs by country, but simple producer protection appears to be the most promising initial hypothesis in most cases.[9]

In an attempt to sort out general societal concerns from special interests, the discussion that follows will consider the relation of protection to three foreign economic policy goals that have been found useful in other contexts: prosperity, autonomy, and security (Kudrle and Davis, 1987, pp. 353–79; Kudrle, 1991). It will be particularly important to see if the declared or apparent motivation really holds up under close analysis. For example, if a sector bound up with national security is suddenly opened to foreigners as the result of bargaining that does not itself involve explicit defence assurances, then the earlier rationale becomes highly suspect. The official explanation may then have been largely a pretext to defend interests tied to the previous order – with a passive public accepting the protection until another configuration of political forces overcame the temporary stasis. Breton argued persuasively that appeals to nationalism may be a particularly effective means of softening up public opinion to support policies preferred by a small group of highly concentrated beneficiaries (Breton, 1964).

The discussion that follows will treat protected sectors by examining them against national goals and apparent special interests. Any attempt to draw conclusions will necessarily be tentative and complicated by the very different situations of the polities under observation. The states differ somewhat in per capita income and greatly in absolute economic size. Not independent of those factors, but more immediately relevant, are variations in resource endowments, foreign and defence policies, attitudes to the role of the state, and cultural vulnerability.

BANKING, FINANCIAL SERVICES, AND INSURANCE

Banking, while never organised as monopoly, is everywhere a highly regulated industry in which foreigners are typically treated exceptionally. Only five of the 23 reporting countries fail to provide special regulations for foreign-controlled operations, yet countries as diverse as Spain, New Zealand, and Belgium appear to have functioned satisfactorily for extended periods without any special controls on the participation of foreigners.

Consideration of the history of banking in the United States suggests how attitudes can be unique to a country's history. Banking instability and panics in the nineteenth century led to the establishment of the Federal Reserve System and state regulation typically based on a fear of concentration and 'foreign' control, where 'foreign' meant out of state ownership, particularly from the metropolitan financial centres. Banking collapse during the Depression reinforced attitudes that highlighted both the centrality and the vulnerability of the system.

Even today state control of many aspects of banking have prevented the levels of concentration and perhaps the scale economies necessary for efficient production.[10] Most important, there is nothing about the differential motives or authority of foreign banks in most countries that provide them with any special leverage over the welfare of host countries. So long as they are obliged to provide their depositors with the same expectation of safe operations as their purely domestic competitors, national favouritism cannot be justified from a national interest point of view. And while parochial prejudices run very strongly in public opinion about banking, and protectionism undoubtedly benefits thereby, numerous bilateral arrangements have been established to provide sectoral reciprocity (OECD, 1987a, pp. 31–65). No negative results are known to the author. (Similar fears have arisen in the innately more innocuous financial services sector.) In the US case the increasing competitive power of European banks as a result of Europe-wide banking following 1992 has been predicted by many observers to force a major restructuring of the US banking system, including system changes not yet fully palatable to political opinion (Golembe and Holland, 1990, ch. 2, p. 88).

Quite similarly, insurance worldwide has been heavily regulated, and some government monopoly elements obtrude, particularly in health insurance. While fewer governments control foreign participation, those that do frequently include sectoral reciprocity as a requirement. The insurance industry in many countries has generated politics similar to that in banking, although generally with less intensity.[11] Like banking, insurance was early seized upon by the internationalists at the OECD as a service industry to be promoted. And now, like banking, insurance is subject to a web of international agreements based mainly on reciprocity. In the United States where insurance

regulation is fully a state responsibility, state postures towards foreign
firms turn frequently on the treatment of US insurance firms in the
home country.

Current state and federal policy in the United States towards both
banking and insurance seems typical of the industrial countries. The
multinational firms are anxious to extend their business abroad while
smaller firms use regulation wherever possible to protect themselves
from competition.[12]

BROADCASTING

Table 10.2 suggests that broadcasting is one of the most restricted of all
industries, and the role of government monopoly looms virtually as
large as in the postal service and the railways. The literature reveals an
amalgam of three declared motivations for these monopolies: national
security, cultural autonomy, and public edification.

Investigation of the historical record reveals a deep concern with
national security issues from the beginning of mass radio broadcasting
in the inter-war period (Acheson *et al.*, 1989, pp. 515–24). And the
power of alien voices in many subsequent periods is undisputed,
although hostile broadcasting seems to have seriously damaged only
authoritarian states.[13]

It is very difficult to defend national exclusivity today on national
security grounds in the liberal developed states, if indeed it ever was.
Leaving aside partial or complete public operation, all stations on
national soil could be immediately commandeered in times of national
emergency anyway, and extreme abuse of a licence for direct political
purposes could cause it to be lost in all countries with private
broadcasting, whatever the nationality of the controlling party. This
is apparently recognised by those German *Länder* that allow private
broadcasting: They do not discriminate against foreigners. None the
less, despite the thousands of private radio and television stations in the
United States and the access of nearly everyone to a multitude of
outlets, the American government continues to insist that no more than
20 per cent of a company with a broadcasting licence or 25 per cent of a
company controlling such a company can be foreign-owned.[14] Many
other countries, including Britain and Canada, have similar restrictions.

Some states see national control of broadcasting as an instrument of
autonomy perhaps more than security. The United States and Britain

may fear little in this regard, but Canada and Australia fear the United States and Britain. Significantly, these smaller countries are among the only OECD countries that control foreign penetration in publishing as well as broadcasting.

Australia and Canada reinforce their restrictions on ownership by attempting to control the nationality of broadcast content. Guidelines written for 'EC 1992' suggest the same thing. And, although regulations vary by country, the identification of nationality is typically done on the basis of the citizenship of those participating in the production rather than by any characteristics of the production itself.[15] Such controls could preserve the technical capacity to produce broadcasts; their contribution to cultural integrity must be indirect at best. The issue becomes more doubtful when the culture that is defended is not national but 'European', which, logically but not politically, can easily be extended to 'Atlantic'.[16]

Recent technological developments have dramatically lowered the monopoly value of much of the electromagnetic spectrum to private enterprises and governments alike. Satellite and cable broadcasting along with VCRs have generated cosmopolitan alternatives to the old regulated outlets, and the political price paid by a seriously interfering authority would be prohibitive. Recognition of the problem may lie behind the EC directive suggesting that a majority of programmes shown should be 'European . . . where practicable'.[17]

Rent can be sought at various stages in the production and sale of differentiated products.[18] In broadcasting, the ability of governments to preserve such rents for their nationals through direct monopoly control or prejudicial licensing has been weakened beyond repair by dramatically increased substitute production involving factors of a variety of nationalities combined at the will of a myriad of cosmopolitan producers. And the same forces that have removed monopoly in broadcast entertainment have removed monopoly elements in news and public affairs as well. The protectionist preoccupation with broadcast licences by national governments makes little sense for any purpose.

POST, TELEPHONE AND TELECOMMUNICATIONS

The amalgam of these sectors into a single category fits the situation of most countries except the United States. Throughout most of the world, the state postal monopoly has controlled the telephone system from its beginnings, and the latter system in turn typically serves as the central agency making decisions relevant to the bulk of the country's telecommunication hardware and software purchases.

The extent of 'natural monopoly' characteristics of postal delivery remains in dispute in the academic literature. None the less, virtually all countries assign a level of postal service for every citizen at a higher level than would be provided by a profit-maximising firm; hence, extensive regulation would be necessary even if the postal service were privatised. In fact, while private firms continue to gnaw away at some profitable parts of what were previously monopoly services, only minor sentiment exists anywhere to abolish the core public monopoly. At the margin of private service provision, foreign firms have frequently been granted non-discriminatory market access. These firms have provided no national security or autonomy threat, and it is difficult to see how they would if they controlled an even larger share of mail and package delivery.

The major international economic relations problem in this sector lies not in postal delivery, of course, but in telephones and other telecommunications. As a monopsony buyer, the central authority in the larger countries has historically yielded to myriad pressures to nurture domestic equipment manufacturers. Now, because of the increasing commonality of telecommunications and computer technology, telecommunications cannot be left alone by any government considering virtually any kind of industrial policy. Whatever the outcome of the Uruguay Round or subsequent bargaining, several necessary ingredients for an international regime of effective competition stand out: mutually acceptable parameters must be established for switching, transmission, and terminal equipment for both hardware and software procurement by government and all regulated purchasers. Outside of technical standards, thorny issues abound in matters of intellectual property rights, dumping and subsidies.[19]

Issues related narrowly to IFDI pale by comparison to these problems but are tightly bound to their solution (or substantial amelioration). Only if the parameters of acceptable telecommunications behaviour can be agreed will most states become more willing to give up enough control to allow greater foreign participation in service production within their borders. The United States did offer some liberalisation with the breakup of AT&T. The regional phone companies are theoretically open to operation by foreigners – but only those that do not use FCC-licenced microwave common carriers (which are controlled as broadcasting stations).

The prosperity motive looks at least as important as any other in this sector, and national security may be affected only indirectly: many states are attempting to maintain their technological edge through telecommunications protection, and that attempt has national defence implications. Unfortunately, those implications sometimes include isolated inferiority rather than autonomous capacity.[20]

OTHER PUBLIC UTILITIES AND ENERGY PRODUCTION

The situation in public utilities and energy production bears a strong resemblance to the cluster just examined. Energy production itself is very often a government monopoly. Where it is not, incumbent firms are usually closely regulated. As a practical matter it may not make much difference today whether or not foreign firms are denied ownership participation because demand in most sectors in most countries is easily handled by existing firms whose ownership changes very infrequently (McGowan and Thomas, 1989). None the less, where utilities are not publicly owned, restrictions well short of banning foreign ownership could assure safe operation, and the national interest in prosperity would seem to call for the greatest market discipline that local conditions allow. Moreover, some new theories of public utility regulation that rely on term bidding for the operation of publicly owned facilities call for a substantial group of experienced bidders. Foreign competition, particularly in smaller markets, might greatly brighten the prospects for this solution to the 'natural monopoly problem'. Much national legislation that bars foreign ownership also precludes alien operation.

Just as in the case of post and telecommunications, political concerns impelling nationalism in this cluster do not plausibly turn on any threat from foreign ownership *per se* but rather on the extent to which that ownership would thwart national favouritism in the use of complementary goods and services. One recent study suggests that the powerplant equipment industry (consisting mainly of boilers and turbine generators) focuses government interest because of its 'perceived strategic importance' (McGowan and Thomas, 1989, p. 542). The only possible 'strategic' motive the study subsequently discerns, however, concerns prosperity: the relatively advanced engineering industry that undergirds production of such goods may be deemed important for the country's overall technological health.

Preparations for 1992 have included strong measures to open public procurement in power generation equipment within the Community, but the small number of firms in the global industry and their network of strategic alliances leave considerable doubt about the level of effective competition (McGowan and Thomas, 1989, p. 553). None the less, unless commercial users of the services provided from the energy system can detect a substantial negative impact on cost or quality as a result of nationalism in either utility ownership restrictions or procurement, major liberalising forces from within the purchasing economies are unlikely to emerge. Where feasible, governments are likely to continue to yield to specific pressures to maintain engineering jobs and to protect 'our' engineering industries.

TRANSPORTATION

Land, air, and maritime transportation can be treated together because their regulation has developed from some of the same historic roots. When national security was considered largely as a matter of physical invasion, prudence suggested that transportation be kept in the hands of nationals. Moreover, railroads were often originally close to natural monopolies, and usually passed into public hands.

For a number of reasons, including a complex pattern of politically mandatory cross-subsidisation of routes and services, the privatisation wave of the eighties left the railroads largely untouched. By contrast, road transport in many countries was liberalised and sometimes opened to foreigners on the basis of reciprocity. Europe is now removing the last vestiges of internal discrimination in road haulage.

Coastal navigation in most countries became so entangled with military preparedness that, even in a world in which the military significance of such activity has much diminished, sorting out an appropriate role for foreigners would present a great challenge. But it remains to be attempted. The United States, for example, links US ship production, special insurance, and requirements about the nationality of crews to protect several types of providers simultaneously while producing an unknown contribution to national security (Seitzinger, 1989, pp. 12–16). In the United States, as elsewhere, however, navigation in domestic waters is neither a large, profitable nor expanding activity.

Air transportation quite appropriately draws virtually all attention. A look at the data underlying the tables presented earlier finds that nearly all countries restrict foreign operation of air services within their borders.

US airline deregulation had a dramatic effect on air transport around the world; America's already powerful carriers became even stronger in international competition while the US government worked to deregulate the most important international routes (Kasper, 1988, p. 92). At the same time, the US traded access to its US market for comparable access abroad in a series of bilateral agreements because US domestic deregulation did not extend to foreign firms. Domestic traffic is reserved exclusively for US carriers, and this means that three-quarters of the ownership must be by US citizens.[21] Other countries – even those few that permit free domestic entry – maintain similar restrictions.

Bilateral liberalisation of domestic aviation has foundered on the unwillingness of US carriers to face competition from foreign firms that are frequently subsidised in various ways by their governments ('a bleeding contest with a blood bank' as described by one airline authority (Kasper, 1988, p. 97)). This factor combines with the inability of any single foreign government to extend potential benefits as potentially rich as open access to US domestic operations, even if they could make domestic openness otherwise credible.

Despite the national security origins of transportation controls in the industrial countries, the literature on airline ownership deregulation scarcely reveals persuasive security concerns today (McGowan and Seabright, 1989, pp. 284–335). Countries instead focus on reciprocal benefit and, especially in some European countries, on the possible fiscal and employment impacts of a more competitive domestic marketplace.[22]

LAND AND NATURAL RESOURCES

Table 10.2 reveals widespread protection of land and natural resources, and Table 10.4 indicates how large a part of the economy is accounted for by the industries in Sector 6. The restrictions in this sector come in a wide variety of forms: reciprocity, maximum equity ownership, maximum size of holding, and many others. One gets the impression that it is the extent of foreign participation rather than its very existence that often generates concern.

Economists have always had particular difficulty understanding popular concerns about the alienation of natural resources. Modern

theories of international trade may contain some support for previously heretical views about trade and investment in high technology
products; they contain no new defences for a hesitation to sell
undifferentiated products, or the resources that produce them, for
the highest possible price.

What harm can come from alienating the national 'patrimony?'[23]
Developing countries traditionally railed against foreign ownership
essentially on grounds of asymmetric information. Simple people sold
their resources because of ignorance of their true value. This argument
scarcely seems plausible now, even in most developing countries; it is
wholly implausible for the countries considered here. Another formally
possible but highly implausible motive would foresee foreign access to
resources somehow depressing prices internationally to the detriment
of national producers.[24] Third, alienation might produce social
outcomes unique to foreign ownership. For example, foreign management practices could be objectionable, but then why are they thwarted
only in resource industries? Perhaps it is the very presence of foreigners
that offends; this suggests that if only absentee landlords purchased
resources, all would be well. But that is not the way the laws are
typically written.

A satisfactory explanation may lie where it frequently does in
protection cases: public predisposition exploited by those with large
stakes. A certain xenophobia may exist in all societies. As Kindleberger
(1966, p. 107) has argued: 'There is an element of the peasant in all of
us.' Most people regard foreigners with mixed feelings. They do things
differently, and they do not 'fit in'. And the general public regards
foreign 'control' as intolerable.[25] Tourists are usually welcomed
because they so clearly increase the demand for current output, but,
as the rhetoric about purely domestic 'paper transactions' during the
eighties suggests, most people may not see the link between the sale of
assets and increased national well being. This may also explain the
otherwise strange behaviour of US state governments that simultaneously encourage most foreign business investment, while restricting
investment in land.

A vitally interested group may take advantage of the latent antipathy
towards foreign ownership for its own purposes. David Laband (1984)
has offered evidence of such a group in the United States. His 1984
study of inter-state variation in the control of foreign investment in
farmland identifies the desire by smaller operators to obtain land at
lower prices than they could otherwise. This tentatively supported
hypothesis is highly plausible because of the relative numbers (voters)

in the two groups, but its possible application to resources more generally remains to be established. The basic argument suggests either that domestic exploitation firms are more powerful than private resource owners or, in cases where the resources are publicly owned, that domestic exploitation firms effectively prevent the state from maximising publicly-owned wealth.

Interest explanations for land and resource ownership restrictions may take us a long way, but one suspects they cannot explain everything. It might be remembered that one argument in the United States against selling MCA to Matshusita turned on MCA's control of concessions in Yosemite National Park. However misguided, an antipathy for foreign participation in the homeland can be regarded partly as an autonomy concern.[26]

CONCLUSIONS FROM THE SECTORAL REVIEW

Several important conclusions emerge from the foregoing review. First, despite the frequently repeated claims that sectors are mainly reserved for national security reasons, that explanation does not stand up under close scrutiny. Except in circumstances in which personnel, organisational, and subsidy questions have become conflated beyond untangling, such as in the maritime policy, most blocked sectors lack a core national security rationale on both analytic and empirical grounds. Analytically, one cannot confect a 'nightmare scenario' in which French ownership of a clear-channel radio station in Kansas City or a microwave relay transmitter in Atlanta poses any kind of national threat. And in sectors in which foreign ownership privileges are granted on the basis of nothing more than the other country's willingness to open the cognate sector, national danger can scarcely be a primary motive for restriction.

The dismissal of serious national security concerns about closed sectors does not by any means suggest that some foreign acquisitions of US-owned firms might not constitute a national security threat. The President was mandated to reject such acquisitions by the Exon-Florio Amendment of 1988 (Graham and Krugman, 1991, pp. 121–8), but this law's major concern with high technology firms in a variety of industries scarcely touches the territory directly guarded by the sectoral restrictions. Moreover, many of the best analyses of the problems of militarily-relevant industries have determined that encouragement of foreign investment for purposes of keeping production on US soil with possible additional requirements for the use of US personnel constitutes a far wiser policy than nationally-owned facilities that duplicate foreign capacities at high cost. Moreover, no one has yet pointed to crucial weaknesses in security arrangements for sensitive production by foreign-owned firms. Some combination of security clearances for personnel and Special Security Arrangements or non-voting trusts seem to have worked effectively (Graham and Krugman, 1991, p. 115). Some sectoral controls seem to be held in place on national autonomy grounds. Australian and Canadian media controls function in this way, although their effect may protect local production capacity more than they promote national cultural consciousness. In land and resources, the xenophobia that incubates restrictive policy frequently serving special interests is apparently more bound up with autonomy than security or prosperity.[27]

Many of the most extensive controls seem to relate almost entirely to the prosperity goal, although precise motives are difficult to descry. An outsider cannot know whether a policy decision is taken mainly to keep engineers employed or out of conviction that the protectionist investment will pay off in a more prosperous future. Whatever the precise mix of motives in a particular case, protection in telecommunications and public utilities serves as a linchpin for national favouritism in procurement. The author has not seen an explicit detailed argument on any other grounds. Moreover, in all of the sectors reviewed, concentrated group interests seem to play an important role in policy formation. Employees and stockholders in the protected sectors and other affected industries lobby actively either to maintain protection or to permit liberalisation only in response to increased market opportunities from reciprocal liberalisation.

A dimension of the political problem, worth noting but impossible to treat fully, concerns the national economic loss resulting from sectoral investment protection. Politically potent studies employing various methodologies estimating the costs of trade protection have been produced in the United States (various studies of the Congressional Budget Office and the Office of Management and Budget), Europe (the Cecchini Report), and Canada (the Macdonald Commission reports). The losses resulting from the kind of protectionism reviewed here are extremely difficult to assess, however. One must attempt to develop a counterfactual scenario in which the foreign package of capital, management and technology are fitted into a specific niche in a national economy. Only when existing protection produces grossly inadequate results in product or service cost or quality are such stories likely to be convincing.

POLICY IMPLICATIONS

Future policy developments can be discussed under four headings: unilateral, multilateral, plurilateral, and bilateral. The discussion so far has suggested the limits of the unilateral pursuit of additional liberalisation. With no strong user interest pushing for liberalisation in any of the protected sectors, incumbent beneficiaries have maximum latitude to maintain their position at least until reciprocity can be achieved. Some essentially unilateral liberalisation will develop in the EC: every time an industry is privatised, it will be open to all Community firms (or else will be subject to challenge). And especially within Europe, but increasingly elsewhere, the distribution of national gains from such an action may be difficult to estimate: a mainly Belgian-owned firm with high value added in France (in term of personnel and other purchases) might be the chief probable beneficiary of French liberalisation where the other possible principal winner is likely a French-owned firm with larger Belgian content. Who is us? (Reich, 1990).

If further unilateral liberalisation is unlikely, how feasible is a genuine GATT for investment? This is a question that goes back to the postwar discussions of the ill-fated International Trade Organisation and revived by Goldberg and Kindleberger in 1970. The prospects for such an organisation have recently been examined again by McCulloch (1990), and Graham and Krugman (1991, pp. 155–9). Most observers have concluded that such an organisation is presently impossible for at least three reasons: substantial differences in attitudes towards IFDI among nations and particularly between richer and poorer countries,[28] the innate complexity of government policies bearing on IFDI, and increasing restiveness about 'free-riding' in the GATT.

If a universal scheme is not possible, could a regime for investment be hammered out among the 'like-minded'? To perhaps oversimplify the problem, this approach removes only the North–South gap, while leaving other major problems. Some difficulties are implied by issues already examined, such as the reality that a much higher percentage of output in closed sectors is produced by government monopoly in some countries than in others. And how does one calculate the putative gains of liberalisation? Some combination of the size of nominally opened new markets and the probable scale of profitable foreign investment by home country firms (yet another meaning for 'competitiveness'!) would measure opportunity for a single country with corresponding estimates gauging vulnerability. When such uncertain gains and losses are compounded with complications such as the effective meaning of Japanese 'openness' to IFDI, rapid progress along this path is difficult to predict.

Another path of 'likemindedness' would concentrate attention on specific sectors. Some progress may be made here, but the difficulties are still formidable. Airline services provide an example. The US industry has resisted foreign entry into domestic service because no single state abroad was large enough to offer a sufficiently attractive market in return. But even the ability of a united Europe to strike a bargain appears problematic: takeovers provide an efficient form of market entry and are perfectly legal in the US, but many of Europe's leading airlines are nationally owned and therefore not for sale.

A final issue in any comprehensive agreement would involve the role of subnational governments. The United States government has been continually unwilling to grasp this political nettle, responding to excessively restrictive state policy with only as much constitutional ammunition as necessary.[29] The United States and other countries must also develop positions about how much authority it wants the European Commission to exercise over individual national policies towards foreign investors (Kline and Wallace, 1991, p. 22).

One is driven back to prospects for bilateral agreement. Commentators sometimes miss an important point about the current IFDI situation: bilateral reciprocity has become accepted as a reasonable standard in a range of controlled industries from banking and insurance to airlines. Many industries in a variety of countries now see only some form of sectoral reciprocity as 'fair' – if they accept liberalisation at all.

In the United States such thinking goes back a very long way. Some of the same legislation that allows foreigners to operate only in return for reciprocal access also treats firms located in other US states in the same way (e.g., insurance). Much of the focus on sectoral reciprocity lies in the very nature of IFDI, which largely serves as a vehicle for the entry of a subset of producers to an industry of differentiated products. Consequently, as noted above, advantages of firms based in particular regions or countries, the competitive results of openness, and the calculations of national gains (and possibly losses) all elude precise estimation. This very uncertainty, coupled with restrictions lacking the quantitative gradation of tariff protection, may go far to explain the political salience of sectoral reciprocity.

This line of argument suggests the importance of developments such as the US–Canada Free Trade Agreement and the incipient agreement of those countries with Mexico. These regional accords provide the occasion for packaging concessions together into broad, complex bargains in which recalcitrant sectors are bowled over by those inspired by greater optimism. Significant IFDI sectoral liberalisation in the near future may come largely from agreements such as these.[30]

CONCLUSION

This assessment has rested mainly on secondary sources. Careful national examinations of the implications of opening currently restricted sectors would certainly precede further major liberalisation. These studies could well provide persuasive justifications for some sectoral protection that the broad overview presented here has over-looked. None the less, the central conclusion of this study is unlikely to be overturned: National security claims for sectoral restrictions have been too often taken at face value. Autonomy fears ranging from fears of cultural submersion to mild but general xenophobia propel a large amount of protection. Another major part arises from an ambition for prosperity that seems linked to national ownership or capital goods use in certain sectors. Together, these impulses drive many more restrictions than does any plausible security concern. Overall, bargaining problems and special interests, not the national welfare, appear to underlie most sectoral protection.

Notes

1. The author thanks Susan Bloom and Uday Lohani for excellent research assistance and editorial advice.
2. Japan also claims to be as open as the rest of its trading partners to IFDI, but foreign penetration has remained very slight. This issue is discussed below.
3. Graham and Krugman, like most contemporary analysts, take the position that 'free market outcomes are innocent until proven guilty'. See Graham and Krugman (1991, p. 144). Raymond Vernon has expressed the general issue thus: 'The presumption against restricting foreign direct investment, in my opinion, rests largely on the residual power of the liberal classical model. And even if the proof is softer and

spongier than their most vociferous proponents will allow, arguments based on that model lead in short order to the conclusion that extensive autarkic measures hurt those who practice them' (Vernon, 1992, p. 19).

4. The term is not defined. The sparing use of the Exon–Florio process by Presidents Reagan and Bush have given heart to proponents of investment openness. Others, however, have stressed the possible elasticity of 'national security' if a chief executive were determined to increase restrictiveness.

5. For a review of such overall screening as it was practised in the mideighties in the industrial countries, see Organisation for Economic Cooperation and Development (1987a).

6. OECD (1987a, p. 11). The USTR's *1990 National Trade Estimate Report on Foreign Trade Barriers* complained about general screening by one OECD country, France.

7. Because foreign investment raises the spectre of foreign domination, it may be significant that the smallest of the OECD countries, Iceland, maintains a posture of 'derogation' towards all investment liberalisation activities, OECD (1987a, p. 71).

8. Inertial policy determinism reigns in some places: Salt provision remains a government monopoly in Japan and Switzerland.

9. Vernon highlighted the difficulty of distinguishing special from general interests in the determination of MNC policy: 'The insistence of some governments that foreign-owned subsidiaries should be subject to special rules of the game is sometimes motivated by questions of public policy. At other times, however, the object is simply to show preference for a national group over foreigners. . .' (Vernon, 1971, p. 242).

10. Some scholars such as Ryan ascribe the greater international competitiveness of Japanese over American banks to weaknesses instilled by populist banking regulation. The present regime may thus be damaging American prosperity, not because of its special treatment of foreigners but rather because of its basic character. See Ryan (1990, pp. 349–66).

11. Absent the tight link with the macroeconomy, most damage from inadequate or otherwise inappropriate regulation has been less spectacular than in banking.

12. The BCCI scandal may cast doubt on the innocuousness of foreign banking, but it resulted from inadequate international cooperation that has been largely amended.

13. Lord Haw-Haw and Tokyo Rose provided something between minor annoyance and almost ghoulish diversion. In sharp contrast, the Voice of America and the BBC provided Mikhail Gorbachev with vital information while he was under house arrest, a fitting coda for forty years of undermining official broadcast monopoly.

14. In the latter case, however, the Federal Communications Commission can issue a variance if it finds such action to be 'in the public interest', in OECD (1987a, p. 65).

15. For a general discussion, see Kudrle and Lenway (1990, ch. 7).

16. This conclusion is drawn by no less a cultural authority than André Malraux. See Acheson *et al.* (1989, p. 522).

17. Ibid.

18. Economic rent is a payment to a factor of production in excess of the amount necessary to have it supplied.
19. See Roseman (1988, pp. 135–49) for an excellent summary of the problems to be overcome; for a detailed view of European developments, especially as they relate to the United States, see Cowley (1990).
20. For a discussion of the general problem, see Moran (1990).
21. In a hearing in 1991, Secretary of Transportation Samuel Skinner advocated increasing the share to 49 per cent to provide the airlines with new sources of capital but at the same time warned of the dilution of US bargaining power that would result from excessive leniency (Golich, (1992, p. 11).
22. In many controlled regimes higher fares substitute for explicit government subsidies (Kasper, 1988, p. 97).
23. One suspects that Bergsten and Graham may have chosen to use a unique and emotive word to avoid having to rationalise the precise motivation and attendant behaviour. See Bergsten and Graham (1991).
24. The opposite has historically been far more frequent; cosmopolitan oligopolies have protected rents internationally, while unintegrated national producers have 'broken' the market.
25. However 'irrational' from some perspectives, attitudes similar to xenophobia have long been dealt with in economic theory. See Becker (1971).
26. As treated here, policy linkage of goals to more specific objectives and policy instruments is not bounded by any kind of rationality constraint. For example, large parts of the Republican party well into the 1950s believed that moderate tariff protection contributed to general prosperity, despite the rejection of such a conclusion by virtually all of the economics profession.
27. Autonomy is apparently important for the psychic income that it produces directly, but it also facilitates pursuit of security and prosperity. See Kudrle (1991).
28. This remains true despite the spectacular *volte face* of many major developing countries including Argentina and Mexico – building on Chile's example.
29. It does act in egregious cases, such as the Supreme Court case of *Zscherning* v. *Miller*, which essentially involved an attempt by the State of Oregon to pursue its own foreign policy toward East Germany (Seitzinger, 1989, p. 6).
30. The sometimes extreme openness that has characterised the recent investment policies of some formerly Soviet bloc countries conforms with the basic analysis of this chapter. The vested interests in sectors traditionally closed in other states are scarcely more sacrosanct than the other remnants of a discredited economic structure, and bargaining issues scarcely obtrude because the former socialist states have little to offer in return.

11 Marketing Strategies to Attract Foreign Investment

Louis T. Wells Jr and Alvin G. Wint

INTRODUCTION

Although the decade of the 1980s has seen a major increase in a range of efforts by both developing and industrialised countries to market themselves as attractive locations for foreign direct investment, existing research has been biased toward the role of investment incentives and policy reform in these activities.[1] Current efforts, however, include not only the use of investment incentives and attempts to improve the investment climates of countries, but also marketing techniques such as advertising, missions, seminars, direct marketing of various forms, and service activities. The goal of these marketing techniques is to inform prospective investors about a country's potential as an investment site, and to persuade them to set up operations in that country. For this study, we defined these marketing efforts as 'investment promotion'. We set out in this research to add to the existing knowledge by focusing on aspects of investment promotion, especially the effectiveness of particular promotional techniques, that remain under-researched.

PREVIOUS STUDIES

Perhaps the earliest published study was the 1966 work of Aharoni (1966, pp. 41–9). He separated image building and service as parts of the promotion programmes of countries, and he noted that 'a program for attracting US investors should be very similar to one for marketing a new industrial product' (Aharoni, 1966a, p. 222). We substantially build upon these concepts. Since Aharoni's study was not based on a wide sample of countries, he had little empirical basis for describing the behaviour of governments, for assessing how similar their programmes were to the programmes of industrial marketers, or for estimating the effectiveness of various promotion activities.

Goodnow, in a 1970 study (Goodnow, 1970, pp. 6–11), reported the results of a mail survey, and several interviews, of American state and port authorities that were making efforts to attract foreign business. The study reports on budgets, staffing, functions performed, promotion methods used, and control systems. Although it is not focused entirely on investment promotion, it provides useful base data, but admits an inability to evaluate performance and makes no effort to explain behaviour.

Watzke and Mindak, from 1981 to 1987 add to knowledge with a series of studies. In the first, Watzke (1982, pp. 33–9) reports on the activities of the Irish Industrial Development Authority, and explicitly introduces the concept of targeting and the need for analysis of organisational structure and management. A second article by Watzke (1981, pp. 53–60) adds three European agencies and begins the process of searching for typologies to describe the structures and behaviours of promotional organisations by proposing four classes of organization: prospectors, defenders, analysers, and reactors. Later Watzke, with Mindak (Watzke and Mindak, 1987, pp. 153–92), produced a normative paper that emphasises targeting, marketing mix, the need for marketing skills, and the need for control mechanisms in promotion organisations, points that would again emerge in our work (Wells and Wint, 1991) and in an SRI study. The SRI study on promotion broke promotion activities into two categories, publicity and investor assistance, and classified promotion agencies according to their relationships with ministries (International Policy Analysis, 1984).

In sum, previous work has established a good basis for further research on promotional activities. This study adds to previous work by:

1. Explicitly identifying the marketing strategy used by a number of agencies, and explaining the usefulness of these strategies by analogy to industrial marketing;[2] and
2. Providing measurements of effectiveness that differentiate the impact of investment promotion by the promotion tool used and by the type of investment project.

METHODOLOGY

To conduct this research we first interviewed investment promotion representatives of twenty countries with offices on the East Coast of the

United States.[3] From these interviews we selected a sample of countries for more intensive examination, including on-site visits. In choosing a sample of countries we sought a mix of countries that varied along the dimensions of level of development, size, and geographical region. We chose ten investment locations: Britain, Canada, Costa Rica, Indonesia, Ireland, Jamaica, Malaysia, Scotland, Singapore, and Thailand. We interviewed over 100 people in the investment promotion or related agencies of these ten countries, using an interview guide. We also gathered archival data on the promotional efforts of these countries.

We also conducted interviews with managers from US corporations involved in thirty investment decisions. We sought in these interviews to determine the impact of promotion efforts on these investment decisions. We focused on firms that had actually invested in these countries because we were particularly interested in identifying which promotional techniques were effective in influencing investors. In all cases we chose firms that had invested recently, so that recall would be reliable. We divided our sample into firms that invested for the domestic market and firms that invested to serve export markets. We used a guide to interview managers who had been involved in the company's decision to invest. For some companies the responsible manager was the general manager, managing director, or CEO; in others it was a VP of marketing or international, a plant manager, a director of special products, or a manager of new markets.

TYPES OF INVESTMENT PROMOTION TECHNIQUES

Although all investment promotion is, of course, ultimately aimed at attracting investors, various promotion activities appear to have different short-term objectives:

(1) Some aim primarily to improve a country's image within the investment community as a favourable location for investment (image-building activities);
(3) Others aim to assist prospective and current investors by providing them with services (investment service activities);
(2) and finally, some activities are aimed quite directly at generating investment (investment-generating activities).

Interviews with officials from promotional agencies identified at least thirteen different promotional techniques that were in use by at

Table 11.1   Taxonomy of promotional techniques

---

(1)   Advertising in general financial media.
(2)   Participating in investment exhibitions.
(3)   Advertising in industry- or sector-specific media.
(4)   Conducting general investment missions from source
       country to host country or from host country to source country.
(5)   Conducting general information seminars on investment opportunities.
(6)   Production and distribution of brochures.
(7)   Engaging in direct mailing or telemarketing campaigns.
(8)   Conducting industry/sector-specific investment missions from source
       country to host country or vice versa.
(9)   Conducting industry/sector-specific information seminars.
(10)   Engaging in firm-specific research followed by 'sales' presentations.
(11)   Providing investment counselling services.
(12)   Expediting the processing of applications and permits.
(13)   Providing post-investment services.

---

least some of the countries that we studied. These thirteen techniques are listed in Table 11.1.

These techniques represent a continuum of activities, but they also coalesce into three more or less disparate clusters. The first six techniques were frequently directed toward building a particular image for the country; in contrast, techniques 7 to 10 were usually used to generate investment directly; and techniques 11 to 13 were first and foremost investment-service techniques. These techniques overlap to some extent, and so to do the goals of the techniques; nevertheless, this classification scheme seems to capture reasonably well the objectives that typically lay behind the use of the various techniques.

Image-building Techniques

All promotional agencies in the sample were using, or had used in the past, one or more image-building techniques (see Table 11.2).

Most (at least 60 per cent) of the agencies used image-building techniques simply with the objective of changing the image of the country as a place to invest. These countries had no expectation that these activities would generate investment directly.[4]

Another, smaller group of agencies did expect image-building techniques to generate investment directly, but they were eventually

Table 11.2 Primary image-building techniques used by agencies (see Table 11.1 for key)

Location techniques	Promotional agency	Image-building
Britain	Invest in Britain Bureau (IBB)	1, 2, 4, 5, 6
Canada	Investment Canada	1, 3, 6
Costa Rica	Costa Rican Investment Promotion Program (CINDE)	2, 3, 4, 6
Indonesia	Investment Coordinating Board (BKPM)	4, 5, 6
Ireland	Industrial Development Authority (IDA)	1, 3, 6
Jamaica	Jamaica National Investment Promotion (JNIP)	2, 3, 4, 5, 6
Malaysia	Malaysian Industrial Development Authority (MEDA)	2, 4, 6
Scotland	Locate in Scotland (LIS)	1, 2, 6
Singapore	Economic Development Board (EDB)	1, 6
Thailand	Board of Investment (BOI)	1, 6

disappointed that these activities were not effective in generating investment.[5]

Investment-generating Techniques

Nine of the ten agencies we studied used what we have called investment-generating techniques[6] (see Table 11.3). These techniques tended to differ from image-building techniques by the greater focus they placed on direct and personal contact with particular, targeted groups of potential investors. For instance, whereas distributing brochures in a passive manner, when requested by companies, or at general missions and seminars, was viewed as an image-building activity (technique 6), the use of these same brochures to provide information to specific companies an agency was seeking to attract through a direct mailing or telemarketing campaign was considered an investment-generating activity (technique 7).

Table 11.3 Primary investment-generating techniques used by agencies (see Table 11.1 for key)

Location	Promotional agency	Investment-generating techniques
Britain	Invest in Britain Bureau (IBB)	7, 10
Canada	Investment Canada	10
Costa Rica	Costa Rican Investment Promotion Program (CINDE)	7, 10
Ireland	Industrial Development Authority (IDA)	10
Jamaica	Jamaica National Investment Promotion (JNIP)	7, 9
Malaysia	Malaysian Industrial Development Authority (MIDA)	7
Scotland	Locate in Scotland (LIS)	7, 10
Singapore	Economic Development Board (EDB)	10
Thailand	Board of Investment (BOI)	8

Most agencies considered that these techniques were effective only if they helped to identify decision makers in companies likely to invest and if they helped to generate personal contacts with these managers. Thus, techniques 7, 8, and 9 were preparatory techniques for personal selling, technique 10. They were not viewed as techniques that were likely to be successful without follow-up.

Investment Service

All the investment promotion agencies in the sample viewed investment services as integral components of the investment promotion function. Thus, all agencies participated in one or more of these service activities (techniques 11–13 in Table 11.1). There is, however, no evidence that these activities serve directly to generate new investment interest, or are a primary force in building or changing images. Nor did agencies expect such results. Rather, agencies expected investment service activities to hold already interested investors, to help keep investors that have already invested, and to induce such firms to reinvest rather than move to a new investment site.

The Mix of Techniques

All the agencies we interviewed engaged to some extent in all three of these distinct types of promotional activities to accomplish their broader goal of attracting foreign direct investment. The relative weights which agencies gave to one type of promotional activity relative to the other two, however, seemed often to follow a certain pattern: the pattern reflected a strategy toward marketing the country. We do not argue that the sequence we observed in these experienced agencies is necessarily right in all circumstances for all countries; we do, however, believe that there is a logic underlying the sequence that can be helpful to countries that are trying to design an appropriate mix of activities.

STRATEGIES OF INVESTMENT PROMOTION PROGRAMMES

Although governments tend to engage in all three types of investment promotion activities to varying degrees most of the time, in their attempts to promote their countries as investment sites, they tend to concentrate their mix of promotional activities at any one time toward image-building or investment-generation. Thus we were able to classify the investment promotion programme of a country, according to its focus at a particular time, as an image-building or an investment-generation programme.

One factor that influenced the mix of promotional techniques used by an agency was recent government policy changes. In three cases, when government policy changed to encourage foreign investment the promotional organisation focused on image-building with the objective of advising the investment community about the government's new attitude toward foreign investment and its interest in attracting investors. When government managers from these organisations believed that an appropriate image had been formed in the minds of prospective investors, they made a shift in focus to investment-generation.

One can readily conceive of situations where image-building need not be the initial step in a promotional programme. For instance, if a country does not have a negative image as a potential site for inward investment, and if its strengths as an investment site are already well known in the international investment community, then there would be little need for the investment promotion agency to develop a promotional strategy that features an initial period of image-building activity. Indeed, the sequence of image-building and then investment-generation was not followed by all agencies. Three agencies did not appear to begin investment promotion operations by focusing on image-building (the other four agencies began with such a focus but not necessarily for the reasons we describe above). Nevertheless, the sequence of image-building followed by investment-generation was the most common pattern.

One could argue that the common sequence of image-building and investment-generating techniques was not one based on logical needs, but rather was simply the result of a learning process. According to this argument, countries begin their promotion efforts with an easy technique: advertising, or conducting a general mission. When they learn that it does not generate investment, they begin to use one of the techniques that we have labelled as investment-generating. Three of the countries in our sample provide evidence for this view. But there is also evidence against this interpretation. Part of the evidence comes from our interviews; but equally important the literature on industrial marketing suggests a logic for a promotional sequence where investment generation follows image-building. The parallels between industrial marketing and investment promotion are quite close.

Motivation For, and Timing of, Changes in the Mix of Promotional Techniques

We examined the cases where there was a shift from a focus on image-building to a focus on investment-generation. Where there was such a shift, we ascertained when the changes took place, and sought the reasons for the changes. The changes, and the time that they went into effect, are recorded in Table 11.4.

Six of the agencies that we studied exhibited the expected pattern by starting investment promotion operations with a focus on image-building, and then shifting thereafter to a focus on investment-generation. Three of these agencies, Investment Canada, Britain's IBB, and Ireland's IDA, also verified the logic we ascribed to this pattern, since they started investment promotion operations with a focus on image-building because of their stated intention of changing the image of their respective countries as a site for foreign direct investment.

With the arrival of a new government in Canada in 1985, Investment Canada was formed with the mandate to attract investors to Canada.

Table 11.4   Changes in the focus of investment promotion programme

Promotional agency	Current focus	Past focus
Invest in Britain Bureau (IBB)	Investment generation	Image-building (1980–2)
Investment Canada	Investment generation	Image-building (1985–6)
Costa Rican Investment Promotion Program (CINDE)	Investment generation	Image-building (1982–4)
Indonesian Investment Coordinating Board (BKPM)	Investment generation	*
Irish Industrial Development Authority (IDA))	Investment generation	Image-building (1969–1971)
Jamaica National Investment Promotion (JNIP)	Investment generation	Image-building (1981–4)
Malaysian Industrial Development Authority (MIDA)	Investment generation	+
Locate in Scotland (LIS)	Investment generation	+
Singapore Development Board (EDB)	Economic Investment generation	+
Thailand Investment (BOI)	Board of Investment generation	Image-building (1980–3)

Key
*: Agency started with an image-building programme and has not yet shifted to a focus on investment-generating activities.
+: No evidence was obtained to suggest that the agency started by focusing on image-building activities.

The agency's first annual report stated the need to change Canada's investment image.[7] By the agency's second year of operation, in 1986, the relevant officials felt that the awareness campaign had been successful and a clear shift in focus was made to attempts to generate investment.

Ireland's IDA began active promotional efforts in 1969–70 with an image-building campaign.[8] IDA continued to advertise over time but the focus of its promotional programme clearly shifted during the early 1970s to promotion, principally through the use of a direct selling technique in which IDA personnel abroad personally contacted executives of foreign firms and promoted Ireland as a place to invest during presentations with corporate executives.

Britain's IBB was given the mandate of attracting internationally mobile investment to all areas of the United Kingdom in 1980, in the aftermath of the election of the Thatcher government. The organisation started investment promotion operations with advertising campaigns. The IBB made a transition from a focus on image-building activities to a focus on investment-generating activities in 1982.

The other three agencies that began investment promotion operations with a focus on image-building activities, and then moved to a focus on investment-generating activities provide some evidence for the alternative proposition, that agencies initially focus on image-building activities because they are not aware of more effective promotional techniques. The Thai BOI, and Costa Rica's CINDE and Jamaica's JNIP in the early years of their operations, all used image-building techniques but expected these techniques also to generate investment. The lack of success of the image-building techniques led to changes to an investment-generating focus. The change in focus turned CINDE, for instance, into what is widely perceived of as a successful promotion agency.

Four agencies had not followed the sequence of the others. Indonesia's BKPM started with a focus on image-building activities, in practice, but not by design. This agency, had, however, not shifted to a focus on investment-generating activities in 1988. The other three agencies, Singapore's EDB, Malaysia's MIDA, and Scotland's LIS, all seemed to have started their investment promotion activities in an investment-generating mode.

In sum, seven of the ten agencies that we studied began investment promotion operations in an image-building mode. Of these seven agencies, six shifted, over time, to an investment-generating mode. More important, there is also evidence to support the logic that we propose as an explanation for this particular sequence of stages. Some countries, however, do seem to have stumbled on a useful pattern of promotion as much by trial and error as by design. Whatever the motivation of the agencies, their shifts follow a pattern that seems to reflect marketing strategies in other, similar environments.

Promotional Strategies in Industrial Marketing

The foreign investment decision is similar in several respects to the industrial buying decision. This similarity suggests that much can be understood about the process by which corporations make foreign investment decisions by examining the work of researchers in industrial marketing on the subject of how corporations decide to make large purchases.

Researchers have divided purchases by industrial buyers into several categories. Of these, it is the first purchase from a particular vendor that is most similar to the foreign investment decision, and thus of primary interest for this study.[9] To explain the process by which corporations and institutions make decisions on their first purchases of industrial products, researchers in industrial marketing have used a hierarchy of effects of communications model. This model suggests that individuals within buying centres of corporations go through the following five mental stages when making a first purchase decision: awareness, interest, evaluation, trial, and adoption.[10] Of course, not all buyers make purchases in as rational a manner as this model would suggest, but nevertheless, researchers have demonstrated that the model does have empirical validity.

Most important to our interest in the promotion activities of countries, several researchers found that different information sources were more effective at different stages of the purchase or adoption process. During the awareness and the interest stages the most effective information sources were impersonal sources such as advertising. However, during the evaluation, trial, and adoption stages, the most effective information sources in gaining adoption of the innovation or purchase of the industrial product were sources such as direct contact from salesmen, or from individuals in other firms, that is, some form of 'personal promotion' (Rodgers, 1962, p. 307; Ozanne and Churchill, 1968, p. 353).

Based upon the parallels between industrial buying and foreign direct investment decisions, we suggest that many corporations probably go through similar stages in deciding to make an investment decision.[11] Further, we observed that some promotional programmes have, in fact, made assumptions about the decision processes of investors, and tried to match their promotional programmes to these decision processes. They have used impersonal promotional techniques to interest investors likely to be in the awareness stage of an investment decision; and personal promotional techniques to influence investors likely to be further along in the investment decision process. Of course, since no agency will, at any particular time, be dealing with investors who are all at the same stage of the investment decision process, every agency might profitably use some mix of impersonal and personal promotional techniques.

Interviews with managers of firms investing abroad provided more direct evidence that supported the usefulness of research in industrial marketing in understanding investment promotion activities.

Assessing the Influence of Promotion on the Investment Decision

In order to determine which techniques were more effective in influencing investors to invest, we interviewed managers from US manufacturing firms involved in thirty recent investment decisions in at least one of the countries that we studied. We asked the managers about the nature of their contact with the promotional organisation prior to the firm's investment, and the factors that influenced the firm to make the particular investment decision. Those managers that indicated that they had been contacted by promotion agencies, or had been exposed to a country's promotional material, were asked to indicate the degree of influence the promotional agency had on the firm's investment decision: whether promotional agencies had a 'significant influence', 'some influence', or 'no influence' on the investment decision.[12]

First, we tried to determine which techniques were effective. Of the thirty investment decisions we examined, in eleven decisions managers indicated that the investment promotion agency had a significant influence on the firm's investment decision. In ten out of these eleven cases managers indicated, prior to assessing the degree of influence of the promotional agency, that they had been personally contacted by investment promoters who had continued to work with their companies throughout the investment decision process. We conclude from these findings that, similar to the industrial purchase decision, the techniques most useful in influencing individuals to make decisions to invest are 'personal promotion' techniques.

Next we set out to determine what kind of projects were influenced by promotion. Consistent with previous work on the impact of investment incentives, we divided the sample of investment decisions into investments oriented toward export markets and investments oriented toward a country's domestic market. Our sample was biased toward investment decisions targeted for export markets. Of the thirty investment decisions we studied, eight represented investment decisions geared toward a particular domestic market, and 22 represented investments targeted at export markets. Even taking into account the bias in our sample toward export projects, however, the degree of influence by market orientation of projects was striking. Of the projects influenced by promotion agencies, there was not a single case (out of a total of eleven) of projects oriented toward domestic markets being 'significantly influenced', and only one case (out of a total of nine) of these projects being subject to 'some influence' by promotional agencies. All eleven cases of 'significant influence' were export-oriented investments, and in 19 of the 22 export-oriented investments studied, promotional agencies exerted influence on the investment decision (see Table 11.5).

Since we examined only a few investment decisions oriented toward domestic markets our findings must be considered tentative. Nevertheless, these findings do suggest that the greatest impact of investment promotion, like that of tax incentives (Wells, 1986, pp. 58–60), is on a particular class of investors: those that will produce for the export market. This seems to be the case regardless of the fact that some of the agencies we studied devoted as much effort to attracting investors to serve the local market, and that none of the agencies that we examined discriminated by the market orientation of projects when deciding which techniques to use to seek to influence firms.

Table 11.5 The influence of promotion on investment decisions by market orientation of investment decision

	Level of influence			
	Significant influence	*Some influence*	*No influence*	*Total*
Market orientation of project				
Domestic	0	1	7	8
Export	11*	8	3	22
Total	11	9	10	30

* The eleven cases of significant influence were split among five investment agencies according to the following distribution of number of significant influence decisions/number of decisions studied: 3/5, 3/5, 3/5, 1/3, 1/2.

Countries involved in investment promotion are, however, not only interested in identifying whether investment promotion is effective in influencing investors, but also whether it is a cost-effective technique for attracting investors. We assessed the cost-effectiveness of investment promotion by comparing the costs of an efficient investment promotion programme with the direct employment benefits of the foreign investment generated through such a programme, and with the costs of an alternative marketing technique – the tax holiday.

To make these calculations, we used figures from Costa Rica's promotion programme. This programme was generally viewed as an efficient one; more important for our purposes, Costa Rica had made the most serious effort to document the number of investors, and the associated jobs, that could be directly attributed to promotion efforts. Since even Costa Rica's numbers could be challenged as inaccurate or atypical, however, we then examined the impact of alternative assumptions on our conclusions. We estimated, based upon data from the promotional programme of Costa Rica, with additional data from the promotional programmes of Ireland, Canada, and Britain, that an efficient investment promotion programme could be conducted at an approximate cost of $570 per job attracted. We compared this cost with an estimate of the direct benefits resulting from one job and with the cost of a typical cost holiday. Our illustrative calculations suggest that promotion is cost-effective both with respect to the benefits accruing from it, and in comparison to increased expenditures on alternative policies for attracting investment such as the tax holiday (see appendix for calculations).

CONCLUSION

We conclude that the model discussed in this chapter provides a framework for understanding the mix of personal and impersonal techniques used by the promotional agencies that we studied. Research in industrial marketing suggests that impersonal promotional techniques are most effective during the early stages of the industrial buying decision process, and personal techniques are more effective during the later stages of the industrial buying decision process. Our findings suggest that a similar relationship seems to hold in investment promotion.

Agencies at times begin active promotion efforts by focusing on image-building through impersonal techniques. In several cases this focus resulted from limited knowledge about, and a limited search for, effective techniques. In three cases, however, we identified that this was done as a deliberate strategy by agencies. These agencies assumed that during the early years of active promotion, or in the aftermath of dramatic changes in foreign investment policy, many of the investors they could hope to attract were probably in the early stages of the investment decision process. As these agencies developed an image, or,

APPENDIX

Table A-1   The costs of an efficient promotion programme

Assumptions

An average efficient programme consists of:
Image-building activities:
  $2 million campaign for one year[*]
  $3 m per year thereafter[†]

Investment-generating activities	$440 per job[†]

Programme attracts 5000 jobs per year.[†]
Government's discount rate 10%
Image-building campaign amortised over nine years.

Analysis

Annual amortised cost of image-building campaign ($2m over 9 years at 10%)	$347 000 per year
Annual actual cost of image-building activities 300 000	
Image-building activities: cost per job (647 000/5000 jobs)	$130 per job
Total cost per job: investment generating and image-building	$570 per job

---

[*]This estimate is for a relatively large-scale image-building programme conducted over a one or two year period, but with results that carry over to successive years, which is why the cost of the programme is amortised over nine years. It was derived, in part, from estimates of the cost of the image-building programmes of Canada, Britain, and Ireland. Canada's 1985 programme cost about $3m; Britain's 1983 programme cost about $1m; and Ireland's 1986 programme cost about $5m (the cost for Ireland includes the cost of printing and promotion expenses).

[†]These figures are all taken from the operations of CINDE in Costa Rica. CINDE's total annual budget of $2.5m included about $300 000, for advertising and public relations. This agency helped to attract about 5000 jobs per year. This leads to a cost for investment-generating activities of about $440 per job ($2.2m/ 5000 jobs).

in the case of other agencies, as they simply gained more experience, there was a shift to a focus on investment-generation through the use of more personal promotional techniques. Our research findings suggest that the personal promotional techniques used by agencies can be effective and cost-effective in influencing investment for export markets.

Table A-2 Cost of promotion versus the direct employment benefits of investment[*]

Assumptions
  $570 to attract one job via investment promotion[†]
  An investment life of 10 years
  A discount rate for the government of 10%
  Investment is export-oriented and all market prices = shadow prices except for the price of labour.
  Shadow price of labour = 70 per cent of its market price
  Market price of labour = $.50 per hour; shadow price = $.35[‡]

Analysis
  Cost of promotion per job $570

  Direct employment benefits to country
  Direct benefits per job per year $312 ($.15 × 40 hours × 52 weeks)
      (market price − shadow price)
  Benefits over life of investment $1917 ($312 discounted at 10%
      for 10 years)

---

[*] Discussion of assumptions and sensitivity calculations are available from the authors.
[†] This promotional cost was obtained from Table A-1.
[‡] This wage rate represents an average wage for low to medium wage countries.

Table A-3   The cost of promotion versus the costs of tax holidays

---

Assumptions
   $570 to attract one job via investment promotion (see Table A-2)
   $1 million of investment
   A capital/labour ration of $20 000/worker[*]
   A rate of return on investment of 15%
   A tax rate of 40%

Analysis
   Cost of promotion
   Number of people employed   50 ($1 000 000/ $20 000)
   Cost of promoting jobs $28 500 (50 × $570)

   Cost of tax holidays
   Annual profits $150 000 ($1 000 000 × 15%)
   Annual taxes forgone $60 000 ($150 000 × 40%)

   Cost of promotion in terms of tax holidays
   $28 500/60 000 = 5.7 months of tax holidays

---

[*] The research uncovered widely varying capital/labour ratios, with ranges of $10 000 to $60 000 per worker. An average ratio of $20 000 per worker was used.

Notes

1. It is useful to view competition among governments for foreign investment as analogous to competition among firms for market share, allowing one to assess the marketing of a country from the perspective of corporate marketing strategies. In this context, product represents the intrinsic advantages, including the effect of government policies, of a country as an investment site; price, represents the cost to the investor of locating in such a site, including incentives such as tax relief, grants, and tariff protection; and promotion represents the marketing mix activity we define and examine in this chapter. For the literature on incentives, see Guisinger and Associates (1985), which adds to and summarises the literature on incentives. For literature on policies that affect a country's desirability as an investment location, see Reuber *et al.* (1973); Lall and Streeten (1977); Robinson (1980).
2. Some of the studies already mentioned had, of course, drawn on the literature of marketing, and others have written on marketing for government activities. See, for example, Mokwa and Permut (1981).
3. These twenty countries were chosen from thirty countries listed in the *Business Facilities Magazine* as those countries most active in seeking investment from US-based companies.

4. Britain's IBB, Investment Canada, Ireland's IDA, Singapore's EDB, Locate in Scotland, and Malaysia's MIDA all fell into this category.

5. The early years of Jamaica's JNIP, and of Costa Rica's Cinde, and the efforts of Indonesia's BKPM illustrate this second group of agencies.

6. Indonesia's BKPM was the exception.

7. Investment Canada's Annual Report stated: 'Canada has always had much to offer investors', but inside and outside the country its business climate was perceived as being unfavourable to business. Creating a positive perception of Canada as a place to do business and as a preferred location for investment was, therefore, Investment Canada's priority during its first nine months of operation. See Investment Canada (1986), p. 21.

8. The IDA's 1970/1971 annual report stated that: 'The U.S. and British advertisements were aimed at presenting Ireland as a country with a modern industrial economy and correcting outmoded impressions of Ireland.' See Industrial Development Authority of Ireland, *Annual Report* (Dublin, 1971, p. 5).

9. This is the most common typology in industrial marketing, and is credited to the work of Robinson *et al*. This study develops a typology of buying situations or 'buy classes', namely, the 'new task' (first purchase), the 'straight rebuy' (routine reorder from seller of first purchase), and the 'modified rebuy' (modified buying specifications with competition for reorder from several sellers). See Robinson *et al*. (1967) and Wind and Robinson (1985) for a complete discussion of this typology.

10. This area of research has developed within behavioural explanations of the organisational buying process. It began with the innovation-adoption paradigm that sought to explain how organisations adopted new products and services. For this original model, see Rodgers (1962), p. 306. The paradigm was extended to explain how industrial buyers purchase new products, and to identify the sources of information most appropriate at each stage of the purchase decision. For the application of this model to industrial marketing, see Ozanne and Churchill (1971, pp. 7–13) and Martilla (1971, pp. 173–8).

11. Researchers have suggested that some foreign investment decisions are not made in a completely rational manner. Nevertheless, even those proponents of limited rationality on the part of investors have also suggested that there is sufficient rationality to the investment decision that one can identify factors that systematically influence an investor's decision to invest. Yair Aharoni in his seminal research on the foreign investment decision, for instance, points both to the limited rationality of foreign investors, see 'The Foreign Investment Decision Process', and to the possibility of foreign investment being systematically influenced by the marketing programmes of governments, see 'How to Market a Country' (Aharoni, 1966b). This paper does not assume perfect rationality on the part of investors, but it does seek to assess empirically whether the marketing efforts of governments might, notwithstanding the limited rationality of investors, be a factor that influences investment.

12. For an agency to have a 'significant influence', the manager would have to so indicate, and would also have to be able to identify the particular

promotional technique that made the agency's influence significant. For us to have considered the role of the agency to have been significant, the agency must have played an important role in attracting a company to a particular country, but not necessarily in attracting the company to that region of the world. In contrast, to qualify as having 'some influence' an agency did not have to influence a company to consider a country, but the firm did have to indicate that the agency was visible, available, and helpful once the firm began the process of examining a country's attractiveness as an investment site. This methodology follows that used by Basi in a survey study to identify the possible determinants of foreign direct investment. See Basi (1963).

References

Acheson, Keith, Christopher Maule and Elizabeth Filleul (1989) 'Folly of Quotas on Films and Television Programmes'. *World Economy*, vol. 12, no. 4 (December) pp. 515–24.

Acheson, Keith and Christopher Maule (1991) 'International Dimensions of the Film and Television Industry' (Ottawa: Carleton University Department of Economics. Mimeograph).

Aharoni, Yair (1966a) *The Foreign Investment Decision Process* (Boston: Division of Research, Harvard Business School).

Aharoni, Yair (1966b) 'How to Market a Country'. *Columbia Journal of World Business*, vol. 1, no. 2, pp. 41–8.

Amin, S. (1976) *Unequal Development* (Hassocks: Harvester).

Anderson, Erin and Hubert Gatignon (1986) 'Modes of Foreign Entry: A Transactions Cost Analysis'. *Journal of International Business Studies*, vol. 17, no. 3, pp. 1–26.

Bartlett, Christopher A. (1986) 'Building and Managing the Transnational: The New Organizational Challenge'; in M. E. Porter (ed.) *Competition in Global Industries* (Boston: Harvard Business School Press), pp. 367–401.

Bartlett, Christopher A. and Sumantra Ghoshal (1989) *Managing Across Borders: The Transnational Solution* (Boston: Harvard Business School Press).

Basi, Raghbir S. (1963) *Determinants of United States Private Direct Investments in Foreign Countries* (Kent, Ohio: Kent State University Press).

Beamish, Paul W. (1988) *Multinational Joint Ventures in Developing Countries* (London and New York: Routledge).

Becker, Gary (1971) *The Economics of Discrimination*. Second Edition (Chicago and London: University of Chicago Press).

Behrman, J. and R. Grosse (1990) *International Business and Government: Issues and Institutions* (Columbia, South Carolina: University of South Carolina Press).

Bergsten, C. Fred and Edward M. Graham (1991) *Global Corporations and National Governments: Are Changes Needed in the International Economic and Political Order in Light of the Globalization of Business?* (Washington, DC: Institute for International Economics. Mimeograph).

Bergsten, C. Fred, T. Horst and T. Moran (1978) *American Multinationals and American Interests* (Washington DC: The Brookings Institution).

Bessant, J. (1991) *Managing Advanced Manufacturing Technology* (Oxford: Basil Blackwell).

Best, Michael (1990) *The New Competition: Institutions of Industrial Restructuring* (Cambridge: Polity Press).

Blomström, Magnus (1990a) 'Competitiveness of Firms and Countries', in John Dunning, Bruce Kogut and Magnus Blomström (eds), *Globalization of Firms and Competitiveness of Nations*. Cranfoord Lectures 2 (Lund: Lund University Institute of Economic Research).

Blomström, Magnus (1990b) *Transnational Corporations and Manufacturing Exports from Developing Countries* (New York: United Nations).

Blomström, Magnus, Irving B. Kravis and Robert E. Lipsey (1988) 'Multinational Firms and Manufactured Exports from Developing Countries'. NBER Working Paper 2493, January.

Blomström, Magnus, and Robert E. Lipsey (1989) 'The Export Performance of U.S. and Swedish Multinationals'. *Review of Income and Wealth*.

Breton, Albert (1964) 'The Economics of Nationalism'. *Journal of Political Economy*, vol. 70, no. 4.

Bull, Hedley (1977) *The Anarchical Society: A Study of Order in World Politics* (London: Macmillan).

Business International (1988) *Organizing for International Competitiveness: How Successful Corporations Structure their Worldwide Operations* (New York: Business International).

Cantwell, John (1989) *Technological Innovation and the Multinational Corporation* (Oxford: Basil Blackwell).

Cantwell, John (1990) 'A Survey of Theories of International Production'. University of Reading Department of Economics. Mimeograph.

Caporaso, James (ed.) (1987) *A Changing International Division of Labour* (Boulder, CO: Lynne Reiner Publishers).

Casson, Mark (1982) 'Transactions Costs and the Theory of the Multinational Enterprise' in Alan Rugman (ed.) *New Theories of the Multinational Enterprise* (London and Canberra: Croom Helm).

Casson, Mark (1986) *Multinationals and World Trade: Vertical Integration and the Division of Labour in World Industries* (London: Allen and Unwin).

Casson, Mark (1987) *The Firm and the Market: Studies in Multinational Enterprise and the Scope of the Firm* (Oxford: Basil Blackwell and Cambridge, Mass.: MIT Press).

Casson, Mark (1990) *Enterprise and Competitiveness: A Systems View of International Business* (Oxford: Clarendon Press).

Caves, Richard (1982) *Multinational Enterprises and Economic Analysis* (Cambridge: Cambridge University Press).

Cecchini, P. M. Catinat and A. Jacquemin (1988) *The European Challenge: The Benefits of the Single Market* (Aldershot: Wildwood House).

Chandler, Alfred (1986) 'Technological and Organizational Underpinnings of Modern Industrial Multinational Enterprise: The Dynamics of Competitive Advantage' in Alice Teichova, Maurice Levy-Leboyer and Helga Nussbaum (eds), *Multinational Enterprise in Historical Perspective* (Cambridge: Cambridge University Press).

Chandler, Alfred (1990) *Scale and Scope: The Dynamics of Industrial Capitalism* (Harvard: Belknap Press of Harvard University).

Chesnais, Francois (1988) 'Multinational Enterprises and the International Diffusion of Technology' in Giovanni Dosi *et al.* (eds), *Technical Change and Economic Theory* (London and New York: Pinter Publishers).

Cohen, Benjamin (1990) 'The Political Economy of International Trade'. *International Organization*, vol. 44, no. 2 (Spring) pp. 261–81.

Contractor, Farok and Peter Lorange (1988) *Cooperative Strategies in International Business* (Lexington: Lexington Books).

Cowley, Peter F. (1990) 'Telecommunications', Chapter 3 in Gary Clyde Hufbauer (ed.), *Europe 1992: An American Perspective* (Washington, DC: The Brookings Institution).

Cox, Robert (1981) 'Social Forces: States and World Order'. *Millennium: Journal of International Studies*, vol. 10, no. 2, pp. 126–55.

Cox, Robert (1987) *Production, Power and World Order: Social Forces in the Making of History* (New York: Columbia University Press).

Crichton, Michael (1991) *Rising Sun* (New York: Alfred Knopf).

Doz, Yves (1986) *Strategic Management in Multinational Enterprises* (Oxford: Pergamon Press).

Drucker, Peter F. (1988) 'The Coming of the New Organization'. *Harvard Business Review*, January–February, pp. 45–53.

Dunning, John (1988) *Explaining International Production* (Boston and London: Unwin Hyman).

Dunning, John (1989a) 'The Theory of International Production', in Khosrow Fatemi (ed.), *International Trade: Existing Problems and Prospective Solutions* (New York: Taylor and Francis).

Dunning, John (1989b) 'Governments, Economic Organization and International Competitiveness'. University of Reading Discussion Papers in International Investment and Business Studies, no. 130, March.

Dunning, John (1989c) 'The Study of International Business: A Plea for a More Interdisciplinary Approach'. *Journal of International Business Studies*, Fall, pp. 411–36.

Dunning, John (1990a) 'The Globalization of Firms and the Competitiveness of Countries' in John Dunning, Bruce Kogut and Magnus Blomström, *Globalization of Firms and Competitivenss of Nations*. Cranfoord Lectures (Lund: Lund University Institute of Economic Research).

Dunning, John (1990c) 'Multinational Enterprises and the Globalization of Innovatory Capacity'. University of Reading Discussion Papers in International Business Studies. No. 143, September.

Dunning, John (1991a) 'Dunning on Porter: Reshaping the Diamond of Competitive Advantage'. University of Reading Discussion Papers in International Investment and Business Studies. University of Reading.

Dunning, John (1991b) 'Governments–Markets–Firms: Towards a New Balance'. *The CTC Reporter*, No. 31, Spring.

Dunning, John and J. Cantwell (1987) *The IRM Directory of Statistics of International Investment and Production* (London: Macmillan Reference Books).

Dunning, John and Robert D. Pearce (1988) 'The Nature and Growth of MNEs' in C. W. Nobes and R. H. Parker (eds), *Issues in Multinational Accounting* (London and New York: Philip Allan and St Martin's Press).

Eden, Lorraine (1985) 'The Microeconomics of Transfer Pricing', in Alan Rugman and Lorraine Eden (eds), *Multinationals and Transfer Pricing* (London and New York: Croom Helm and St Martin's Press).

Eden, Lorraine (1989) 'Pharmaceuticals in Canada: An Analysis of the Compulsory Licensing Debate' in Alan M. Rugman (ed.) *International Business in Canada: Strategies for Management* (Toronto: Prentice-Hall).

Eden, Lorraine (1990) 'Two Steps Forward, One Step Back: Into the 1990s', in Maureen Molot and Fen Hampson (eds), *Canada Among Nations. 1989: The Challenge of Change* (Ottawa: Carleton University Press).

Eden, Lorraine (1991a) 'Multinational Responses to Trade and Technology Changes: Implications for Canada', in Don McFetridge (ed.) *Foreign Investment, Technology and Growth* (Ottawa: University of Calgary Press and Investment Canada).

Eden, Lorraine (1991b) 'Bringing the Firm Back In: Multinationals in International Political Economy'. *Millennium: Journal of International Studies*, vol. 20, no. 2, pp. 197–224.

Eden, Lorraine and Fen Hampson (1990) 'Clubs Are Trumps: Towards a Taxonomy of International Regimes'. Centre for International Trade and Investment Policy Studies Discussion Paper, 1990, no. 2 (Ottawa: Carleton University).

Encarnation, Dennis J. and Louis T. Wells Jr. (1985) 'Sovereignty en garde: Negotiating with Foreign Investors'. *International Organization*, vol. 39, no. 1 (Winter) pp. 47–78.

Encarnation, Dennis J. and Louis T. Wells, Jr. (1986) 'Competitive Strategies in Global Industries: a View from Host Governments', in Michael E. Porter (ed.), *Competition in Global Industries* (Boston: Harvard Business School Press) pp. 267–90.

Erdlick, Asim (ed.) (1985) *Multinationals as Mutual Invaders: Intra-industry Direct Foreign Investment* (New York: St Martin's Press).

Evans, Peter, Dietrich Rueschemeyer and Theda Skocpol (1985) 'On the Road to a More Adequate Understanding of the State' in Peter Evans *et al.* (eds), *Bringing the State Back In* (Cambridge: Cambridge University Press).

Ferdows, K. (1989) 'Mapping International Factory Networks', in K. Ferdows (ed.), *Managing International Manufacturing* (Amsterdam: North-Holland).

Fieldhouse, D. K. (1986) 'The Multinational: A Critique of a Concept', in Teichova *et al.* (eds), *Multinational Enterprise in Historical Perspective* (Cambridge: Cambridge University Press).

Frieden, Jeffery and David Lake (eds) (1987) *International Political Economy* (New York: St Martin's Press).

Frobel, Folker, Jurgen Heinrichs and Otto Kreye (1978) 'The World Market for Labour and the World Market for Industrial Sites'. *Journal of Economic Issues*, vol. 12, no. 4 (December) pp. 843–58.

Frobel, Folker *et al.* (1980) *The New International Division of Labour: Structural Unemployment in Industrialised Countries and Industrialisation in Developing Countries* (Cambridge: Cambridge University Press).

Giddy, I. and Young, S. (1982) 'Conventional Theory and Unconventional Multinationals: Do New Forms of Multinational Enterprise Require New Theories?', in A. Rugman (ed.), *New Theories of the Multinational Enterprise* (London: Croom Helm).

Gilpin, Robert (1975) 'Three Models of the Future', in C. F. Bergsten and L. B. Krause (eds), *World Politics and International Economics* (Washington, DC: The Brookings Institution).

Gilpin, Robert (1987) *The Political Economy of International Relations* (Princeton: Princeton University Press).

Gill, Robert and David Law (1988) *The Global Political Economy: Perspectives, Problems and Policies* (Baltimore: Johns Hopkins University Press).

Globerman, Steven and Aidan Vining (1983) 'Bilateral Cultural Free Trade: The U.S.–Canadian Case', in Fred Thompson (ed.) *Canadian–U.S Interdependence in Cultural Industry*. Proceedings of a conference held at Columbia University, New York. Mimeograph.

Goldberg, Paul M. and Charles P. Kindleberger (1970) 'Toward a GATT for Foreign Investment: A Proposal for Supervision of the International Corporation'. *Law and Public Policy in International Business*, Summer.

Golembe, Carter H. and David S. Holland (1990) 'Banking and Securities'. Chapter 2 in Gary Clyde Hufbauer (ed.), *Europe 1992: An American Perspective* (Washington, DC: The Brookings Institution).

Golich, Vicki (1992) 'Liberalizing International Air Transport Services'. Paper delivered to the annual meeting of the International Studies Association.

Goodnow, James D. (1970) 'American Overseas Business Promotion Offices'. *Michigan Business Review*, January, pp. 6–11.

Graham, Edward M. and Paul R. Krugman (1991) *Foreign Direct Investment in the United States*. Second Edition (Washington, DC: Institute for International Economics).

Grimwade, Nigel (1989) *International Trade: New Patterns of Trade, Production and Investment* (London and New York: Routledge).

Guisinger, Stephen E. and Associates (1985) *Investment Incentives and Performance Requirements* (New York: Praeger).

Guisinger, Stephen E. (1986) 'Host Country Policies to Attract and Control Foreign Investment', in Theodore H. Moran *et al.*, *Investing in Development: New Roles for Private Capital?* (Washington, DC: Overseas Development Council) pp. 157–172.

Heininger, Horst (1986) 'Transnational Corporations and the Struggle for the Establishment of a New World Order', in Alice Teichova *et al.* (eds), *Multinational Enterprise in Historical Perspective* (Cambridge: Cambridge University Press).

Hoekman, Bernard (1991) 'Market Access and Multilateral Trade Agreements: The Uruguay Round Services Negotiation'. Paper delivered to the National Bureau of Economic Research Conference on the Political Economy of International Market Access. February 7–8. Mimeograph.

Hoffman, Kurt and Raphael Kaplinsky (1988) *Driving Force: The Global Restructuring of Technology, Labour and Investment in the Automobile and Components Industries* (Boulder: Westview Press).

Hunt, Shelby D. (1976) 'The Nature and Scope of Marketing'. *Journal of Marketing*, vol. 40 (July) pp. 17–28.

Hymer, Stephen (1971) 'The Multinational Corporation and the Law of Uneven Development', in Jagdish Bhagwati (ed.), *Economics and World Order* (New York: Macmillan).

Hymer, Stephen (1979) 'The International Division of Labour', in R. B. Cohen, N. Felton, J. van Liere and M. Nkosi (eds), *The Multinational Corporation: A Radical Approach, Papers by Stephen Herbert Hymer* (Cambridge: Cambridge University Press), IDS Bulletin, vol. 20, no. 1.

International Policy Analysis (1984) *An Assessment of Investment Promotion Activities* (Washington, DC: SRI International).

Investment Canada (1990) 'The Business Implications of Globalization'. *Investment Canada Working Paper Series.* No. 1990–V (Ottawa: Government of Canada).

Investment Canada (1991) 'International Investment: Canadian Developments in a Global Context'. *Investment Canada Working Paper Series* No. 1990-VI (updated) (Ottawa: Government of Canada).

Investment Canada (1986) *Annual Report* (Ottawa: Ministry of Supply and Services).

Isaak, Robert (1991) *International Political Economy: Managing World Economic Change* (Englewood Cliffs, New Jersey: Prentice-Hall).

Jenkins, R. (1987) *TNCs and Uneven Development: The Internationalization of Capital and the Third World* (London: Methuen).

Junne, Gerd (1987) 'Automation in the North: Consequences for Developing Countries Exports', in James Caporaso (ed.), *A Changing International Division of Labour* (Boulder: Lynne Reiner Publishers).

Kaplinsky, Raphael (1990) 'Post-Fordist Industrial Restructuring: Policy Implications for an Industrially Advanced Economy'. Presented at the Conference on Canadian Political Economy in the Era of Free Trade, Carleton University, April 6–8, 1990.

Kaplinsky, Raphael (1990) *The Economics of Small* (London: Intermediate Technology Press).

Kasper, Daniel M. (1988) 'Liberalizing Airline Services: How to Get from Here to There'. *World Economy.* vol. 11, no. 1 (March) pp. 91–107.

Keohane, Robert (1983) 'The Demand for International Regimes', in Stephen Krasner (ed.) ,*International Regimes* (Ithaca: Cornell University Press).

Kiljunen, Kimmo (1989) 'Toward a Theory of the International Division of Labour'. *World Development,* vol. 17, no. 1, pp. 109–39.

Kindleberger, Charles (1969) *American Business Abroad: Six Lectures on Direct Investment* (New Haven: Yale University Press).

Kindleberger, Charles (ed.) (1970) *The International Corporation* (Cambridge, Mass.: MIT Press).

Kindleberger, C.K. and P.M. Goldberg (1970) 'Towards a GATT for Investment: A Proposal for Supervision of the International Corporation'. *Law and Policy in International Business,* vol. 2, pp. 295–323.

King, Robert L. (1968) *Marketing and the New Science of Planning* (Chicago: American Marketing Association, Fall Conference Proceedings).

Kline, John M. and Cynthia Day Wallace (1991) *EC-92 and Changing Global Investment Patterns: Implications for the U.S.–EC Relationship* (Washington DC: Center for Strategic and International Studies).

Kobrin, Stephen J. (1987) 'Testing the Bargaining Hypothesis in the Manufacturing Sector in Development Countries'. *International Organization,* vol. 41, pp. 609–38.

Kosnik, Thomas J. (1988) 'Corporate Positioning: How to Assess and Build a Company's Reputation'. Unpublished working paper (Boston: Harvard Business School).

Kravis, Irving B. and Robert E. Lipsey (1992) 'Sources of Competitiveness of the U.S. and Swedish Multinationals'. *Review of Economics and Statistics,* vol. LXXIV, May.

Kudrle, Robert T. (1985) 'The Several Faces of the Multinational Corporation: Political Reaction and Policy Response', in W. Ladd Hollist and F. LaMond Tullis (eds), *An International Political Economy*. The International Political Economy Yearbook volume 1 (Boulder, Co: Westview Press).

Kudrle, Robert T. (1991) 'The Challenger Within: Direct Investment in Europe and the United States', in Earl Fry and Lee H. Radebaugh (eds), *Investment in the North American Free Trade Area* (Provo: Brigham Young University Press).

Kudrle, Robert T. and Davis B. Bobrow (1987) 'U.S. Policy Towards Foreign Direct Investment'. *World Politics*, vol. 34, pp. 353–79.

Kudrle, Robert T. and Stefanie Ann Lenway (1990) 'Progress for the Rich: The Canada–U.S. Free Trade Agreement'. Chapter 7 in Emanuel Adler and Beverly Crawford (eds), *Progress in Post-War International Relations* (New York, NY: Columbia University Press).

Laband, David N. (1984) *Foreign Ownership of U.S. Farmland* (Lexington, Mass.: Lexington Books).

Lall, Sanjaya (1990) *Building Industrial Competitiveness in Developing Countries* (Paris: OECD).

Lall, Sanjaya (1992) 'Technological Capabilities and Industrialization'. *World Development*, vol. 20, no. 2, 1992.

Lall, Sanjaya and George Kell (1991) 'Industrial Development in Developing Countries and the Role of Government Interventions'. *Banca Nazionale del Lavoro Quarterly*. September.

Lall, Sanjaya and Paul Streeten (1977) *Foreign Investment, Transnationals and Developing Countries* (Boulder, Col.: Westview Press).

Lenway, Stefanie Ann and Thomas P. Murta (1991) 'The Idea of the State in the International Business Literature'. University of Michigan, School of Business Administration, Working Paper no. 656, April.

Leyton-Brown, David (1990) 'The Roles of the Multinational Enterprise in International Relations', in David Haglund and Michael Hawes (eds), *World Politics, Interdependence and Dependence* (Toronto: Harcourt, Brace, Jovanovich).

Lipsey, Robert, and Irving B. Kravis (1985) 'The Competitive Position of U.S. Manufacturing Firms'. *Banca Nazionale del Lavoro Quarterly Review*, no. 155, June.

Lipsey, Robert, and Irving B. Kravis (1987) 'The Competitive and Comparative Advantage of U.S. Multinationals, 1957–1984'. *Banca Nazionale del Lavoro Quarterly Review*, no. 161, June.

Martilla, John A. (1971) 'Word of Mouth Communication in the Industrial Adoption Process'. *Journal of Marketing Research*, vol. 8 (May) pp. 173–8.

McCulloch, Rachel (1990) 'Investment Policies in the GATT'. *World Economy*, vol. 13, no. 4, (December) pp. 541–53.

McGowan, Francis and Paul Seabright (1989) 'Deregulating European Airlines'. *Economic Policy*, October, pp. 284–335.

McGowan, Francis and Stephen Thomas (1989) 'Restructuring in the Power-Plant Equipment Industry and 1992'. *World Economy*, vol. 12, no. 4 (December) pp. 539–56.

McKinlay, R. D. and R. Little (1986) *Global Problems and World Order* (Madison: University of Wisconsin Press).

Milner, Helen (1988) *Resisting Protectionism: Global Industries and the Politics of International Trade* (Princeton: Princeton University Press).

Milner, Helen and David Yoffie (1989) 'Between Free Trade and Protectionism: Strategic Trade Policy and a Theory of Corporate Trade Demands'. *International Organization*, vol. 43, no. 2 (Spring) pp. 239–72.

Ministry of International Trade and Industry (MITI) (1980) *Waga-Kuny Kigyo no Kaigai Jigyo Katsudo* (Japanese Firms' Activities Abroad, 1977).

Ministry of International Trade and Industry (MITI) (1989) *Kaigai Jigyo Katsudo Kihon Chosa: Kaigai Toshi Tokey Soran* (Basic Survey of Firms' Activities Abroad, 1986), May.

Migdal, J. (1988) *Strong Societies and Weak States: State–Society Relations and State Capacities in the Third World* (Princeton: Princeton University Press).

Mokwa, Michael P. and Steven E. Permut (eds) (1981) *Government Marketing: Theory and Practice* (New York: Praeger).

Moran, Theodore H. (ed.) (1985) *Multinational Corporations: The Political Economy of Foreign Direct Investment* (Lexington, Mass.: Lexington Books).

Moran, Theodore H. (1990) 'The Globalization of the Defense Industry'. *International Security*, Summer.

Moriarty, Rowland T. (1983) *Industrial Buying Behavior: Concepts, Issues and Applications* (Lexington, Mass.: Lexington Books).

Morrison, A. and Roth, K. (1989) 'International Business-Level Strategy: The Development of a Holistic Model', in Anant Negandhi and Arun Savara (eds), *International Stategic Management* (Lexington, Mass.: Lexington Books).

Murphy, Craig and Roger Tooze (1991) *The New International Political Economy*. IPE Yearbook vol. 6 (Boulder, Col.: Lynne Reiner Publishers).

Musgrave, P. B. (1975) *Direct Investment Abroad and the Multinationals: Effects on the U.S. Economy* (Washington, DC: Senate Foreign Relations Committee-Subcommittee on Multinational Corporations).

Mytelka, Lynn K. (1987) 'Knowledge-Intensive Production and the Changing Internationalization Strategies of Multinational Firms', in James Caporaso (ed.), *A Changing International Division of Labour* (Boulder, Col.: Lynne Reiner Publishers).

Mytelka, Lynn K. (1990) 'Strategic Partnering Activity by European Firms through the ESPRIT Program'. *KIEP Working Paper*, no. 2 (Korea Institute for International Economic Policy).

Negandhi, Anant and Arun Savara (1989) (eds) *International Stategic Management* (Lexington, Mass.: Lexington Books).

Newfarmer, Richard (ed.) (1985) *Profits, Progress and Poverty* (Notre Dame: University of Notre Dame Press).

Nicolaides, Phedon (1991) 'Investment Policies in an Integrated World Economy'. *World Economy*, vol. 14, no. 2 (June) pp. 121–137.

Nye, Joseph (1990) *Bound to Lead: The Changing Nature of American Power* (New York: Basic Books).

Ohmae, Kenichi (1985) *Triad Power: The Coming Shape of Global Competition* (New York: The Free Press, Macmillan).

Ohmae, Kenichi (1989) 'Managing in a Borderless World'. *Harvard Business Review*, May–June, pp. 152–61.

Ohmae, Kenichi (1990) *The Borderless World: Power and Strategy in the International Economy* (New York: Harper Business).

Oman, Charles (1990) *New Forms of Investment in Developing Countries: Mining, Petrochemicals, Automobiles, Textiles, Food.* Development Center of the OECD (Paris: OECD).

O'Neal, C. R., H. B. Thorelli and J. M. Utterback (1973) 'Adoption of Innovation by Industrial Organizations'. *Industrial Marketing Management*, vol. 2, pp. 235–48.

Organisation for Economic Co-operation and Development (1986) *Code of Liberalisation of Capital Movements* (Paris: OECD).

Organisation for Economic Co-operation and Development (1987a) *Controls and Impediments Affecting Inward Direct Investment in O.E.C.D. Member Countries* (Paris: OECD).

Organisation for Economic Co-operation and Development (1987b) *Recent Trends in International Direct Investment* (Geneva: OECD).

Organisation for Economic Co-operation and Development (1987c) *Structure and Organization of Multinationals* (Geneva: OECD).

Ostry, Sylvia (1990) *Governments and Corporations in a Shrinking World: Trade and Innovation Policies in the United States, Europe, and Japan* (New York: Council on Foreign Relations).

Ozanne, U. G. and G. A. Churchill (1968) 'Adoption Research: Information Sources in the Industrial Purchase Decision', in R. L. King (ed.), *Marketing and the New Science of Planning* (Chicago: American Marketing Association), Fall Conference Proceedings, Series 28.

Ozanne, U. G. and G. A. Churchill (1971) 'Five Dimensions of the Industrial Adoption Process'. *Journal of Marketing Research*, vol. 8, pp. 322–8.

Perez, C. (1985) 'Microelectronics, Long Waves and Structural Change: New Perspectives for Developing Countries', *World Development*, vol. 13, no. 1.

Piore, Michael J. and Charles F. Sabel (1984) *The Second Industrial Divide: Possibilities for Prosperity* (New York: Basic Books).

Porter, Michael E. (1980) *Competitive Strategy: Techniques for Analyzing Industries and Competitors* (New York: The Free Press, Macmillan).

Porter, Michael (ed.) (1986) *Competition in Global Industries* (Cambridge, Mass.: Harvard Business School Press).

Porter, Michael (1987) 'Changing Patterns of International Competition', in David Teece (ed.), *The Competitive Challenge: Strategies for Industrial Innovation and Renewal* (Cambridge, Mass.: Ballinger Publishing Co.).

Porter, Michael (1990a) *The Competitive Advantage of Nations* (New York: The Free Press, Macmillan).

Porter, Michael (1990b) 'The Competitive Advantage of Nations'. *Harvard Business Review*, March–April, pp. 73–93.

Prahalad, C. K. and Yves L. Doz (1987) *The Multinational Mission: Balancing Local Demands and Global Vision* (New York: The Free Press).

Prahalad, C. K. and Gary Hamel (1990) 'The Core Competence of the Corporation'. *Harvard Business Review*, May–June, pp. 78–91.

Radice, Hugo (ed.) (1975) *International Firms and Modern Imperialism* (London: Penguin).

Ramstetter, Eric D. (1991) *Regional Patterns of Japanese Multinational Activities in Japan and Asia's Developing Countries* (Institute of Economic and Political Studies, Kansai University).

Reich, Robert (1990) 'Who Is Us?'. *Harvard Business Review*, January–February.

Reich, Robert (1991) *The Work of Nations: Preparing Ourselves for 21st Century Capitalism* (New York: Knopf).

Reuber, Grant *et al.* (1973) *Private Foreign Investment in Development* (Oxford: Clarendon Press).

Richardson, David (1990) 'The Political Economy of Strategic Trade Policy'. *International Organization*, vol. 44, Winter, pp. 107–35.

Robinson, Patrick J., Charles W. Faris and Yoram Wind (1967) *Industrial Buying and Creative Marketing* (Boston: Allyn and Bacon).

Robinson, Richard D. (1980) *Foreign Investment in the Third World: a Comparative Study of Selected Developing Country Investment Promotion Programs* (Washington, DC: Chamber of Commerce of the United States).

Robock, Stefan H. and Kenneth Simmonds (1989) *International Business and Multinational Enterprises*. Fourth Edition (Homewood and Boston: Irwin).

Rodgers, Everett M. (1962) *Diffusion of Innovations* (New York: The Free Press).

Roseman, David (1988) 'Towards a GATT Code on Trade in Telecommunication Equipment'. *World Economy*, vol. 11, no. 1, pp. 135–49.

Rugman, Alan M. (1981) *Inside the Multinationals: The Economics of Internal Markets* (London: Croom Helm; and New York: Columbia University Press).

Rugman, Alan M. (1988) 'The Multinational Enterprise', in Ingo Walter (ed.) and Tracy Murray (ass. ed.), *Handbook of International Management* (New York, NY: John Wiley & Sons) pp. 1.3–1.18.

Rugman, Alan M. and Andrew Anderson (1987) *Administered Protection in America* (London and New York: Routledge).

Rugman, Alan M. and Joseph D'Cruz (1991) *Fast Forward: Improving Canada's International Competitiveness* (Toronto: Kodak Canada Inc.).

Rugman, Alan, Don Lecraw and Lawrence Booth (1985) *International Business: Firm and Environment* (Toronto: McGraw-Hill).

Rugman, Alan M. and Alain Verbeke (1987) 'Trade Policy in the Asia–Pacific Region: A U.S.–Japan Comparison'. *Journal of Business Administration*, vol. 17, pp. 1/2, 89–107.

Rugman, Alan M. and Alain Verbeke (1989) 'Strategic Management and Trade Policy'. *Journal of International Economic Studies*.

Rugman, Alan M. and Alain Verbeke (1990) *Global Corporate Strategy and Trade Policy* (London and New York: Routledge).

Ryan, Cillian (1990) 'Trade Liberalisation and Financial Services'. *World Economy*, vol. 13, no. 3 (September), pp. 349–66.

Samuels, Barbara (1990) *Managing Risk in Developing Countries* (Princeton: Princeton University Press).

Schiffman, Leon G., Leon Winer and Vincent Gaccione (1978) 'The Role of Sources of Information in the Institutional Buying Decision-making Process', in Arch G. Woodside *et al.* (eds), *Foundations of Marketing Channels* (Austin, Texas: Lone Star Publishers), pp. 248–63.

Schneider, Friedrich and Bruno Frey (1985) 'Economic and Political Determinants of Foreign Direct Investment'. *World Development*, vol. 13, no. 2, pp. 161–75.

Seitzinger, Michael V. (1989) *Foreign Investment in the United States: Major Federal Restrictions*. Congressional Research Service Report for Congress (Washington, DC: The Library of Congress).

Services of the Commission of the European Community (1991) *Report on United States Trade Barriers and Unfair Practices: Problems of Doing Business with the U.S.* Mimeograph.

Shapiro, Helen and Lance Taylor (1990) 'The State and Industrial Strategy'. *World Development*, vol. 18, no. 6, pp. 861–78.

Spero, Joan (1990) *The Politics of International Economic Relations*. Fourth Edition (New York: St Martin's Press).

Stopford, John and Susan Strange (1991) *Rival States, Rival Firms: Competition for World Market Shares* (Cambridge: Cambridge University Press).

Strange, Susan (1988) *States and Markets: An Introduction to IPE* (London: Pinter).

Strange, Susan (1990) 'An Eclectic Approach to International Monetary and Trade Relations'. Paper presented at the International Studies Association annual meeting, Washington DC, April 10–14.

Strange, Susan (1991) 'Big Business and the State'. *Millennium: Journal of International Studies*, vol. 20, no. 2, (Summer), pp. 245–50.

Tanzi, Vito and Isaias Coelho (1991) 'Barriers to Foreign Investment in the U.S. and Other Nations'. *The Annals of the American Academy of Political and Social Science*, 516 July, pp. 154–68.

Teece, D. J. (1985) 'Transaction Cost Economics and the Multinational Enterprise: An Assessment'. *Journal of Economic Behavior and Organization*, vol. 7, pp. 21–45.

Teece, D. J. (1987) 'Profiting from Technological Innovation', in D. Teece (ed.), *The Competitive Challenge: Strategies for Industrial Innovation and Renewal* (Cambridge, Mass: Ballinger).

Tiechova, Alice, Maurice Levy-Leboyer and Helga Nussbaum (eds) (1986) *Multinational Enterprise in Historical Perspective* (Cambridge: Cambridge University Press).

Tooze, Roger (1984) 'Perspectives and Theory: A Consumer's Guide', in Susan Strange (ed.), *Paths to International Political Economy* (London: Allen and Unwin).

United Nations Centre for Transnational Corporations (UNCTC) (1988) *Transnational Corporations in World Development: Trends and Prospects* (New York: United Nations).

United Nations Centre for Transnational Corporations (UNCTC) (1989) *List of Sales Publications of the UNCTC, 1973–1989*. October (New York: United Nations).

United Nations Centre for Transnational Corporations (UNCTC) (1991) *World Investment Report 1991: The Triad in Foreign Direct Investment* (New York: United Nations).

US Department of the Treasury (1988) *Survey of G–7 Laws and Regulations on Foreign Direct Investment* (Washington, DC: US Department of the Treasury).

198 *References*

US Department of Commerce. (1975) *U.S. Direct Investment Abroad, 1966: Final Data* (Bureau of Economic Analysis, Washington, DC).

US Department of Commerce (1981) *U.S. Direct Investment Abroad: 1977 Benchmark Survey Data* (Bureau of Economic Analysis, Washington, DC).

US Department of Commerce (1985) *U.S. Direct Investment Abroad: 1982 Benchmark Survey Data* (Bureau of Economic Analysis, Washington, DC).

US Department of Commerce (1988) *U.S. Direct Investment Abroad: Operations of U.S. Parent Companies and Their Foreign Affiliates, Revised 1985 Estimates* (Washington, DC).

US Department of Commerce (1989) *U.S. Direct Investment Abroad: Operations of U.S. Parent Companies and their Foreign Affiliates, Revised (1986) Estimates* (Washington, DC).

US Department of Commerce (1991) *U.S. Direct Investment Abroad: Operations of U.S. Parent Companies and Their Foreign Affiliates, Revised 1988 Estimates* (Washington, DC).

US Department of Commerce (1992) *U.S. Direct Investment Abroad: Operations of U.S. Parent Companies and Their Foreign Affiliates, Preliminary 1989 Estimates* (Washington, DC).

United States Trade Representative (Office of) (1991) *National Trade Estimate Report on Foreign Trade Barriers* (Washington DC: U.S. Government Printing Office).

Van Tulder, Rob and Gerd Junne (1988) *European Multinationals in Core Technologies* (New York: John Wiley).

Vernon, Raymond (1966) 'International Investment and International Trade in the Product Cycle'. *Quarterly Journal of Economics*, vol. 80, no. 2, May.

Vernon, Raymond (1971) *Sovereignty at Bay: The Multinational Spread of U.S. Enterprises* (New York: Basic Books).

Vernon, Raymond (ed.) (1974) *Big Business and the State: Changing Relations in Western Europe* (London: Macmillan).

Vernon, Raymond (1977) *Storm over the Multinationals* (Cambridge, Mass: Harvard University Press).

Vernon, Raymond (1979) 'The Product Cycle Hypothesis in the New International Environment'. *Oxford Bulletin of Economics and Statistics*, vol. 41, no.4, November.

Vernon, Raymond (1981) 'Sovereignty at Bay: Ten Years After'. *International Organization*, vol. 35, no. 3 (Summer) pp. 527–37.

Vernon, Raymond (1983) 'Organizational and Institutional Responses in International Risk', in R.J. Herring (ed.) *Managing International Risk* (Cambridge: Cambridge University Press).

Vernon, Raymond (1991) 'Sovereignty at Bay: Twenty Years After'. *Millennium: Journal of International Studies*, vol. 20, no. 2 (Summer) pp. (191–6).

Vernon, Raymond (1992) 'Are Foreign-owned Subsidiaries Good for the United States?'. Occasional Paper no. 37 (Washington, DC: Group of Thirty).

Vernon, Raymond and Debora Spar (1990) *Beyond Globalism: Remaking American Foreign Economic Policy* (New York: Macmillan).

Wade, Robert (1990) *Governing the Market* (Princeton, NJ: Princeton University Press).

Wallace, Cynthia Day (1982) *Legal Control of the Multinational Enterprise* (The Hague: Martinus Nijhoff Publishers).

Waltz, Kenneth Neal (1979) *Theory of International Politics* (Reading, Mass.: Addison-Wesley).

Watzke, Gerard E. (1981) 'Four European Development Agencies in the U.S.'. *Management International Review*, Fall, pp. 53–60.

Watzke, Gerard E. (1982) 'An Irish Sweepstakes for American Corporations'. *Journal of General Management*, Summer, pp. 31–9.

Watzke, Gerard E. and W. A. Mindak (1987) 'Marketing-oriented Planning in Public Administration: The Case of the State Development Agency'. *International Journal of Public Administration*, vol. 9, no. 2, pp. 153–92.

Webster, F. E., Jr (1968) 'Interpersonal Communication and Salesmen Effectiveness'. *Journal of Marketing*, vol. 3 (July) pp. 7–13.

Weigand, Robert (1983) 'International Investments: Weighing the Incentives'. *Harvard Business Review*, July–August 1983, pp. 146–52.

Wells, Louis T. Jr. (1986) 'Investment Incentives: An Unnecessary Debate'. *The CTC Reporter*, No. 22 (Autumn) pp. 58–60.

Wells, Louis T. Jr. and Alvin G. Wint (1991) 'The Public–Private Choice: the Case of Marketing a Country to Investors'. *World Development*, vol. 19, no. 7.

Wind, Yoram and Patrick J. Robinson (1968) 'Simulating the Industrial Buying Process', in Robert L. King (ed.), *Marketing and the New Science of Planning* (Chicago: American Marketing Association) Fall Conference Proceedings.

Williamson, Oliver (1975) *Markets and Hierarchies: Analysis and Antitrust Implications* (New York: Free Press).

Womack, James, Daniel Jones and Daniel Roos (1990) *The Machine that Changed the World* (New York: Rawson Associates).

Yarbrough, Beth and Robert Yarbrough (1989) 'International Institutions and the New Economics of Organization', *International Organization*, vol. 44, no. 2 (Spring) pp. 235–59.

Yuan, Jing-dong and Lorraine Eden (1992) 'Export Processing Zones in Asia: A Comparative Study'. *Asian Survey*, vol. 32, no. 11 (November), pp. 1026–45.

Index

Advertising: contribution to export shares of US MNEs, 139; impact on MNE competitiveness, 140

Africa, 51, 88, 103, 119

Agricultural industries, 110, 148–9

Aharoni, Y., 168

aircraft industry, 45

Albania, increasingly open to FDI in 1980s, 103

Alberta, 93; *see also* Canada, Sub-national

American Telephone and Telegraph Co. (AT&T), 156

Anti-dumping laws, 95, 98; *see also* Countervail

Anti-trust policies, 7, 69; US policy on, 49; *see also* Sovereignty at bay

Apple Corporation, 108

Argentina, 118

Association of Southeast Asian Nations (ASEAN), 119–20

Australia: historic domination of by UK and US, 150–1; media controls in, 14, 162; restrictions by sector, 146–9; restrictions on FDI in broadcasting, 155; *for comparison see* Canada

Austria, restrictions by sector, 146–1

Automation, *see* Flexible manufacturing systems

Automobile industry: MNE strategies in, 31, 45; inter-firm relations in, 113; relation to scale, 115–16; simultaneous engineering in, 113

Balance of payments: relation to outward foreign direct investment, 68; Third World problems with, 109

Banking sector: bilateral reciprocity in, 164; restrictions on IFDI, 14, 145–50, 152, 154

Basques, 86; *see also* Decentralization

Beggar-thy-neighbour policy, 23

Belgium, as major outward investor, 68; IFDI restrictions by sector, 146–9, 151, 153

Bergsten, C. Fred and Graham, Edward M., 152

Blomström, Magnus, 4, 12–13, 18

Board of Investment (BOI): central investment agency of Thailand, 172–3; promotional techniques of, 176–7

Brazil, 118, 126; automobile industry of, 119; impact of Law of Similars on FDI, 106; reaction to US MNCs, 22

Bridgestone, 96

Broadcasting industry: national security implications of, 154; restrictions on IFDI in, 14, 145–50, 154; Canadian restrictions in, 154–5

California, 60; *see also* US

Canada, 150, 170; decentralisation of political power in, 8, 92–4; impact of economic nationalists on FDI, 96; industrial policy in, 98; Investment Canada as national investment agency of, 15, 96, 172–3, 175–6; investment image of, 175; media controls in, 14, 162; restrictions on IFDI, 96, 142, 146–9, 151; *see also* Broadcasting, Investment Canada